Eric Clapton

THE MAN THE MUSIC THE MEMORABILIA

Eric Clapton

THE MAN THE MUSIC — THE MEMORABILIA

MARC ROBERTY

Paper Tiger
An imprint of
Dragon's World Limited
Limpsfield
Surrey RH8 0DY
Great Britain

First published by Dragon's World 1994

EDITOR: Fiona Trent
DESIGN AND ART DIRECTION: Dave Allen
TEXT STYLIST: Stuart Green
DTP MANAGER: Keith Bambury
SPECIAL PHOTOGRAPHY: Graham Bush
EDITORIAL DIRECTOR: Pippa Rubinstein

The catalogue record for this book is available from the British Library

ISBN 1 85028 247 1

Printed in Spain

Over the years the Royal Albert Hall

concerts have become an essential part of

Eric Clapton's annual curriculum: *page 2*

1994 *page 5* 1989 *page 9* 1990

For Verushka, Aslan and Chyna

Contents

INTRODUCTION   8

1   From a Rooster To a Yardbird 10
TOUR DATES 1963-1966 25

2   Top of the Milk 30
TOUR DATES 1966-1968 50

3   Blind Faith, Derek and Friends 58
TOUR DATES 1968-1970 77

4   EC Was Here…Or Was He? 80
TOUR DATES 1971-1979 111

5 *Another Ticket, Another Ride*   118
TOUR DATES 1980-1984   131

6 *Plugged in: The Albert Hall Years*   136
TOUR DATES 1985-1994   167

7 *Moonlighting*   178

8 *The Bootlegs*   204

DISCOGRAPHY   214
INDEX   222
ACKNOWLEDGEMENTS   224

Introduction

This book represents a lifetime of collecting and traces the thirty-year-plus career of one of the most influential guitarists of our time.

Eric's guitar playing has always come from the heart rather than the head. There may be some who are faster or technically more proficient, but no one is more emotionally charged and fluid.

While everyone around him was smashing or burning guitars, he never resorted to gimmicks to put his music across and this may well go some way to explain his longevity. He has certainly survived mistakes and near death experiences to arrive in the 'nineties with his dignity still intact.

Yet, despite our long acquaintance with him, Eric Clapton remains an enigma. His total honesty in interview situations still fails to reveal the real inner man and very few people, if any, have got really close to him.

As a tribute to a great musician, this book offers a visual feast of Clapton memorabilia from his early days to the present, supplemented with rare and, in many cases, previously unpublished photographs. It is by no means complete, nor does it pretend to be. To do so would take up another two volumes! However, it does feature the rarest and most appealing of Eric's associated artifacts from around the world.

Most of the material can be tracked down at various collectors shops around the world, but be warned, some of it will cost you a small fortune!

Do not forget, though, that at the end of the day that it's the music that counts.

Marc Roberty, 1994

1 *From a Rooster To a Yardbird*

Eric Clapton was born in 1945 to an unmarried woman in the tiny village of Ripley, in the Surrey countryside. Unable to cope with rearing a child by herself in a rural community of the forties, his mother went abroad soon after he was born, leaving Eric to be raised as one of their own by his grandparents. His mother reappeared, to devastating effect, in time for his thirteenth birthday. 'I was raised by my grandparents under the illusion that they were my parents. But when my mum came back we had to go through this whole thing of pretending she was my sister. From the moment she came back they say I was moody and nasty and wouldn't try.' A difficult stage in anyone's development, Eric was to find the passage from boy to man tough, particularly because of his illegitimacy. 'Throughout my teens I was very confused, angry and lonely.'

Like millions of teenagers around the world in the late fifties Eric was to hear the echo of his alienation in the incendiary music that was burning up the charts for the first time. Rock 'n' roll was to provide the perfect outlet for his angst, but it wasn't until he heard the music of the legendary founding-father of the blues, Robert Johnson that Eric felt he had found a true soul mate. Johnson's background — the extreme poverty of the deep south — couldn't have contrasted more with Eric's comfortable Surrey upbringing, but the pain and sorrow expressed in Johnson's tunes connected instantaneously with this disturbed English teenager.

Eric had discovered the guitar, and his grandmother bought him his first guitar, an acoustic Hoya, for his thirteenth birthday. He mastered the instrument quickly, experimenting with different sounds that could be achieved in various rooms, and working everything out by ear. He poured

FACING PAGE The Yardbirds take a slowboat to success in 1963. From the back, left to right: Jim McCarty, Eric Clapton, Keith Relf. Front, left to right: Paul Samwell-Smith, Chris Dreja.

Early promo shot taken in Richmond Park, Surrey. Left to right: Eric Clapton, Jim McCarty, Chris Dreja, Paul Samwell-Smith, Keith Relf.

all his energies into music, with a particular emphasis on the blues.

He often recorded himself playing on his reel to reel, quarter inch Grundig Cub, and compared the results to the records he was attempting to reproduce. Even at this stage he was a perfectionist, and he would spend hours trying to get it right. However, he also enjoyed the more usual boyhood pastimes such as building model aircraft and using his air rifle in the garden. His school days were not particularly studious ones, but he was interested in art and won a number of competitions for his originality and attention to detail. He moved on from St Bedes Secondary Modern in Woking to Hollyfield Road School in Surbiton to study a basic design course with a view to going to Kingston Art College. His entry to art college was relatively easy. He had built up a large enough portfolio of his work to impress the entry panel sufficiently, and even though Eric did not have the necessary academic qualifications, they put him on a year's probation. However, he was by this time well and truly addicted to music, with a particular love of the blues, and consequently his mind was on playing his guitar and definitely not on his art studies.

His first exposure to live audiences came from busking and playing in the small pubs and clubs of local Surrey towns such as Kingston and Richmond. He played acoustic folk-blues numbers by, for example, Big Bill Broonzy and Ramblin' Jack Elliott. 'It was the beat scene then, so if you sat in a pub and played 'San Francisco Bay Blues' and stuff like that you'd get a sandwich and perhaps even somewhere to sleep for the night.'

Eric first heard the influential electric blues of Muddy Waters, Jimmy Reed and Bo Diddley in 1961 at the home of Mike Vernon. A true blues aficionado, Vernon was later to become a major force on the British blues scene of the sixties when he formed the legendary Blue Horizon record label. He held regular blues parties at his home, where a select number of blues purists would discuss the merits of each new record; picking out their favourite bits and trying to figure them out. It was during such a session that Eric decided he needed an electric guitar, and his grandmother once again willingly obliged and bought him a double cutaway Kay. He then joined fellow folk-blues guitarist Dave Brock and the duo played the local coffee bar circuit, occasionally venturing out as far as Fulham. 'We felt honoured to be members of this sort of club of people who just liked rhythm and blues records: for me the blues were very serious and I could only listen to them with people who were equally serious.'

Eric takes five in Hyde Park during a promotional shoot for The Yardbirds. Several other photos from the same session also survive.

Eric was still supposed to be studying at Kingston Art School, but his consuming passion for music left little time for art and soon resulted in expulsion. 'There was a test at the end of the year where you had to walk in with your folder and show them how much work you'd done, and I was the one with the least amount of work done.' Following his expulsion, Eric worked for a while as a manual labourer on building sites.

It was around this time, January 1963, that Eric was introduced to Tom McGuiness. Eric had known Tom's girlfriend at art school, and when Tom was looking for a guitarist to join his band, she suggested Eric. The Roosters, as they called themselves, also comprised Ben Palmer on piano, Robin Mason on drums and Terry Brennan on vocals, but no bass player. After a quick audition-come-rehearsal at The Prince of Wales pub in New Malden, Eric was offered a place in the band.

Together they learnt different R & B covers from various singles and albums in their individual collections, including numbers by B.B. King, John Lee Hooker, Larry Williams and Freddie King. Although never remotely successful, the Roosters were a valuable stage in the learning process for Eric. 'Tom brought in the 'Hideaway' single by Freddie King and the B side was 'I Love That Woman', which is still one of the greatest. And that's the first time I heard that electric lead-guitar style, with the bent notes; T-Bone Walker, B.B. King and Freddie King, that style of playing. Hearing that Freddie King single was what started me on my path.'

The Yardbirds play Britain's TV pop show, the prestigious *Ready Steady Go*. Left to right: Paul Samwell-Smith, Chris Dreja, Keith Relf, Eric Clapton.

The Roosters were a purist blues band for like-minded fanatics. However, there wasn't much demand for R & B, trad jazz was still very popular and venues were not too thrilled at the prospect of amplified instruments. What gigs they could get – and the Roosters would play anywhere for any fee including weddings – were often disastrous. Ben Palmer recalls one night when members of the audience menacingly brandished hangman's nooses at the band. Understandably, they soon became disillusioned and they disbanded in August 1963, although they remained friends.

But it *was* 1963, and the British music scene was about to explode with a force that was to send shock waves throughout the world. The fuse was lit in November when a group from Liverpool released their first single,

'Love Me Do'. The Beatles basic grasp of R & B, married to a fine-tuned Tin Pan Alley pop sensibility, heralded a new sound that had been nurtured over the past few years in small clubs up and down the country. Merseybeat took the nation, and then the world, by storm. It even picked Eric Clapton up in its wake for a while. He was hanging out at the Scene, a club in London's Soho, when he was approached by Ray Stock, the drummer of long-forgotten Merseybeat band, Casey Jones and the Engineers. The band, led by Brian Casser, needed two guitarists and although it wasn't much of a gig, Eric and Tom McGuinness decided to take the job. Eric's time as an Engineer was short lived, but he was grateful for the few weeks touring experience. 'It got my chops together,' he said, but the commercial nature of the band, including the wearing of matching uniforms and confederate caps, proved too much for him. 'It was a really heavy pop show, you know, and I couldn't stand that for very long.'

Meanwhile, over in the west of London, a man named Giorgio Gomelsky was writing himself into pop history as one of the pioneers of the early British blues scene. Gomelsky shrewdly foresaw the end of traditional jazz, and recognizing the potential of authentic blues music, had been promoting Sunday R & B sessions in a Richmond pub, the Station Hotel, since early 1963. Gomelsky re-named his venue the Crawdaddy Club, and transformed it into a landmark of Rock 'n' Roll in London. His first resident band was the Rolling Stones.

BELOW The Yardbirds's first single 'I Wish You Would' on EMI's Columbia label, released in November 1963.
BELOW RIGHT Sleeve that all The Yardbirds' and contemporary Columbia singles were released in.
BELOW LEFT Music press advert for their first single.

Left to right: Eric Clapton, Chris Dreja, Jim McCarty, Keith Relf, Paul Samwell-Smith. The Yardbirds turn mean and moody after noting the hideous orange backdrop.

Their high-octane blues and bad-boy image attracted a strong and loyal following, making them a very viable proposition. But, just as they were poised to follow the Beatles into the charts, the Stones were pinched from under Gomelsky's nose by a zoot-suited, nineteen-year-old hustler, Andrew Loog-Oldham. Gomelsky had only a verbal agreement to manage the Stones, and he was determined to find and own his next band completely.

A local Kingston group, the Yardbirds, was to be that band. The Yardbirds, formed in August 1963, originally comprised Keith Relf on vocals and harmonica, Jim McCarty on drums, Paul Samwell-Smith on bass, Chris Dreja on rhythm guitar and Anthony 'Top' Topham on lead guitar. Top, however, left them in October 1963 when he bowed to parental pressures to finish his education. Keith vaguely remembered Eric from

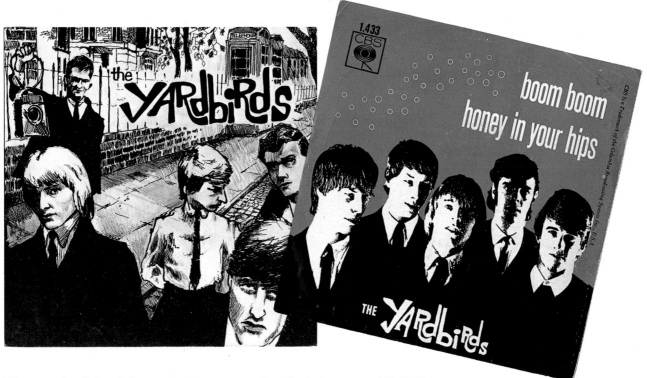

Kingston Art School days as having a reputation for being a good R & B player, so asked him to join the band for a rehearsal, during which he offered him the job as lead guitarist. Jim McCarty remembers Eric's confident appearance, 'he had all his style worked out, his clothes, his hair. We were quite relaxed about what we wore, but Eric was different. Wearing something was quite important to him.' Furthermore, he also 'seemed to have this aura about him, a certain magnetism,' added Jim.

Their early gigs were held at Ken Colyer's Studio 51 in Leicester Square, as well as in local venues, such as the Toby Jug in Surbiton. It was at one of these shows that Hamish Grimes, a partner in Giorgio's organization, saw them play and immediately recognized their potential as replacements for the departing Stones at the Crawdaddy. Giorgio signed the Yardbirds and took control of everything – gigs, recording, publishing and wages.

Eric was already into quality guitars by this time. He had given his prized Kay to Roger Pearce, a friend of Keith's and now owned some of the best guitars money could buy. These consisted of a Cherry Red Gibson ES335, a white Fender Telecaster and a Fender Jazzmaster, which enabled him to add various dimensions to his sound and growing reputation. Slowly, the Yardbirds built up a loyal following on the Crawdaddy circuit, both in Croydon at the Star on Saturday nights, and in Richmond at the Station Hotel on Sundays. Not an envious, nor indeed, an easy task after the Rolling Stones. It was at one of these early gigs that their first recordings were made. They were playing support to American bluesman Sonny Boy Williamson, as well as backing him. Both sets were recorded, but they weren't released till 1966. They backed Sonny Boy on a number of other occasions at various other gigs up and down the country. Eric remembers Sonny Boy's love of whisky as being a problem, and how one night he collapsed through the

ABOVE LEFT Rare Yardbirds bootleg single of 'Boom Boom' backed with 'Honey In Her Hips'. Both tracks taken from demo sessions at R.G. Jones Studios in Morden, Surrey.

ABOVE RIGHT This rare official Yardbirds single, featuring the same tracks as the bootleg (above left) was only released in the Netherlands.

The first Yardbirds album, FIVE LIVE YARDBIRDS, was recorded live at the Marquee in March 1964. Their raucous live set was memorably captured, without the benefit of digital technology, with the aid of a microphone suspended above the stage from a fishing rod.

curtain and lay in a heap as the spotlight hit him. But Eric acknowledged that he learnt a great deal from playing with the 'genuine article'.

Clearly, the next move was for the Yardbirds to secure a record contract, and to that end they recorded seven songs at R.G. Jones Studios in Morden. These were played to Decca and EMI and although both labels showed interest, Giorgio signed them to EMI. Soon after, they recorded their first single, 'I Wish You Would', and took up a Friday-night residency at London's Marquee Club. These 'rave-ups' became legendary for the intensity of the band's performance and the rabid reaction of the crowd, all of which is preserved on the band's debut album, FIVE LIVE YARDBIRDS. The album, now a widely acknowledged classic, captures brilliantly the raw excitement of the early 1960s British blues clubs.

The Yardbirds had a good year in 1964, and established themselves in the forefront of the British scene. They toured all over England; made their first TV appearances; played at the National Jazz and Blues Festival in Richmond; and were featured in influential music papers such as *Melody Maker* and *New Musical Express*. The Yardbirds had joined pop's elite, and all seemed to be going well for them, but Eric was beginning to feel disenchanted. He felt that certain members of the band were prepared to sacrifice musical integrity in exchange for popularity. 'When the Stones came out of all that whole scene, it sparked ambition in some members of the band. The Stones were getting on big package tours, they were on TV, they got a Chuck Berry song on to the charts. And some of the Yardbirds and Giorgio began to see a future in being internationally famous. I couldn't see what was so wonderful about competing with the Liverpool sound and all that, trying to jump on the bandwagon.' Eric felt the call of his roots. 'There was still a great part of me that was very much the blues purist, thinking, "Music is this, it's not that".'

Paul Samwell-Smith, the group's official musical director, was particularly influential in steering the Yardbirds towards a more commercial sound. They were offered a Graham Gouldman song called 'For Your Love' to record as their next single. As Eric recalls, 'Giorgio came up with a number by Otis Redding. I thought it would make a great single because it was still R & B and soul, and we could do it really funky.' But, much to Eric's chagrin, things did not go as planned. 'Paul got the 'For Your Love' demo, and he heard it with harpsichord! Where does that leave me? Twelve-string guitar I suppose.' It basically boiled down to the fact that Eric either had to do what Paul Samwell-Smith said, or leave the band.

Therefore, it was no great surprise when, in March 1965, Eric announced his departure. He helped establish the Yardbirds as one of the seminal bands of the period and left a legacy of superb guitar solos (though

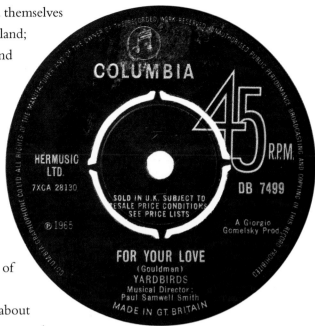

ABOVE 'For Your Love', Eric's final single with The Yardbirds, which reached number three in the UK charts and stayed in the top forty for twelve weeks. By the time it was released in February 1965, Eric had left the group to explore less commercial sounds.

BELOW LEFT THE SHAPES OF THINGS, a four CD compilation set, which is now deleted.
BELOW RIGHT Another cover to another anthology. Just one among many.

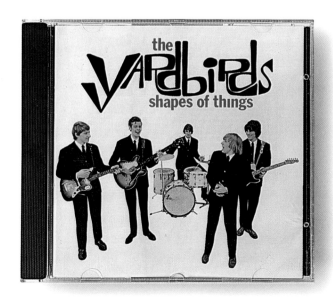

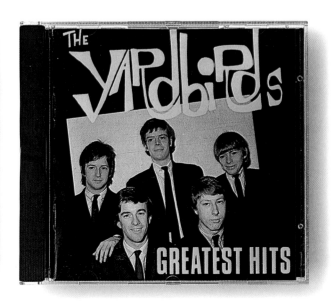

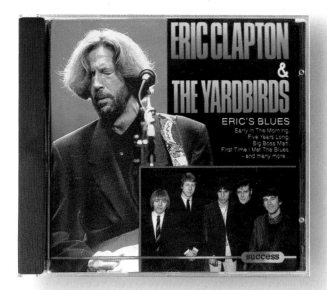

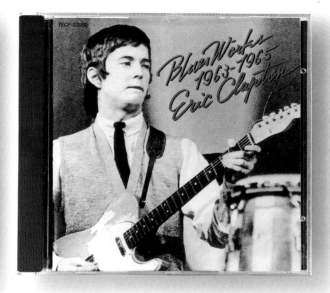

ABOVE LEFT ERIC CLAPTON & THE YARDBIRDS, another compilation of the old tunes, this one with a photo taken in 1990.

ABOVE RIGHT A Japan-only release, THE BLUES WORKS 1963-1965, gathered Eric's early Yardbirds material together with some blues he recorded for the Immediate label.

ABOVE A rare double US Yardbirds compilation album, simply called THE YARDBIRDS on the Epic label. It features all three of their famous guitarists, Eric Clapton, Jimmy Page and Jeff Beck.

they were largely relegated to B sides of their singles). The B side of 'For Your Love' featured his first composition entitled 'Got To Hurry'. This scorching instrumental was the perfect swan song; its blistering solo hinting at what was to come.

In the days that followed his departure, without any clear idea of what he was going to do next, Eric began to doubt his abilities. 'I was all screwed up about my playing. I decided that I was not playing well and was really brought down. Playing with the Yardbirds had put me in a very strange frame of mind. I had lost a lot of my original values.'

Eric spent some time with Ben Palmer, his friend from the days of the Roosters, in Oxford. They talked about the possibility of doing a blues album together, but Ben wanted to concentrate on his woodcraft. John Mayall, in the meantime, having read of Eric's departure from the Yardbirds, was trying to track him down for an audition with his Bluesbreakers. By April 1965, only a month after he left the Yardbirds, Eric had joined another major British band, the Bluesbreakers. As John recalls, 'He didn't take much persuading, he was a blues player and I ran a blues band.'

When Eric first went to John's house, he walked into an Aladdin's Cave of blues records. Here were records by blues giants, such as Freddie King, Otis Rush and Buddy Guy, playing with real fire. These records were an inspiration to Eric and helped him develop a new sound. 'They sounded like they were really on the edge, like they were barely in control, that at any time they could hit a really bad note and the whole thing would fall apart – but of course, they didn't.' Eric's new style was also due, in part, to his decision to swap the Fender Telecaster and 30 watt Vox amp, which he had used in the Yardbirds, for a Gibson Les Paul and 50 watt Marshall, the traditional arsenal of any dedicated follower of the British blues boom. Eric made this change after spotting a Les Paul guitar on the cover of a Freddie King album.

Eric became a key figure in the band as soon as he joined, choosing material for them to do. Both the Bluesbreakers and Eric's reputations flourished rapidly on the club circuit; and their storming sets at London's Flamingo attracted their contemporaries in droves. John recorded one of

The Yardbirds make a corn circle in Richmond Park, Surrey. Left to right: Paul Samwell-Smith, Keith Relf, Jim McCarty, Eric Clapton, Chris Dreja.

The seminal British Blues album of the sixties, JOHN MAYALL'S BLUESBREAKERS WITH ERIC CLAPTON was released in July 1966 to great critical acclaim. It reached number six in the UK album charts and had a chart presence for seventeen weeks. Many feel Eric has yet to surpass his guitar playing on this album, so they still regard it as the pinnacle of his career. The cover is equally infamous for featuring Eric reading the classic British comic, The Beano.

these shows on his own two-track reel-to-reel recorder and was eventually released in the early eighties as PRIMAL SOLOS. Although primitive sounding by today's digital standards, it is, nevertheless, an exciting document from the height of the British blues scene in the mid sixties.

By August 1965, Eric already felt that the job with Mayall had become a job, and he wanted to go and have some fun. The fun in question was a madcap adventure involving Eric and a few friends travelling to Australia over land and paying their way by playing songs. They dubbed themselves the Glands and made it as far as Greece where they were taken on at a nightspot called the Igloo as support for a local Greek band, who played cover versions of songs by the Beatles and Rolling Stones. The Glands played in the interval while the headliners were taking a break.

Fate took a turn for the worst when members of the local group were involved in a fatal car crash. Eric was called in by the club's manager as a replacement, but soon saw the futility of such eccentricities. However, leaving was to prove difficult. The autocratic Greek club owner realized he had an ex-Yardbird working for him and was not prepared to let him go and, to prevent him from doing so, he held his guitar under lock and key. Finally, Eric used the excuse that he needed new strings for his guitar and left his amp with the manager as collateral. Ben Palmer was waiting outside in the car and together they headed to Athens and then home to England. The others carried on with their adventure, but Eric and Ben were only too happy to make their way home.

John Mayall, realizing what he was losing, was prepared to give Eric some leeway during his escapade and kept Eric's 'job' open for him. Eric did go back, but things were not the same on his return: 'When I got back with Mayall, Jack Bruce was on bass, and we hit it off really well.' The experience was to be short-lived though as Jack left to go with Manfred Mann, and Mayall got John McVie back. But even in the short time Eric played with Jack Bruce, he realized that 'there was something creative there'. He was stimulated by his improvisatory style; it stood in strong contrast to the bland copying of various blues musicians and records that the rest of the band had been doing. In Jack, he saw a like-minded musician.

The seeds of doubt, which had been planted in Eric's mind about his future, were still growing. But in the meantime, the band embarked on a heavy schedule of live concerts and recording sessions. By March 1966 Eric

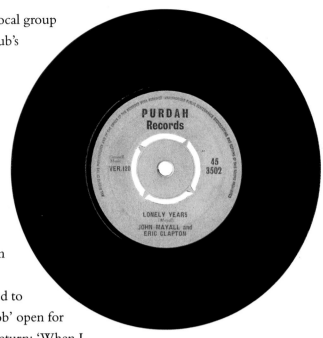

ABOVE John Mayall and Eric Clapton's first recording for Mike Vernon's Purdah label. Only 500 copies were pressed.
BELOW Two seventies compilations of sixties material documenting Eric's involvement with such Decca artists as John Mayall, Champion Jack Dupree and Otis Spann. Both were withdrawn because the cover photographs implied they were contemporary recordings.

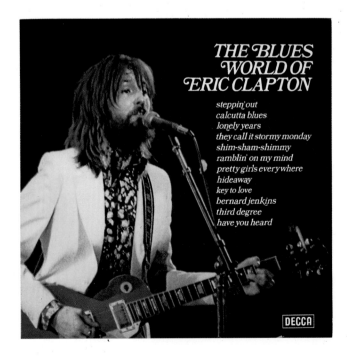

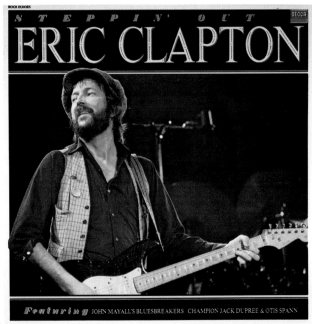

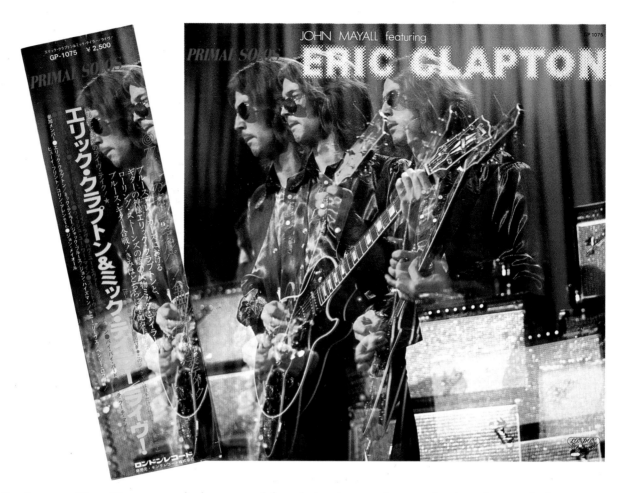

ABOVE Rare Japanese edition of the wonderful PRIMAL SOLOS album with a slip sleeve. This release features a side's worth of live material recorded at The Flamingo in London with John Mayall in 1966. The cover photo of Eric was taken during a Delaney and Bonnie concert 1969 and features Eric playing a Gibson Les Paul.

had progressed from being just another good guitar player to being a great one. This new status was acknowledged by John Mayall when he gave Eric top billing on the next Bluesbreakers' album, something John had never done before, or for that matter since. The album, called BLUESBREAKERS FEATURING ERIC CLAPTON is a classic of its time, with Eric's playing still hailed as a major influence by many guitarists today. The album also marked the beginning of the media-hype surrounding Eric, which was eventually to build to such intolerable levels, particularly during his time with Cream. Eric Clapton was no longer an unknown from the Surrey countryside, but 'God' according to his growing legion of fans. Eric, however, views the album rather modestly, 'it's just a record of what we were doing every night in the clubs with a few contrived riffs we made up kind of as afterthoughts to fill out some of the things. It isn't any great achievement.'

Before leaving the Bluesbreakers, Eric recorded his first vocal on the album RAMBLING ON MY MIND. John liked Eric's singing, which gave him more confidence, but as John points out, Eric was extremely shy when it came to singing. 'He didn't want anybody in the room, so it was one that we did as a separate session after the others had gone home.'

By May 1966, Eric was feeling trapped and frustrated; he wanted a new outlet for his creative force. So when Graham Bond Organisation's drummer, Ginger Baker, approached him about starting a new band, Eric was more than a little interested.

THE YARDBIRDS CLUB TOUR

The Yardbirds were:

Eric Clapton (guitar), Keith Relf (vocals, harmonica), Jim McCarty (drums), Paul Samwell-Smith (bass), Chris Dreja (guitar).

The set list was taken from:

'Boom Boom', 'Louise', 'Smokestack Lightning', 'Honey In Your Hips', 'Baby What's Wrong', 'Carol', 'I Wish You Would', 'Let It Rock', 'You Can't Judge A Book By The Cover', 'Who Do You Love', 'Little Queenie', 'I'm A Man'.

SEPTEMBER 1963

20, 27, 29

  Studio 51, Leicester Square, London

OCTOBER 1963

4, 6, 13	Studio 51, Leicester Square, London
20	Studio 51, Leicester Square, London (4.00–6.30pm)
20	Crawdaddy Club, Richmond, Surrey (7.45pm)
27	Crawdaddy Club, Richmond, Surrey

NOVEMBER 1963

2	Star Club, Croydon, Surrey
3	Crawdaddy Club, Richmond, Surrey
8	Edwina's Club, Finsbury Park, London
9	Star Club, Croydon, Surrey
10	Crawdaddy Club, Richmond, Surrey
15	Edwina's Club, Finsbury Park, London
16	Star Club, Croydon, Surrey
17	Crawdaddy Club, Richmond, Surrey
20	Ricky Tick, Windsor, Berkshire
22	Edwina's Club, Finsbury Park, London
23	Star Club, Croydon, Surrey
24	Crawdaddy Club, Richmond, Surrey
29	Edwina's Club, Finsbury Park, London
30	Star Club, Croydon, Surrey

DECEMBER 1963

1	Crawdaddy Club, Richmond, Surrey
6	Edwina's Club, Finsbury Park, London
7	Star Club, Croydon, Surrey
8	Crawdaddy Club, Richmond, Surrey
	Live recording of the Sonny Boy Williamson And The Yardbirds album
13	Edwina's Club, Finsbury Park, London
14	Star Club, Croydon, Surrey
15	Civic Hall, Guildford, Surrey
17	Ricky Tick, Windsor, Berkshire
20	Plaza Ballroom, Guildford, Surrey
21–22	Star Club, Croydon, Surrey
23	Olympia Ballroom, Reading, Berkshire
24	Ricky Tick, Windsor, Berkshire
28	Star Club, Croydon, Surrey
29	Crawdaddy Club, Richmond, Surrey

JANUARY 1964

3	Marquee Club, London
4	Star Club, Croydon, Surrey
5	Crawdaddy Club, Richmond, Surrey
10	Marquee Club, London
11	Star Club, Croydon, Surrey
12	Crawdaddy Club, Richmond, Surrey
14	Ricky Tick, Windsor, Berkshire
17	Plaza Ballroom, Guildford, Surrey
18	Star Club, Croydon, Surrey
19	Crawdaddy Club, Richmond, Surrey
20	Toby Jug Hotel, Tolworth, Surrey
21	Ricky Tick, Windsor, Berkshire
23–24	Marquee Club, London
25	Star Club, Croydon, Surrey
26	Crawdaddy Club, Richmond, Surrey
27	Toby Jug Hotel, Tolworth, Surrey
28	The Flamingo, London
30	Marquee Club, London
31	St John's Ambulance Hall, Reading, Berkshire

FEBRUARY 1964

1	Pearce Hall, Maidenhead, Berkshire
2	Crawdaddy Club, Richmond, Surrey
4	Plaza Ballroom, Guildford, Surrey
6	Marquee Club, London
8	Pearce Hall, Maidenhead, Berkshire
9	Crawdaddy Club, Richmond, Surrey
11	Coronation Hall, Kingston, Surrey
13	Marquee Club, London
15	Star Hotel, Croydon, Surrey
16	Crawdaddy Club, Richmond, Surrey
18	Plaza Ballroom, Guildford, Surrey
20	Marquee Club, London
22	Pearce Hall, Maidenhead, Berkshire
23	Crawdaddy Club, Richmond, Surrey
25	Coronation Hall, Kingston, Surrey
27	Marquee Club, London
28	Town Hall, Birmingham, Midlands
	First Rhythm and Blues Festival. Live recording.

The set list was taken from:

'Too Much Monkey Business', 'Got Love If You Want It', 'Smokestack Lightning', 'Good Morning Little Schoolgirl', 'Respectable', 'Five Long Years', 'Pretty Girl', 'Louise', 'I'm A Man', 'Here Tis", 'I Wish You Would', 'Little Queenie', 'Carol', 'Boom Boom', 'I Ain't Got You'.

MARCH 1964

1	Crawdaddy Club, Richmond, Surrey
3	Coronation Hall, Kingston, Surrey
5	Marquee Club, London

6	Telephone House, Wimbledon, London
7	Pearce Hall, Maidenhead, Berkshire
8	Crawdaddy Club, Richmond, Surrey
13	Marquee Club, London
14	Star Club, Croydon, Surrey
15	Crawdaddy Club, Richmond, Surrey
20	Marquee Club, London
21	Star Club, Croydon, Surrey
22	Crawdaddy Club, Richmond, Surrey
27	Marquee Club, London
28	Star Club, Croydon, Surrey
29	Crawdaddy Club, Richmond, Surrey

APRIL 1964

3	Marquee Club, London
4	St Peter's Hall, Kingston, Surrey
5	Crawdaddy Club, Richmond, Surrey
7	The Refectory, Golders Green, London
10	Marquee Club, London
11	Star Club, Croydon, Surrey
12	Crawdaddy Club, Richmond, Surrey
17	Marquee Club, London
18	Star Club, Croydon, Surrey
19	Crawdaddy Club, Richmond, Surrey
21	Star Club, Croydon, Surrey
24	Marquee Club, London
25	Town Hall Ballroom, Abergavenny, Wales
26	Crawdaddy Club, Richmond, Surrey
27	The Manor House, Harringay, London
28	Star Club, Croydon, Surrey

MAY 1964

1	Marquee Club, London
3	Crawdaddy Club, Richmond, Surrey
4	Bromel Club, Bromley Court Hotel, Bromley, Kent
4	Decca Studios, West Hampstead, London.
	Eric plays his first studio session as a guest musician on two
	tracks for Otis Spann, 'Pretty Girls Everywhere' and 'Stirs Me Up'.
8	Marquee Club, London
10	Crawdaddy Club, Richmond, Surrey
13	Bromel Club, Bromley Court Hotel, Bromley, Kent
15	Marquee Club, London
17	Crawdaddy Club, Richmond, Surrey
22	*Ready Steady Go* television appearance
	They performed 'I Wish You Would'.
22	Marquee Club, London
24	Crawdaddy Club, Richmond, Surrey
27	Beckenham Ballroom, Beckenham, Kent
29	Marquee Club, London
31	Crawdaddy Club, Richmond, Surrey

JUNE 1964

5	Marquee Club, London
7	Crawdaddy Club, Richmond, Surrey
11	Brighton Dome, Brighton, Sussex
12	Marquee Club, London
13	Club Noriek, London (*all-nighter*)
14	Wimbledon Palais, Wimbledon, London
19	Marquee Club, London
20	Jazz Festival, Osterley Rugby Club, Middlesex
21	Crawdaddy Club, Richmond, Surrey
26	Northern Jazz Festival, Redcar, Cleveland
28	Crawdaddy Club, Richmond, Surrey

JULY 1964

3	Marquee Club, London
5	The Cavern, Liverpool
10, 17	Marquee Club, London
18	2nd Scottish Jazz & Blues Festival, Ayr, Scotland
19-23	Lugano Hotel, Switzerland
24	Marquee Club, London
26	Crawdaddy Club, Richmond, Surrey
29	Bromel Club, Bromley Court Hotel, Bromley, Kent
31	Marquee Club, London

AUGUST 1964

2	Crawdaddy Club, Richmond, Surrey
4	(*venue unknown*), Kenton, Middlesex
7	Marquee Club, London
9	Fourth Jazz and Blues Festival, Richmond, Surrey
	Mick O'Neill on vocals and at the end of the set they are
	joined by Georgie Fame, Ginger Baker and Graham Bond for
	a jam session.

SEPTEMBER 1964

4	Marquee Club, London
6	Crawdaddy Club, Richmond, Surrey
11	Marquee Club, London
13	Crawdaddy Club, Richmond, Surrey
18	Granada Theatre, Walthamstow, London

YARDBIRDS PACKAGE TOUR

*Package tour for The Yardbirds, which featured Billy J. Kramer
and the Nashville Teens*

19	Colston Hall, Bristol
20	Odeon Theatre, Lewisham
21	Granada Theatre, Maidstone
22	Granada Theatre, Greenford
23	Gaumont Theatre, Ipswich
24	Odeon Theatre, Southend
25	ABC Theatre, Northampton
26	Granada Theatre, Mansfield
27	Empire Theatre, Liverpool
28	Caird Hall, Dundee
29	ABC Theatre, Edinburgh
30	Odeon Theatre, Glasgow

OCTOBER 1964

1	ABC Theatre, Dublin
2	Adelphi Theatre, Belfast
3	Savoy Theatre, Cork
4	ABC Theatre, Stockton
7	ABC Theatre, Carlisle
8	Odeon Theatre, Bolton
9	Granada Theatre, Grantham
10	ABC Theatre, Hull
11	Granada Theatre, East Ham
13	Granada Theatre, Bedford
14	Granada Theatre, Brixton
15	Odeon Theatre, Guildford
16	ABC Theatre, Southampton
17	ABC Theatre, Gloucester
18	Granada Theatre, Tooting

BELOW Pop star Clapton changes the colour of his hair and proudly clutches a red Fender Telecaster. Left to right: Paul Samwell-Smith, Chris Dreja, Keith Relf, Jim McCarty, Eric Clapton.

THE YARD BIRDS

THE YARDBIRDS CLUB TOUR

23	Marquee Club, London
25	Crawdaddy Club, Richmond, Surrey
26	Glenlyn Club, Forest Hill, London
30	Marquee Club, London

NOVEMBER 1964

1	Crawdaddy Club, Richmond, Surrey
6	Hippodrome, Brighton, Sussex
	With Jerry Lee Lewis and Twinkle
8	Crawdaddy Club, Richmond, Surrey
	The remainder of the month and early December is spent on another package tour

DECEMBER 1964

7	Royal Albert Hall, London
10	Olympia Ballroom, Reading, Berkshire
12	Palais, Peterborough, Cambridgeshire
13	Sheffield (*venue unknown*), S. Yorkshire
14	Grand Pavilion, Porthcawl, Wales
17	Lakeside Ballroom, Hendon, Middlesex
18	(*venue unknown*), Gravesend, Kent
21	Fairfield Hall, Croydon, Surrey

The Yardbirds are on the bill for 'The Beatles Christmas Show' at London's Hammersmith Odeon Cinema. Other acts include Freddie and the Dreamers, Jimmy Saville, Sounds Incorporated, Elkie Brooks. They play 20 concerts with 38 performances in total! The Yardbirds played their regular Sunday evenings at the Crawdaddy in Richmond.

24	Odeon Cinema, Hammersmith, London
26	Odeon Cinema, Hammersmith, London
	(*2 shows at 6.15pm and 8.45pm*)
27	Crawdaddy Club, Richmond, Surrey
28	Odeon Cinema, Hammersmith, London
	(*2 shows at 6.15pm and 8.45pm*)
29	Odeon Cinema, Hammersmith, London
30–31	Odeon Cinema, Hammersmith, London
	(*2 shows at 6.15pm and 8.45pm*)

JANUARY 1965

1–2	Odeon Cinema, Hammersmith, London
	(*2 shows at 6.15pm and 8.45pm*)
3	Crawdaddy Club, Richmond, Surrey
4–9	Odeon Cinema, Hammersmith, London
	(*2 shows at 6.15pm and 8.45pm*)
10	Crawdaddy Club, Richmond, Surrey
11–16	Odeon Cinema, Hammersmith, London
	(*2 shows at 6.15pm and 8.45pm*)
17	Crawdaddy Club, Richmond, Surrey
20	Bromel Club, Bromley Court Hotel, Bromley, Kent
22	Marquee Club, London

FEBRUARY 1965

1, 15	Marquee Club, London
28	Crawdaddy Club, Richmond, Surrey

MARCH 1965

1, 8	Marquee Club, London
8	Marquee Club, London
	This was probably Eric's last show with The Yardbirds

JOHN MAYALL'S BLUESBREAKERS CLUB TOUR

John Mayall's Bluesbreakers were:
Eric Clapton (guitar), John Mayall (guitar, keyboards, vocals, harmonica), John McVie (bass), Hughie Flint (drums).

The set list was taken from:
'Crawling Up A Hill', 'Bye Bye Bird', 'Crocodile Walk', 'Stormy Monday', 'Steppin Out', 'Hideaway', 'On Top Of The World', 'Key To Love', 'Have You Ever Loved A Woman', 'Hoochie Coochie Man', 'It Hurts To Be In Love', 'Maudie'.

APRIL 1965

24	BBC Studios, London
	First recording with Eric. They play 'Crawling Up A Hill', 'Crocodile Walk' and 'Bye Bye Bird'
28	Flamingo Club, Soho, London

MAY 1965

12	Levy's Recording Studio, Bond Street, London.
	Eric, John Mayall, John McVie and Hughie Flint join Bob Dylan for some informal jamming.
15	Flamingo Club, Soho, London (*all-nighter*)
21–22	Flamingo Club, Soho, London
25	Klooks Kleek, Hampstead, London

JUNE 1965

3	Cellar Club, Kingston, Surrey
4–6	Flamingo Club, Soho, London
10	Klooks Kleek, Hampstead, London
18	Pontiac Club, Zeeta House, Putney, London
19	Uxbridge Blues & Folk Festival, Uxbridge, Middlesex

JULY 1965

7	Bromel Club, Bromley Court Hotel, Bromley, Kent
8	Klooks Kleek, Hampstead, London
9–10	Flamingo Club, Soho, London
15	College Of Fashion, London
16	Ricky Tick, Windsor, Berkshire (*8.00pm*) and
16	Flamingo Club, Soho, London (*all-nighter*)
24	Pontiac Club, Zeeta House, Putney, London
29	Klooks Kleek, Hampstead, London
30	Bluesville Club, Harringay, London

AUGUST 1965

4, 11, 25

Pontiac Club, Zeeta House, Putney, London

SEPTEMBER 1965

The Glands play at The Igloo an Athens night-club restaurant for most of the month.

JOHN MAYALL'S BLUESBREAKERS CLUB TOUR
NOVEMBER 1965

11	Pontiac Club, Zeeta House, Putney, London
12	Bluesville, Manor House, London
28	Flamingo Club, Soho, London

DECEMBER 1965

23	Refectory, Golders Green, London
26	Flamingo Club, Soho, London
28	Bluesville Club, Harringay, London
31	Bluesville, Manor House, London

JANUARY 1966

1	Flamingo Club, Soho, London
16	Bromel Club, Bromley Court Hotel, Bromley, Kent
17	Star Club, Croydon, Surrey

FEBRUARY 1966

5	Polytechnic Of Central London, London
6	Woolwich R&B Club, Shakespeare Hotel, London
8	Klooks Kleek, Hampstead, London
12	Polytechnic Of Central London, London
15	Fishmongers Arms, Wood Green, London
18	Bluesville, Manor House, London
19	Flamingo Club, Soho, London
27	Bromel Club, Bromley Court Hotel, Bromley, Kent

MARCH 1966

4, 17	Flamingo Club, Soho, London
	Live recording taken on 17th.
18	Ram Jam Club, Brixton, London
18	Flamingo Club, Soho, London *(all-nighter)*
19	BBC Studios, London
	Live session for radio broadcast. Numbers played are 'Little Girl', 'Hideaway', 'Steppin' Out', 'On Top Of The World', 'Key To Love'.
20	Eel Pie Island, Twickenham, Middlesex
26	Flamingo Club, Soho, London

APRIL 1966

6	Bluesville, Manor House, London
11	Marquee Club. Soho, London
22	Refectory, Golders Green, London
24	Bromel Club, Bromley Court Hotel, Bromley, Kent
27	Castle Club, Tooting Broadway, London
30	Flamingo Club, Soho, London

MAY 1966

7	Ram Jam Club, Brixton, London
9	Klooks Kleek, Hampstead, London
10	Star Hotel, Croydon, Surrey
14	Toft's Club, Folkestone, Kent
17	Fishmongers Arms, Wood Green, London
21	Ricky Tick, Windsor, Berkshire
22	Flamingo Club, Soho, London
27	The Refectory, Golders Green, London
30	Marquee Club, Soho, London

JUNE 1966

3	Flamingo Club, Soho, London
5	Bromel Club, Bromley Court Hotel, Bromley, Kent
10	Ram Jam Club, Brixton, London
16	Marquee Club, Soho, London
23	Fishmongers Arms, Wood Green, London
25	Flamingo Club, Soho, London

2 *Top of the Milk*

ric was excited at the prospect of being involved in a new band with new ideas. The only condition was that it should include Jack Bruce on bass. 'It was strange, telepathic really. I used to think what it would be like to have the ideal group while I was with John Mayall and feeling frustrated and eager to get out on my own. My ideal group was Ginger and Jack. I had played with Jack and knew how good he was, and I used to see Ginger a lot and knew Ginger was perfect. When he said to me how about forming a group I just said "yes, what about Jack Bruce"?'

Eric wasn't aware of any animosity between Ginger and Jack, but soon realized that they 'were chemically opposite, they were just polarized, always getting into fights.' They talked through their problems for the sake of the band, but the results were cosmetic more than anything else. In the meantime, the music press were quick to label the nascent band a 'supergroup'. According to Jack, 'Eric thought of the name Cream. It sounded like a good name, sounded arrogant, names like that were trendy at the time. It seemed good.'

Eric gave John Mayall two weeks notice. John was obviously disappointed, 'Eric was easily the best musician I ever worked with. Quite remarkable.' But he quickly saw that trying to talk Eric round was pointless.

Robert Stigwood, The Graham Bond Organisation's former manager and owner of the Reaction record label, became Cream's manager at Ginger's suggestion, partly because no one could think of anyone else. Rehearsals initially took place at Ginger's home in Neasden before moving to a scout hall in Willesden where, incidentally, Eric's treasured Les Paul was stolen. Their pot-pourri of musical tastes and influences formed the initial

FACING PAGE Cream take a break. Left to right: Ginger Baker, Eric Clapton, Jack Bruce.

FACING PAGE Two of the earliest Cream promotional photographs taken shortly before their first concert at Manchester's Twisted Wheel in July 1966. It is interesting to note that at this stage they were prepared to wear the silly costumes normally associated with pop groups.

basis of those first rehearsals. They hit it off musically right from the word go, and with a combined energy that Robert Stigwood knew was going to blow the whole world away. Ginger still enthuses about those early rehearsals, 'the first time we got together in Neasden was beautiful, unbelievable. It was just so right we knew that was it!' Jack was writing material for the band with lyricist and poet, Pete Brown. Ginger was also writing, but Eric felt more comfortable, at first, in offering country-blues based songs by people such as Son House, Skip James and Robert Johnson.

After a warm-up gig in Manchester, Cream played their first major gig at the 6th National Jazz and Blues Festival in Windsor on 31 July 1966. They didn't, however, record together until September/October time, when they produced a single, 'Wrapping Paper' and an album, FRESH CREAM. While the single spent six weeks in the charts it only ever rose as high as 34, but the album spent over four months in the top forty, peaking at number six. Buoyed by constant touring on the British blues circuit and appearances on the UK's first TV pop show, *Ready Steady Go*, as well as

Eric in meditative mood captured at the Windsor Jazz and Blues Festival. Lovely jacket! Their second live performance took place on 31 July 1966. The trio followed Georgie Fame and the Blue Flames to play a forty minute set.

frequent live sessions, Cream were established as the band to watch.

They were the right group at the right time. Inspired by the sounds coming out of the west coast of America; the increasing availability of mind-expanding psychedelic drugs; and the emergence of a new god – the guitar hero – pop was turning into rock and Cream was well placed to take full advantage. In December 1966 they released their first classic single, 'I Feel Free'. A gorgeous rush of sound it was the first indication of the acid-tinged direction Cream would take with their next album, DISRAELI GEARS.

Sessions for DISRAELI GEARS were held at the legendary Atlantic Studios, New York where artists, such as Otis Redding, Aretha Franklin and Ray Charles, had redefined the meaning of soul. Like many white boys before, and since, this was a journey to the promised land for Eric. To be

reaction

RF

MADE IN ENGLAND

Dratleaf

591007A

℗ 1966

M 45

591007

WRAPPING PAPER
(Bruce/Brown)
CREAM
A Robert Stigwood Production

TOP LEFT Cream's first single 'Wrapping Paper' on the Reaction label. The single spent six week in the UK charts, but only ever reached as high as number thirty four.
LEFT Music press advert for that all-important first single, 'Wrapping Paper'.
BELOW Cream's second single, 'I Feel Free', was their first acknowledged classic. Released in December 1966 it spent twelve weeks in the charts, rising to number eleven.
BOTTOM Music press advert for 'I Feel Free'.

Cream
recording
"WRAPPING PAPER"
reaction 591·007

Managed & distributed by Polydor Records for the Robert Stigwood Organisation Ltd

reaction

RF

MADE IN ENGLAND

Dratleaf

591011 A

℗ 1966

M 45

591011

I FEEL FREE
(Bruce/Brown)
CREAM
A Robert Stigwood
Production

THE **CREAM'S L.P.** IS RELEASED ON DECEMBER 9TH. TH[E TIT]LE IS **'FRESH CREAM'**
THEIR SECOND SINGLE IS ALSO RELEASED ON THE SAM[E D]AY- IT IS CALLED **'I FEEL FREE'**
THE FLIP: **'N.S.U.'** - BOTH ON

reaction

SINGLE: 591 011 / THE L.P.: 593 001 (MONO) & 594 001 (STEREO)

MANAGED & DISTRIBUTED BY POLYDOR RECORDS LTD. FOR THE ROBERT STIGWOOD ORGANISATION.

ABOVE Sleeve for Cream's first album FRESH CREAM with the lads all wearing Second World War flying gear. Recorded at Chalk Farm Studios and Mayfair Studios in London between July and September 1966 it was released in December 1966. FRESH CREAM was in the UK album charts for seventeen weeks peaking at number six, and was mainly promoted on the British club circuit.

LEFT A sought-after French Cream EP, featuring a guitar solo on 'Cat's Squirrel' which is exclusive to this release.

BELOW European sleeve for FRESH CREAM reissue on the RSO label.

BELOW Extremely rare acetates which can now fetch prices as high as $200.00 each. Left to right: 'I'm So Glad', '4 Till Late', 'Sweet Wine', 'Wrapping Paper'.

Cream at the Starlite Ballroom, Greenford on 4 December 1966 during one of their almost nightly club shows. Left to right: Jack Bruce, Ginger Baker, Eric Clapton.

standing in the same building was a thrill in itself, but to actually record there was like a dream come true. The sessions went brilliantly and were superbly produced by Felix Pappalardi and engineered by Tom Dowd. According to Tom, 'they were incredible. I never saw anything so powerful in my life. It was frightening, they recorded at ear-shattering level.'

DISRAELI GEARS was released in November 1967 to confirm Cream's position as one of the biggest and most important bands of the time. The album stayed in the British charts for a Beatlesque forty-two weeks, and made a similarly large dent in the United States. In hindsight, DISRAELI GEARS can be seen as the result of a host of disparate influences on the band. Part of its intensity may be due to the fact that, just prior to recording, Cream took part in the *Murray the K Show* alongside The Who and the Lovin' Spoonful. According to Eric's friend, Ben Palmer, who became Cream's road manager, 'It was a big bill, a lot of acts, and it was supposed to be five shows a day. I think the first curtain was at ten o'clock in the morning – the kids were on holiday – and the last show would go on not far

short of midnight.' Sadly, since the shows weren't broadcast, Cream did not really get much exposure from them.

DISRAELI GEARS eclectic mix of blues, pop and psychedelia has now been acknowledged as one of the first albums in a new genre, heavy metal. It successfully captured Cream's live sound and reflects the advances that were being made in the recording studios. But, at the time, DISRAELI GEARS received only a lukewarm reception from the press, who criticized the band for straying from their blues roots.

Although DISRAELI GEARS came out within the same year as the Beatles' SERGEANT PEPPER, THEIR SATANIC MAJESTIES by the Rolling Stones and the Doors' first album, Cream were expected to tread the same purist path they always had. The guitar playing was a particular target for barbs, but Eric just shrugged, 'I can't play anything else, you know. So everything I play is blues structurally.' A comment that stands true to this day; whatever music Clapton has played over the years, you can be certain that his solos are based on the blues. Perhaps the critics were just too slow to

Jack and Eric share a mike on *Ready Steady Go* for a performance of 'I Feel Free'. Left to right, Jack Bruce, Eric Clapton, Ginger Baker

ABOVE Cream's second album, DISRAELI
GEARS, was released in November 1967
with a distinctive psychedelic cover
designed by Martin Sharp. Considered by
many to be Cream's best and most
consistent album, as reflected by its massive
forty-two week stint in the UK charts.

RIGHT The back of the sleeve for DISRAELI
GEARS features a collage of photos taken in
Kings Road, Chelsea as well as Ben Nevis in
Scotland.

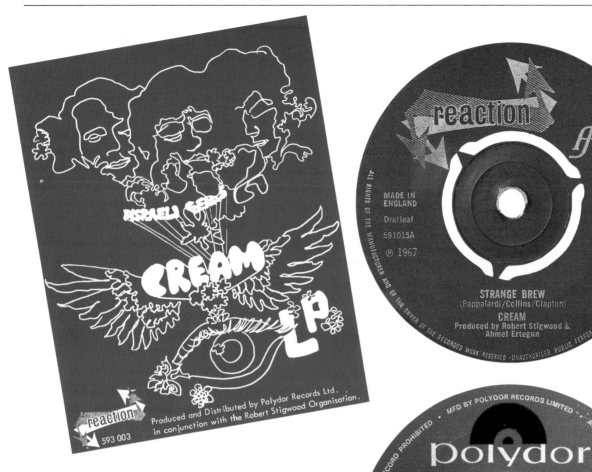

recognize that the straightforward R & B that had characterized pop for the first half of the sixties, was now evolving into something new.

Inevitably, Cream were influenced by the thriving scene in Greenwich Village, New York. Eric jammed with longtime hero B.B. King and saw some early, ground-breaking, shows by Frank Zappa and the Mothers of Invention. It was like coming home for Eric. Well, sort of. 'I made a lot of friends there. New York is incredible, I'd love to live there. Everybody is so much more hip to the music scene. Taxi drivers talking about James Brown – can you imagine that here?'

Another major influence was Jimi Hendrix, whose driven, fuzz-tone blues opened up a whole new world of possibilities for the electric guitar. On arriving in London, one of the first people Hendrix wanted to meet was Eric Clapton. His manager, ex-Animal, Chas Chandler, arranged for Hendrix to see Cream play at the Regent Polytechnic in London on 1 October 1966.

'He was flash, very flash; even in the dressing room,' recalled Eric. 'He stood in front of the mirror combing his hair and asked if he could play a couple of numbers. I said "of course," but I had a funny feeling about him. He came on and did 'Killing Floor' a Howlin' Wolf number that I've always wanted to play, but which I've never really had the complete technique to do. Ginger and Jack didn't like it – they had never heard the

TOP LEFT Music press advert for Cream's DISRAELI GEARS album.

TOP RIGHT 'Strange Brew', Cream's third single, released in June 1967.

ABOVE 'Anyone For Tennis', Cream's fourth single released in May 1968 and their first on the Polydor label.

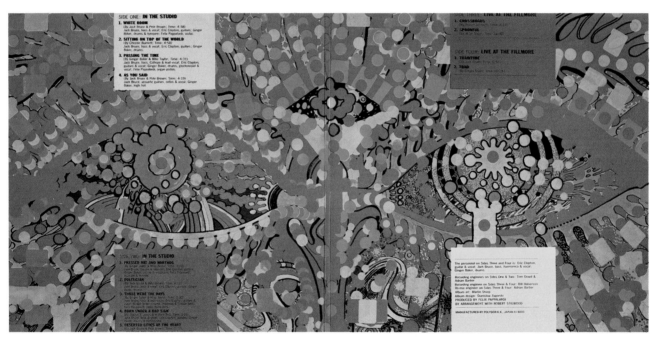

song before. It was just, well, he stole the show. From then on I just started going to watch him.'

In early 1967, Cream were about to embrace psychedelia and flower power, which so often went hand in hand with mind-expanding substances such as LSD. But it wasn't until the photo shoot for the cover of DISRAELI GEARS that Eric first took acid (LSD). 'We went up to Scotland and took it at the bottom of Ben Nevis and then went to the top. It was amazing. We ran down. It took us about half a day to get to the top and then about three hours to run down.' (UFO Records released a limited-edition boxed set of the album in 1992, which included a hilarious book of photos by Robert Whitaker featuring the lads tripping their way down the mountain.)

On their return to England in April 1967, Cream continued to tour and in July, three months before the release of their second album, they started recording possible tracks for their third. But from now until they split, Cream were to concentrate their energies on the biggest record buying market in the world – the United States. They flew over in August 1967, slap bang in the middle of the 'Summer of Love', for their first official live dates at Bill Graham's Fillmore West. A centre for the new music erupting out of Haight Ashbury, Graham's San Francisco venue holds the same place in American rock 'n' roll folklore as the Crawdaddy does in Britain. 'We'd just been doing three, four or five minute versions of our songs before we went to San Francisco,' Jack Bruce remembers. 'We were extremely nervous because this was something really big for us, and it was almost the first time we had played to a full house. The audience were shouting things like "just play anything...just play...we love you," and stuff and the whole thing ended up with us just playing these incredibly long improvised things.' The band walked on stage as paid-up members of the psychedelic generation; Eric and Jack had their guitars covered with acid designs by the Fool design team who had done a similar job for George Harrison. The audience, of course, really loved the band.

WHEELS OF FIRE, the band's third album, saw Cream go global. It stayed in the British charts for six months. Endless touring throughout their brief career saw Cream graduate from poky English pubs and clubs to huge American stadiums. In 1968 they took their place in the pantheon of rock gods; alongside the Rolling Stones; the Doors; the Jimi Hendrix Experience and the fast-disintegrating Beatles. Cream were now one

ABOVE LEFT Cream's fifth single, 'Sunshine Of Your Love', originally released in September 1968. At the time of its release it spent seven weeks in the charts, reaching number twenty five.

ABOVE Front page advert in the *New Musical Express* for Cream's fifth single, 'Sunshine Of Your Love'.

BELOW Cream's sixth single, 'White Room'. Released in January 1969, it reached number twenty eight and stayed in the charts for eight weeks.

RSO reissue of GOODBYE, the last Cream album to feature studio material. It was originally released in March 1969, four months after their final shows at London's Royal Albert Hall. The only difference between this reissue and the original is the presence of RSO's red cow logo as opposed to the Polydor brand name. GOODBYE reached number one and stayed in the UK charts for twenty eight weeks. This was to be Cream's only number one album.

of the biggest bands in the world, but the constant media attention, coupled to the band's massive touring schedule, was taking its toll.

Cream, and Eric Clapton in particular, had become a focal point for the aspirations of the new youth culture. The rock press lionized the individual group members as the best musicians in the world, and their readers agreed. One reader's poll after another found Eric Clapton, Jack Bruce and Ginger Baker voted top in their respective categories (a practice that continued for years after the group split) and Eric found himself an icon. His intense fretwork had burned such an impression into guitar-crazy youth, that the once jokey epithet 'Clapton is God', sprayed on tenement walls as far apart as Glasgow and Detroit (some surviving to this day), became a slogan and a rallying cry for generations of lost hippies.

Their biggest and longest American tour started in February 1968 and continued to the middle of June, with only a short break in April. The problem was, that like many stars before them, the band began to believe their own press. A once-humble group of strolling players had started to look on *themselves* as mini-deities, which resulted in swollen heads and lazy performances. It took a review in *Rolling Stone* by respected rock critic Jon Landau, for Eric to recognize that things were going wrong. 'The magazine ran an interview with us in which we were really praising ourselves,' Eric recalls, 'and it was followed by a review that said how boring and repetitious our performance had been. And it was true!'

Inevitably, relations within the group became strained. 'We split from one another on that tour,' Eric said later about their marathon jaunt. 'We

TOP LEFT AND RIGHT Cream's seventh and final single 'Badge' released in April 1969 and featuring George Harrison on guitar. In the UK 'Badge' spent ten weeks in the charts and reached number eighteen. On the left is the UK Polydor release and on the right the US ATCO version

ABOVE Emphasizing the finality of their split, Cream had the song titles of GOODBYE printed on tombstones on the inside of the sleeve.

RIGHT Extremely rare
programme from Cream's
farewell US tour in 1968
showing an exhausted and
none too happy bunch of
superstars. The logo
illustrated on the back of
the programme (far right)
was the same as that which
appeared on Ginger Baker's
bass drums for a while.

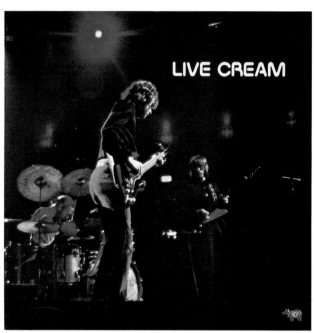

ABOVE LIVE CREAM released in June 1970,
consists of live recordings of the shows at
Fillmore West and Winterland in San
Francisco in March 1968.

ABOVE RIGHT LIVE CREAM VOLUME II
released in July 1972 was largely recorded
on Cream's farewell tour of the United
States.

would hang out on our own with friends we had acquired in cities that we were in. We weren't living as a group at all, there was a lot of conflict.' The conflict Eric was referring to was, of course, the resurrected antics between Jack and Ginger, which, coupled with management pressure on them to tour endlessly, caused the inevitable split.

Once a decision had been made to split it was agreed that they would do a final farewell-tour for the fans in the States. Ending months of rumours and speculation, an official announcement was eventually made that Cream were soon to be no more. So the tour, which began at Oakland's Coliseum Arena on 4 October 1968, was to be their last. The intense pressures of having to live up to the hype of being the world's greatest rock musicians

day in day out, the never ending tours and the endless arguments had burned the group out. Perhaps, if they had been allowed a little more time off, the band might have survived as a unit, but the group's management were determined to exploit Cream as far as they could. 'They worked us to the point of death,' Jack Bruce said bitterly. 'We never had time to write new material, and we'd be given one day off in which we had to fly across to New York from wherever we were and record our next record. We had no time to think, or really experiment in the studio.'

At the end of the American tour Cream announced that they would play two further final shows at London's Royal Albert Hall. But the British rock press and fans, who had followed the band loyally since their earliest

TOP LEFT 'Cream On Top' was only available as a mail-order item for a short time in England and is now very rare.

TOP RIGHT AND ABOVE Rare Japanese picture sleeves of the singles 'Sunshine of Your Love', 'Crossroads', and 'White Room'.

Cream in action for the last time on their farewell date at the Royal Albert Hall in London on 26 November 1968. Two concerts were filmed by Tony Palmer on behalf of BBC television and later broadcast in edited form. Left to right: Jack Bruce, Ginger Baker, Eric Clapton.

days, felt let down by the band for only playing two farewell concerts in their own country. 'Goodbye Eric, Jack and Ginger. We dug your sound, but you kicked us in the teeth,' wailed *Melody Maker*. Despite the press, the Albert Hall shows were a resounding success, and in the post-gig euphoria the band reconsidered their decision to break up – though exactly how seriously any of them took the idea is open to conjecture.

As a finale, Eric Clapton, Jack Bruce and Ginger Baker entered the studio as Cream for one last time. They recorded three songs for inclusion on an otherwise live album, which had been recorded on their farewell tour in Los Angeles. The album was aptly titled GOODBYE and there could be no doubt that this was the end for one of the seminal rock bands of the sixties: the song titles featured on the inside sleeve were inscribed on gravestones.

Twenty-five years later on 12 January 1993, Cream were elected to the Rock 'n' Roll Hall of Fame. The band re-formed for a one-off appearance at the show, and in a nostalgic ten minutes played 'Sunshine Of Your Love', 'Born Under A Bad Sign' and 'Crossroads' to an ecstatic audience. It was an experience that all three enjoyed. 'It was wonderful,' exclaimed Ginger. 'It was like coming home. The rehearsals were especially good. It was the first time we'd all played together since the split in 1968.' He was also particularly proud of the fact that both Eric and Jack told him 'Ah, somebody who can play 'Sunshine Of Your Love'!'

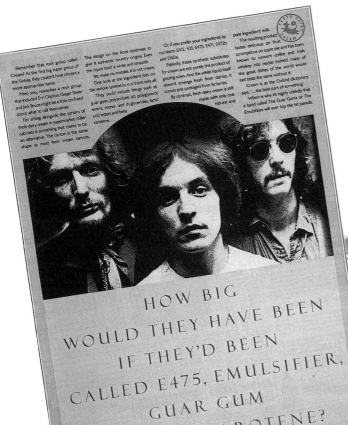

Remember that rock group called Cream? As the first big super group of the Sixties, they couldn't have chosen a more appropriate name.

Mind you, nowadays a rock group that included Eric Clapton, Ginger Baker and Jack Bruce might be a little confused about what to call themselves.

For sitting alongside the cartons of fresh dairy cream in supermarket chiller cabinets is something that claims to be an alternative. The carton is the same shape as most fresh cream cartons.

The design on the front contrives to give it authentic country origins. Even the liquid itself is white and smooth. Yet, make no mistake, it is not cream.

One look at the ingredient lists on the various synthetics out there tells all. They could include things such as guar gum, polysorbate 60, polyglycerol esters, mono- and di-glycerides, lactic acid esters and beta carotene.

Or, if you prefer your ingredients by numbers: E412, 435, E475, E47I, E472b and E163a.

Patently, these synthetic substitutes for cream are not purely the product of grazing cows. And the white liquid itself doesn't emerge fresh from factories. It comes pre-packaged from factories.

By contrast, fresh dairy cream is still made with only one natural and

pure ingredient: milk.

The resulting product tastes delicious on fruit, scrumptious on apple pie and has been known to convert coffee and Irish whiskey into nectar. Indeed, many of the great dishes of the world would not taste the same without it.

Cream is, as the Oxford dictionary says, '... the best part of something.'

Which is why it's highly unlikely that a band called The Guar Gums or The Emulsifiers will ever top the hit parade.

HOW BIG
WOULD THEY HAVE BEEN
IF THEY'D BEEN
CALLED E475, EMULSIFIER,
GUAR GUM
AND BETA CAROTENE?

ABOVE Twenty-five years after their break up Cream re-form to play a short three-song set after being inducted to the Rock & Roll Hall of Fame. This historic event took place in Los Angeles at the Century Plaza Hotel on 12 January 1993. Left to right:, Jack Bruce, Ginger Baker, Eric Clapton.

LEFT Cream appropriated to advertise the real thing in 1992.

BELOW Three older and wiser men happy to smile for the press after the reunion show.

Together again: Eric Clapton, Ginger Baker and Jack Bruce meet up in Los Angeles

Hall of Fame rock honours
for the crème de la Cream

Cream
of the
crock

NOW . . . Clapton, Baker and Bruce in LA to receive their award

CREAM'S FIRST UK TOUR

Cream were:

Eric Clapton (guitar, vocals), Jack Bruce (bass, vocals, harmonica), Ginger Baker (drums).

Cream's set list was taken from:

'Cat's Squirrel', 'Lawdy Mama', 'Meet Me In The Bottom', 'Spoonful', 'Sweet Wine', 'Steppin' Out', 'I'm So Glad', 'Traintime', 'Toad'.

JULY 1966

29   Twisted Wheel, Manchester

31   6th National Jazz and Blues Festival, Windsor, Berks

AUGUST 1966

2   Klooks Kleek, West Hampstead, London

6   Town Hall, Torquay

9   Fishmongers Arms, Wood Green

16   Marquee Club, Soho, London

19   Cellar Club, Kingston, Surrey

27   Ram Jam Club, Brixton, London

27   Flamingo Club, Soho, London

SEPTEMBER 1966

2   Bluesville, Manor House, London

4   Ricky Tick, Windsor, Berks

15   Gaumont Cinema, Hanley

16   Hermitage Halls, Hitchin, Herts

17   Grantham (*venue unknown*)

18   Blue Moon Club, Hayes, Middlesex

19   Woking (*venue unknown*)

23   Corn Exchange, Newbury

26   Star Club, Star Hotel, Croydon

27   Marquee Club, Soho, London

30   Ricky Tick, Hounslow

OCTOBER 1966

1   Regent Polytechnic, London

     Jimi Hendrix joins Cream for Howlin' Wolf's 'Killing Floor'.

2   Kirklevington, *venue unknown (possibly cancelled)*

3   Chester, *venue unknown(possibly cancelled)*

4   Fishmongers Arms, Wood Green (*possibly cancelled*)

5   Reading, *venue unknown (possibly cancelled)*

6   York, *venue unknown (possibly cancelled)*

8   Kings College University, Brighton, Sussex

9   Birdcage, Portsmouth

11   Flamingo Club, Soho, London

21   Bluesville 66, Manor House, London

NOVEMBER 1966

3   Ram Jam Club, Brixton, London

4   Wembley TV studios .

     Debut appearance on Ready Steady Go

5   Town Hall, East Ham, London

7   Gosport, *venue unknown*

8   Marquee Club, Soho, London

9   BBC Studios, London

     Live radio session. Numbers recorded: 'Wrapping Paper',

     'Sweet Wine', 'Steppin' Out'

11   Public Baths, Sutton

12   Liverpool University, Liverpool

13   Coathams Hotel, Redcar

15   Klooks Kleek, West Hampstead, London

18   Village Hall, Hoverton

19   Blue Moon Club, Cheltenham

25   California Ballroom, Dunstable

ABOVE AND BELOW *UK music press advertisements for various shows by Cream.*

DECEMBER 1966

2	Hornsey Art College, Hornsey
3	Birdcage, Porstmouth
4	Starlite Ballroom, Greenford
5	Baths Hall, Ipswich
7	Hull University, Hull
9	Bluesville 66, Manor House, London
	BBC Radios Studios, London
	Live radio session. Numbers recorded: 'Cat's Squirrel',
	'Traintime', 'Lawdy Mama', 'I'm So Glad'.
10	Polytechnic, Isleworth
12	Cooks Ferry Inn, Edmonton
13	Exeter University, Exeter, Devon
14	Bromel Club, Bromley Court Hotel, Bromley
15	Sussex University, Sussex
19	Camberly, *(venue unknown)*
22	Pavilion, Worthing
23	Birmingham, *(venue unknown)*
30	Roundhouse, Chalk Farm, London

JANUARY 1967

7	Ricky Tick, Thames Hotel, Guildford, Surrey
10	Marquee Club, Soho, London
	BBC Radio Studios, London.
	Live session. Numbers recorded: 'Four Until Late', 'I Feel Free',
	'NSU'
13	Guildhall, Southampton
14	Coventry, *(venue unknown)*
15	Ricky Tick, Hounslow
18	Town Hall, Stourbridge
19	Granby Hall, Leiceister
20	Club A Go Go, Newcastle
21	Floral Hall, Southport
24	Corn Exchange, Bristol
25	BBC televison studios
	Live recording for Top Of The Pops
28	Ram Jam Club, Brixton

FEBRUARY 1967

2	Queens Hall, Leeds
4	Technical College, Ewell
5	Saville Theatre, London
9	City Hall, Salisbury
10	Bluesville 66, Manor House, London
11	Baths Pavilion, Matlock
15	Assembly Hall, Aylesbury
18	Tofts Club, Folkestone
19	Starlite Ballroom, Wembley
22	Bromel Club, Bromley Court Hotel, Bromley
24	Beat Club, Bremen, Germany
25	Star Club, Hamburg, Germany
26	Star Club, Kiel, Germany

MARCH 1967

6	KB Halle, Copenhagen, Denmark
7	Konserthuset, Stockholm, Sweden
	Radio broadcast.
8	Gothenburg, Sweden, *venue unknown*
21	Marquee Club, Soho, London

MURRAY THE K SHOW IN US

Cream perform for ten days, five times a day, on Murray The K Show along with various other popular bands of the day: The Who, Lovin' Spoonful, Mitch Ryder and Wilson Pickett.

25–31	RKO 58th street Theatre, New York, USA

APRIL 1967

1–3	RKO 58th Street Theatre, New York, USA
6	Simon Dee Show, London (television)
	Cream mime to 'Strange Brew' with live vocals by Eric.
14	Ricky Tick, Newbury
22	Ricky Tick, Hounslow

MAY 1967

7	Wembley Empire Pool, Wembley, London
	(NME Poll Winners Concert) Cream play two numbers: 'NSU'
	and 'I'm So Glad'.
20	Berlin Stadium, Berlin, Germany
23	Marquee Club, Soho, London
27	Pembroke College May Ball, Oxford
29	Tulip Bulb Auction Hall, Spalding
30	BBC Radio Studios, London
	Live session. Numbers recorded: 'Strange Brew', 'Tales Of
	Brave Ulysses', 'We're Going Wrong', 'Take It Back'.

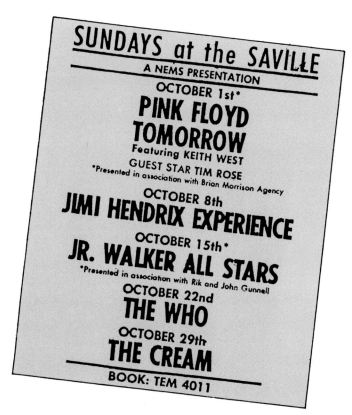

ABOVE *Press advertisement for upcoming show at the Saville Theatre in London. Cream played on 29 December 1967.*

JUNE 1967

1	Palais Des Sports, Paris, France
3	Ram Jam Club, Brixton, London
11	Starlite Ballroom, Greenford

A short tour of Germany followed. Dates and venues are not known.

30	Bluesville 67, Manor House, London

JULY 1967

2	Saville Theatre, London
	Support by the Jeff Beck Group
12	Floral Hall, Southport
14	UFO, London

A short tour of Scotland followed including dates at McGoos in Glasgow, Two Red Shoes in Elgin and Beach Ballroom in Aberdeen.

AUGUST 1967

13	7th National Jazz And Blues Festival, Windsor
17	The Speakeasy, London

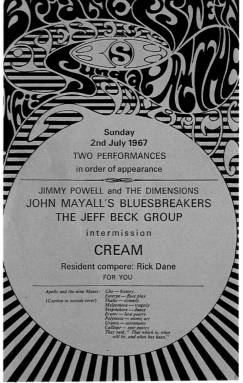

ABOVE *Extremely rare programme for Cream's show at the Saville in London.*
LEFT *Poster for the 7th National Jazz and Blues Festival. This was Cream's second appearance at the festival.*

CREAM'S FIRST US TOUR

Cream's set list was:

'Tales Of Brave Ulysses', 'Sunshine Of Your Love', 'NSU', 'Sitting On Top Of The World', 'Sweet Wine', 'Spoonful', 'Stepping Out', 'Traintime', 'Toad'.

| 22–27 | Fillmore Auditorium, San Francisco |
| 29–31 | Fillmore Auditorium, San Francisco |

SEPTEMBER 1967

1–3	Fillmore Auditorium, San Francisco
4–5	Whisky A Go Go, Los Angeles
7	Psychedelic Supermarket, Boston
8	Cross Town Bus Club, Boston
9	Brandeis University, Waltham

ABOVE *Beautiful US poster for Cream's West Coast concerts in San Francisco in 1967.*

RIGHT *These beautiful tickets were printed in different shades for different nights.*

RIGHT *Underground advertisement for Cream's show at the famous Whisky A Go Go in Los Angeles.*

ABOVE *Posters for Cream's Detroit Grande Ballroom concerts.*

Cream's second-leg set list was:

'Tales Of Brave Ulysses', 'NSU', 'Sitting On Top Of The World', 'Sweet Wine', 'Rollin' And Tumblin'', 'Spoonful', 'Steppin' Out', 'Traintime', 'Toad', 'I'm So Glad', 'Sleepy Time Time'.

23	Village Theatre, New York
26–30	Café Au Go Go, New York

OCTOBER 1967

1, 3–8	Café Au Go Go, New York
11–12	The 5th Dimension Club, Ann Arbor
13–15	Grande Ballroom, Dearborn
24	BBC Radio Studios, London
	Live session. Numbers recorded: 'Outside Woman Blues', 'Born Under A Bad Sign', 'Take It Back'.
29	Saville Theatre, London

ABOVE LEFT *West Coast poster for Cream's 1967 Fillmore concerts in San Francisco.*

ABOVE *Rare programme for another Cream show at London's Saville Theatre.*

TOUR DATES JULY 1966-1968

NOVEMBER 1967

6   Silver Blades Ice Rink, Streatham

A Scandinavian tour followed. Exact dates and venues not known.

23   Club A Go Go, Newcastle
24   Central Pier Ballroom, Morecambe
26   BBC studios, London
        Television appearance on Twice A Fortnight show.
28   Marquee Club, Soho, London

DECEMBER 1967

1   Top Rank, Brighton
20   Private concert for debutant's ball in Chicago.
22–23   Grande Ballroom, Detroit

JANUARY 1968

9   BBC Radio Studios, London
        Live session. Numbers recorded: 'Politician', 'Steppin' Out', 'Swalbr', 'Blue Condition'.
27   St Mary's College, Twickenham

FEBRUARY 1968

Cream play two shows at the Falkoner Hall in Copenhagen. Dates not known.

CREAM'S SECOND US TOUR

Cream's set list was:

'Tales Of Brave Ulysses', 'Sunshine Of Your Love', 'NSU', 'I'm Sitting On Top Of The World', 'Steppin' Out', 'Traintime', 'Toad', 'I'm So Glad'.

23   Civic Auditorium, Santa Monica (*2 shows*)
29   Winterland Auditorium, San Francisco (*2 shows*)
        Live recording

MARCH 1968

1–2   Winterland Auditorium, San Francisco
        2 shows on each date. Live recording
3, 7   Fillmore Auditorium, San Francisco
        2 shows on each date. Live recording
8–10   Winterland Auditorium, San Francisco
        2 shows on each date. Live recording

ABOVE RIGHT *Rare poster for a 1968 concert.*

RIGHT *Beautiful set of concert tickets for the famous Fillmore and Winterland shows in 1968 where the WHEELS OF FIRE album was recorded.*

11	Memorial Auditorium, Sacramento
15–17	Shrine Auditorium, Los Angeles
18	Convention Centre, Anaheim
19	The Family Dog, Denver
21	Beloit College, Beloit
22	Clowes Hall, Butler University, Indianapolis
23	Brown University, Providence
27	Staples High School, Westport
29	Hunter College Auditorium, New York
30	Convention Centre, Dallas
31	Music Hall, Houston

APRIL 1968

5	Backbay Theatre, Boston
6	Commodore Ballroom, Lowell
7	Eastman College Theatre, Rochester
8	Capitol Theatre, Ottawa
12–14	Electric Factory, Philadelphia
16	Paul Suave Arena, Montreal
19–21	Grande Ballroom, Dearborn
22	Massey Hall, Toronto
26	The Cellar, Arlington Heights, Illinois
27	Coliseum, Chicago

MAY 1968

5	The New City Opera House, St. Paul
12	Music Hall, Cleveland
14	Veterans Memorial Auditorium, Columbus
17–18	Convention Centre, Anaheim
19	Exhibit Hall, San Diego
20	'Smothers Brothers Comedy Hour' *Television recording in Los Angeles. Cream mime to their new single 'Anyone For Tennis' and play a live version of 'Sunshine Of Your Love'.*
24	Robertson Gym, University of Ca., Santa Barbara
25	Civic Auditorium, San Jose
27	Swing Auditorium, San Bernadino
28	Pacific Center, Long Beach
29	Eagles Auditorium, Seattle
31	Calgary Stampede, Calgary

BELOW *Canada welcomes the Cream.*

Valid Thursday Only $3.00

Valid Friday Only $3.00

Valid Saturday Only $3.00

Valid Sunday Only $3.00

ABOVE *Legendary Fillmore and Winterland tickets for March 1968.*
BELOW *Beautiful poster for Cream's show at Robertson Gym on 24 May 1968.*

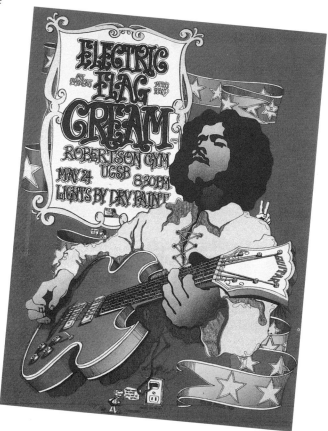

JUNE 1968

1	Sales Pavilion Annex, Edmonton
2	PNE Coliseum, Vancouver
7–8	Grande Ballroom, Dearborn
14	Island Garden, West Hempstead
15	Oakdale Music Theatre, Wallingford
16	Camden Music Fair, Camden

CREAM'S FAREWELL TOUR

Cream's set list was taken from:

'White Room', 'Politician', 'Crossroads', 'Sunshine Of Your Love', 'Spoonful', 'Deserted Cities Of The Heart', 'Toad', 'I'm So Glad', 'Sitting On Top Of The World', 'Traintime', 'Steppin' out'.

OCTOBER 1968

4	Almeda County Coliseum, Oakland *Live recording*
5	University Of New Mexico, Albuquerque
7	Civic Opera House, Chicago
11	New Haven Arena, New Haven
12	Olympia Stadium, Detroit
13	Chicago Coliseum, Chicago
14	Veterans Memorial Auditorium, Des Moines
18–19	The Forum, Los Angeles *Live recording*
20	San Diego Sports Arena, San Diego *Live recording*
24	Sam Houston Coliseum, Houston
25	Memorial Auditorium, Dallas
26	Sports Arena, Miami
27	Chastain Park Amphitheatre, Atlanta
31	Boston Garden, Boston

NOVEMBER 1968

1	The Spectrum, Philadelphia
2	Madison Square Garden, New York
3	Civic Centre Arena, Baltimore
4	Rhode Island Auditorium, Providence *Last US show.*
26	Royal Albert Hall, London *Cream perform two shows.*

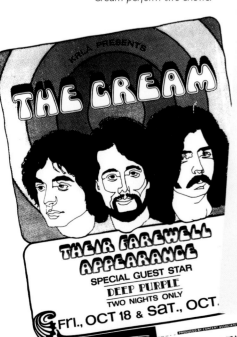

TOP *Cream at UFO Club in London 14 July 1967.*
ABOVE *Rare US poster.*
LEFT *US advertisements for Cream's farewell show.*

3 Blind Faith, Derek and Friends

After Cream split Eric decided to sit back for a while and enjoy the fruits of his labours. He had spent some of his hard-earned fortune on a palatial Italian-style mansion set deep in the Surrey countryside, but due to the never-ending tours since the day he joined the Yardbirds, he'd never really had the chance to live there. Luxurious though the house was, perhaps the best thing about it for Eric was the security and isolation it offered. 'I've tended to withdraw from making contact with people. I'm harder to get to know than I was a few years ago. I don't trust people so readily,' Eric confessed at the time.

But, within months, he was approached to appear in the Rolling Stones' infamous film *Rock and Roll Circus*. Inspired by the Beatles' *Magical Mystery Tour*, and directed by *Ready Steady Go's* Michael Lindsay Hogg, the show was to be an entertainment extravaganza intended for worldwide television broadcast. One of pop's most notorious missing moments, the film, although fully completed, was never released due to the Stones' dissatisfaction with their performance – Brian Jones's drug-addled playing was blamed. The Who turned in a wonderful 'Mini Opera' for the film, and other guest artists included Jethro Tull, Marianne Faithfull, and an eclectic one-off supergroup who called themselves Winston Legthigh and the Dirty Macs. Winston was John Lennon and his 'Dirty Macs' were Mitch Mitchell on drums, Keith Richards on bass and Eric on lead guitar. Yoko Ono also joined in, as did violinist Ivry Gitlis. They played a grinding version of 'Yer Blues' from the Beatles' WHITE album, followed by an instrumental jam with improvised Yoko vocals. Eric and John Lennon certainly enjoyed themselves, even if the Stones didn't. The film is not too hard to locate in

FACING PAGE An unshaven Eric with Gibson ES335 rehearsing at home with Blind Faith.

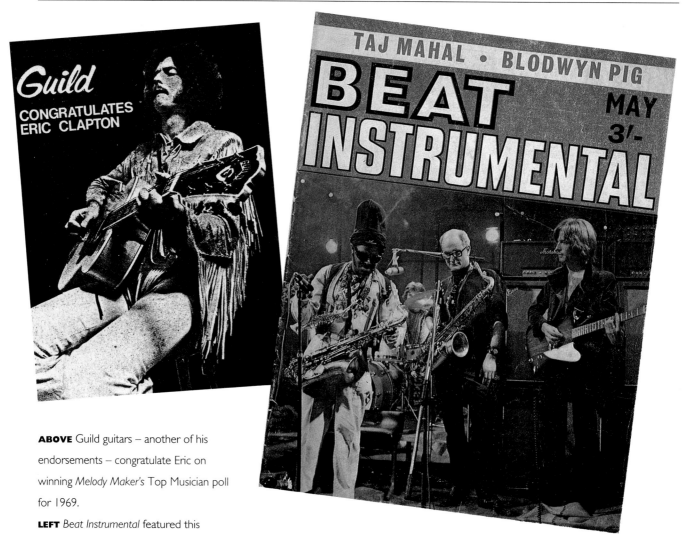

ABOVE Guild guitars – another of his endorsements – congratulate Eric on winning *Melody Maker's* Top Musician poll for 1969.

LEFT *Beat Instrumental* featured this wonderful colour cover of Eric jamming with Ransaan Roland Kirk and Dick Heckstall-Smith during the filming of *Supersession.*

collector circles and will perhaps be released officially at some stage.

Several months after Cream's demise, Eric was ready for a new musical challenge. He knew that Stevie Winwood was at a loose end having left Traffic, and since they thought highly of each other's playing they organized some informal jams to see what, if anything, came out of them. It was a happy time for Eric, and things went so well that in February 1969 they hired Morgan Studios to rehearse and record their ideas. Having overcome some initial reluctance from Eric, Steve invited Ginger Baker to come along to the studio – Eric had wanted to escape from his Cream past as fast as he could. Rick Grech from Family joined them soon after on bass. The early sessions ranged across the genres from blues to rock to jazz, but before they could bond as a unit and settle on a musical direction this informal group of friends and musicians allowed themselves to be overtaken by the music business and the money motive. 'It seemed good enough just to be making the money,' sighed Eric later, 'and that wasn't good.'

The press, aware that ex-members of Cream, Traffic and Family were rehearsing together, dubbed them a 'supergroup' before they had played a single note in public. The record company, Polydor, soon kicked in with a contract, and before the group had been able to mature into a proper working band, the Robert Stigwood management had organized a huge tour of the United States. Under the weight of such expectations it is no wonder the band fell apart so quickly.

In recognition of the devotional press they were getting, and with heavy irony, they called themselves Blind Faith. The hype was intense, and the group, or rather their management, seemed determined to live up to it. They played their first, very public, gig at a huge free concert in London's Hyde Park on 7 June 1969. One of the most eagerly awaited events of the year, the audience in general were disappointed and throughout the show they called out for Cream and Traffic songs. Instead, they got an inspired version of the Stones' hymn to mysogny, 'Under My Thumb' and several numbers from the Blind Faith's forthcoming, eponymously titled album.

Considering the pressures the band were under, the album was very good and is more than just a historical curiosity dating from the 'supergroup' period. Notably, it features 'Presence of the Lord', the first complete song – words and music – that Eric had ever written. Collectors may also note that the original album cover caused a great deal of controversy, particularly in the United States, where objections were voiced about its depiction of a naked girl holding a phallic-looking silver spaceship. It was eventually released in a different sleeve in the States, where Ahmet Ertegun, president of their US label said, 'we haven't withdrawn the other cover by any means…we have just given people a choice. After all we aren't in the art business.'

Blind Faith's problem was that the reputations of the individual band

ABOVE The World's Greatest Guitarist endorses Sound City guitar strings in this 1969 music press advert.

BELOW Blind Faith make their world debut appearance in London's Hyde Park on 7 June 1969. Left to right: Rick Grech, Ginger Baker, Eric Clapton, Stevie Winwood.

The original, controversial cover to Blind Faith's eponymous debut album released in August 1969. It was eventually withdrawn in the States and other countries after numerous objections to the naked girl and the phalic-looking spaceship. The UK inside sleeve (left) became the front cover instead.

members preceded the group as a unit. In a less fraught period, where rock stars were expected to play, and do nothing more than wreck hotel rooms in their time off, the band might have survived. But in the late sixties it was expected that rock would lead the way into the promised land, hence the concept of the 'supergroup' with its comic book hero connotations. Blind Faith never stood a chance and by the time they started their American tour, Eric for one had lost interest. 'The disillusionment came with the concept of the supergroup that we were labelled with, and the immediate hype that was thrust upon us. We were doing a world tour much too soon, and trying to live up to a musical background that we hadn't established.' Towards the end of the American tour they even conceded to audience pressure by playing 'Sunshine of Your Love'. The last show of the tour, in Hawaii, was to be the last show of the band; Blind Faith went their separate ways, never to reunite.

In an effort to get away from Blind Faith and the surrounding hype while on tour, Eric spent much of his spare time with one of the support bands, Delaney and Bonnie. He preferred travelling to gigs in their bus rather than Blind Faith's official limos. 'I started looking for somewhere else to go, an alternative, and they were a godsend.' Delaney encouraged Eric to write and sing his own songs during this period and suggested that Eric should record a solo album on his return home. They discussed the possibility of Eric playing guitar for Delaney and Bonnie, and before long they were writing songs together. On completion of the Blind Faith tour, Eric joined these southern girls and boys in Los Angeles to record some tracks for their new album. The sessions were a great success, and it was agreed that Eric would bring Delaney and Bonnie over to Europe for a tour in November, in return for Delaney producing his solo album.

ABOVE LEFT Rare European sleeve for the BLIND FAITH album.

ABOVE RIGHT European picture sleeve release of 'Presence Of The Lord'.

BELOW Extremely rare single with the same uncredited Blind Faith jam on both sides. Island Records put their change of address on one side of the label and their sales office phone number on the other.

ABOVE Controversial cover to Blind Faith's US tour programme. This programme is now very rare and highly sought after by collectors of EC memorabilia.

BELOW LEFT The complete set from the Plastic Ono Band's London Lyceum show was a free disc with SOME TIME IN NEW YORK CITY.

BELOW RIGHT The live Toronto album.

On his immediate return to England, Eric received a call from John Lennon inviting him to appear with Lennon's new band at a Rock 'n' Roll Revival in Toronto. Lennon had agreed to do the show with only forty-eight hours to curtain, so Eric arranged to meet John and Yoko, bassist Klaus Voorman and drummer Alan White at Heathrow airport.

Some consider the gig itself to have been an embarrassing fiasco. The only rehearsals had taken place on unamplified electric guitars during the flight over, while John Lennon suffered pre-show nerves. During the show the Plastic Ono Band, as they hurriedly called themselves, played some ropey versions of rock 'n' roll standards, such as 'Blue Suede Shoes' and 'Dizzy Miss Lizzy', followed by a grinding slog through 'Yer Blues' and Lennon's forthcoming single, 'Cold Turkey'. The second half was altogether

more *avant garde*, with a free-form jam accompanied by the atonal warbling of Yoko. As a finale, Eric and John simply lent their guitars against their amps and let them feedback for several minutes before turning them off one by one. By the time the band went off stage many in the front rows were hurling obscenities at them, and others had walked out in protest. Fortunately, seeing a Beatle and guitar-god Clapton on stage together was enough for most of the audience.

On their return to England, Eric went into the studio with the Plastic Ono Band to record a couple of tracks for a single. The result, 'Cold Turkey', is a song about Lennon's fight with heroin, and is a highlight in his

Plastic Ono Band and friends, including George Harrison, backstage at London's Lyceum on 15 December 1969 after their Christmas show.

post-Beatles career. A truly cathartic slice of white noise set to a pulsating
bass line, and with Eric's howling guitar and Lennon's tortured vocals, the
single perhaps represents Lennon's screams for release from his addiction.

Delaney and Bonnie duly arrived, as promised, in early November.
Together they rehearsed night and day at Eric's home before heading off on
the European tour. Everything looked promising, but in an effort to cash in
on the superstar, the German promoters advertised the shows as Eric
Clapton gigs. Naturally, people expected to see him centre stage playing his
own songs, and inevitably, a majority felt ripped off to see him at the back of
the stage. Fortunately, in England the shows were better received, possibly
because the band were joined by George Harrison. Delaney and
Bonnie's live album, recorded at Croydon's Fairfield Halls, is fairly
representative of the way they sounded.

Eric, Delaney and Bonnie and also George Harrison,
joined John Lennon and Yoko Ono at London's Lyceum
on 15 December for their 'Peace for Christmas' concert.
This was historic in post-Beatle history for featuring John
and George on stage at the same time.

Eric was happy simply to be a band member with
Delaney and Bonnie for a while. 'That's what I wanted, I
saw a way where I could be a sideman, and on top of that,
they were genuine R & B singers and players from the South.'

He seemed genuinely at ease and in his element playing as their guitarist, and gladly accepted their help when it came to recording his first solo album.

Recording sessions for Eric's eponymously titled album began at Olympic Studios in Barnes during a break in the tour, and were then relocated to Los Angeles. Eric and Delaney had written some songs during the Blind Faith tour, and the rest of the album was made up of songs by Leon Russell and J.J. Cale, with the remainder emerging from studio jams.

Probably for the first time in his career, Eric was doing something he really wanted to, and more importantly, he was in control and free from any real pressure as far as his own career prospects were concerned. He still had a confidence problem when it came to singing, a problem that he often solved by drinking a bottle of peppermint schnapps before starting a session. 'It was Delaney's favourite drink, and I'd go out and sing. Horrible I know but it was like nectar in those days,' remembers Eric. Once they had finished the sessions, Eric went on an American tour with Delaney and Bonnie, who had started to include him in their long-term plans.

Eric soon realized, however, that as much as he enjoyed playing with Delaney and Bonnie, they were becoming too dependent on him for continued exposure. He started to feel trapped, and reluctantly he told them he wanted to leave. 'I started to feel a lot of pressure. Delaney didn't want to let me go, because I had the popularity and the status to carry the whole thing a lot further. It was heart-rending, but finally I extricated myself from

TOP LEFT Delaney and Bonnie's ON TOUR WITH ERIC CLAPTON album recorded on their UK tour and released in June 1970.
TOP RIGHT UK tour Programme for Delaney and Bonnie and friends which featured Eric Clapton.
ABOVE *Beat Instrumental* featured Eric on the cover. The photo was taken on stage at Delaney and Bonnie's concert at London's Royal Albert Hall in 1969.

ABOVE Front of Eric's first solo album. ERIC CLAPTON was released in August 1970 and spent eight weeks in the charts. Most of the tracks were recorded in January 1970 and the album featured Delaney and Bonnie and Friends.

LEFT Rare European sleeve for 'After Midnight' which like the cover for the album (above) sees Eric make his first public appearance in a suit.

it and came back home in March 1970.' Once home he really had no idea
what to do next, but as is generally the case, fate took over. 'It's not as if I
had a life plan. I mean, things happen to me in my life in a very haphazard
way, on the surface of things as you look at it.' A few weeks after his return
Carl Radle and Jim Gordon contacted him; they had been fired from
Delaney's band, along with Bobby Whitlock, for asking for a pay rise, and
were keen to form a band with Eric. 'I thought, why not get them? And
they came to England and we lived together at my house for a year, and we
played night and day and took all kinds of dope.'

The new band called themselves Derek and the Dominos. The name,
as Eric recalls, started off as a joke. 'Tony Ashton suggested it because he
always used to call me Del and he wanted to call it Del and the Dominos...so
it became Derek and the Dominos.' The ridiculous moniker gave Eric
something to hide behind as he went out as the lead singer for the first time.
He didn't feel ready to go out as Eric Clapton and his band. 'We wanted to
be a band and I didn't feel that I had earned enough respect in the public eye
to be the singer. It would have spoiled it for me if I'd had to go out and lead
it, whereas I could lead it from the inside in a subtle way, if it was called
something else.'

During this period Eric was very much in demand as a session player,
making innumerable guest appearances on recordings by musicians such as
Stephen Stills, Howlin' Wolf and Billy Preston. Most notably, however, Eric
and his new band backed George Harrison on the majority of tracks that
eventually made up the triple album, ALL THINGS MUST PASS.

During the recording of ALL THINGS MUST PASS, Clapton had a lot
of spare time on his hands, and sadly, he started to take heroin and cocaine
regularly from the readily available supplies in the studio. He had already
fallen hopelessly in love with Pattie Boyd, George Harrison's wife by this

ABOVE Rare promotional badge given out
at press launch for Derek and the Dominos.
BELOW LEFT European picture single for
'After Midnight'. The photograph is rather
misleading; it was taken the previous year
during Blind Faith's Hyde Park concert.
BELOW RIGHT British release of Eric's first
single 'After Midnight', from his solo album.
Released in October 1970 'After Midnight'
failed to make it into the UK charts.

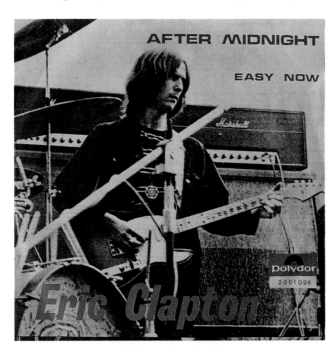

ABOVE US and UK versions of the first Derek and the Dominos single, 'Tell The Truth' backed with 'Roll It Over'. Both are extremely rare now as the band insisted the record company withdraw it in the week of its initial release because they weren't happy with it.

BELOW US music press advert for 'Bell Bottom Blues'. In the UK, 'Bell Bottom Blues' was released only as the B side for Layla.

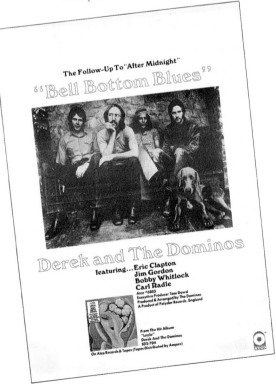

time, and since George was one of his best friends, recording the album cannot have been easy. Eric had often met Pattie over the last couple of years at George's home, and Eric would often dream up excuses to visit George so he could talk to Pattie. She was one of the top models in the sixties and perhaps not surprisingly, had a hugely publicized wedding to George Harrison at Esher's Register Office in 1966. Eric was attracted to Pattie from the moment he set eyes on her. She was attracted to Eric and his mysterious aura when she had seen him performing with Cream, but thought nothing more of it, after all, she was happily married at the time. At the recording of ALL THINGS MUST PASS, Eric and Pattie spent a lot of time together, but Eric had trouble in expressing his feelings to her. Eventually, after a series of embarrassing blunders, he told her. Her reaction was one of shock and she rejected his advances. Perhaps his drug taking increased during this time because he was looking for release from the angst he was feeling?

Eric and the new boys really gelled as a unit during the recording sessions of ALL THINGS MUST PASS, and helped provide George with the biggest-selling album thus far by a solo Beatle. In return, George gave them some free studio time and the services of legendary producer, Phil Spector. They recorded two songs, 'Tell the Truth' and 'Roll it Over' for the band's debut single. It was not however an auspicious debut; the band were unhappy with Spector's production and consequently asked for the record to be withdrawn in the week of its release in September 1970. They re-recorded the number in Florida and were much happier with the result.

Derek and the Dominos gave their first live performance at a one-off charity gig in June 1970, which was followed by a short UK tour in August, before they flew to Miami to record their first album. Although much

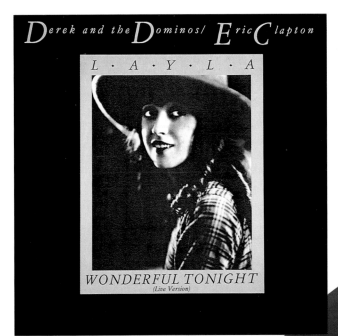

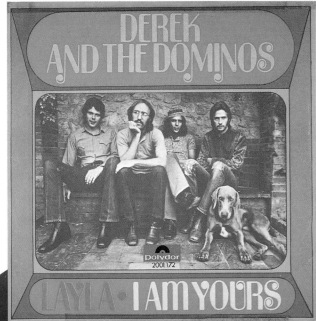

TOP LEFT Yet another re-release of 'Layla'. This one, a 12 inch version, was released in February 1982.

TOP RIGHT European picture sleeve of 'Layla' single.

ABOVE RIGHT Rare US blue vinyl single for 'Layla'.

RIGHT Japan

LAYLA AND OTHER ASSORTED LOVE SONGS, Eric's classic seventies masterpiece, was released in December 1970. But, at the time of its release the reception was cool and the album didn't even make the UK charts.

underrated on its release, perhaps because no one could take a band called Derek and the Dominos seriously, the double-album LAYLA is a Clapton masterpiece and has since been designated a seventies classic. The Dominos were joined on the album by influential guitarist, Duane Allman, whose slide-guitar work with Wilson Picket, Aretha Franklin and his own, Allman Brothers Band, was greatly admired by Eric. The two musicians hit it off immediately; they set their amps up on chairs – Eric using tiny Fender Champ and Pignose amps for the first time, instead of the Marshall stacks that he had been using since Cream days – and they played nose to nose. Jamming night and day, they traded licks, riffs and figures. Eric's toppy, bright Fender, answering and calling to Allman's grungey Gibson's screeching replies, all accompanied by Eric's most emotive vocals to date.

One night after a concert, the Dominos were joined by the rest of the Allman band and together they jammed until six the following night. Engineer Tom Dowd looked on amazed. 'There was no control, you just kept the machines rolling. It was a wonderful experience.' (Many of these jams were later to find their way on to the twentieth-anniversary CD boxed set of LAYLA released in 1990.)

The main source of lyrical inspiration for the album welled up from Eric's heartache at the time, from being rejected by Pattie Boyd, George Harrison's wife. Eric identified with the protagonist of Ganjavi Nizami's poem '*Story of Layla and Majnun*'. In this romantic tale, Qays, a young man, falls helplessly in love with a moon princess, Layla. Sadly, she is married off to another man by her father. Qays' love for her becomes so obsessive that he is deemed insane, and is forbidden from ever seeing his beloved Layla again.

BELOW LEFT Rare promotional CD single featuring an unreleased live recording of 'Little Wing'.

BELOW RIGHT Another live version of 'Little Wing', this time issued free in August 1988 with US magazine, *Guitar Player*.

BOTTOM Special twentieth anniversary edition of LAYLA AND OTHER ASSORTED LOVE SONGS. The three CD set includes the original double album and two further CD's of unreleased outtakes and jams, as well as copies of studio sheets.

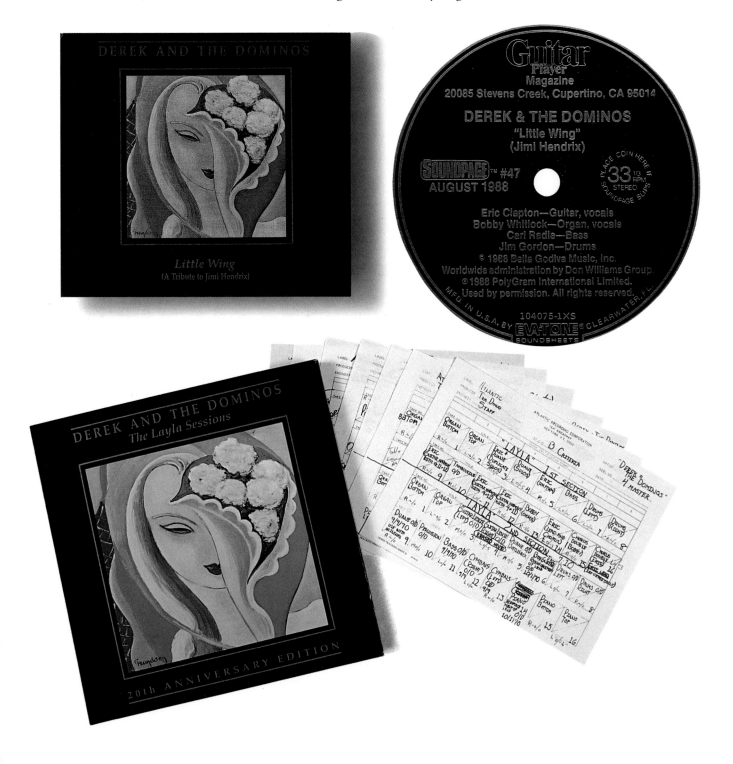

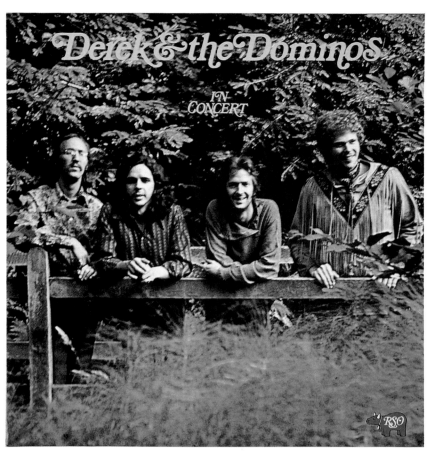

Derek and the Dominos IN CONCERT double album released in March 1973. Recorded at the Fillmore East in New York in October 1970, the album only dipped into the UK charts for one week at number thirty six. The inside sleeve (left) was a poster-style photograph of Eric.

The story ends with Qays roaming the streets, known until his last breath as 'Majnun', which, translated from the Persian, means 'madness'.

Eric formed a tight song-writing team with Bobby Whitlock and they used Qays' declaration of love for Layla in one of the first recorded songs, 'I am Yours', as well as taking the name of the moon princess for the title track. Some tracks were written on the spot and others emerged from the continual improvisation, but almost all were composed, not with the intention of being great songs, but rather as something for this fired-up bunch of musicians to play. On the album itself, the tracks appear in the order in which they were recorded, progressing from the mournful blues of Jimmy Cox's, 'Nobody Knows You When Your Down and Out' to softer ballads such as 'Thorn Tree in the Garden'. More than any other track, it is probably the cover version of Billy Miles's 'Have You Ever Loved a Woman' that most accurately summed up Eric's feelings for Pattie at the time.

The recording of LAYLA was an intimate, relaxed affair; taking advantage of Florida's sub-tropical climate, every day would be divided between the pool and the sauna. However, at night the band would go to the studio and get loaded on heroin and cocaine. Like many notable musicians, before and since, Eric and his friends found these drugs inspirational at first, but as he would find out to his cost, 'it's the way with drugs, they would catch up with you later'. They may not have impaired the playing on LAYLA, but the ensuing trip around the United States was to be

different. 'We scored a massive amount of heroin and cocaine before we left
Florida and took it on tour.' Predictably, some of their performances were
less than satisfactory, and perhaps a sign that Eric Clapton had thrown in the
towel. By the time they flew home, taking heroin had become a daily ritual
for Clapton.

Back home, a chance meeting with Pattie at a theatre resulted in a
night of passion. Further secret romantic rendez-vous were organized at
Eric's house, but before long Pattie's guilt meant she had to end the affair.
Eric was devastated. The poor sales of LAYLA on its initial release; the deaths
of his grandfather and friend Jimi Hendrix within a short space of time; and
his new rejection by Pattie all served to push Eric further into the junk-sick
world of the addict.

In April 1971 the Dominos started recording their second album.
Unsurprisingly, the sessions went badly. 'Money, dope and women were so
involved with our nucleus that we couldn't communicate any more.' After a
few weeks, and hardly any tracks finished, the whole thing came to the
crunch. Jim was playing drums and Eric made some remark about a
drummer in another band. 'I don't even remember making the remark,'
recalls Eric. 'But he got up from behind his kit and said, "Why don't you get
so-and-so in here? He could play it better than I could." And I said, "Oh,
that's it," packed my guitar, walked out of the studio and never came back.'

BELOW LEFT Eric singing during Derek and
the Dominos' US tour in November 1970.
BELOW Bobby Whitlock and Eric Clapton
during the Derek and the Dominos tour of
the United States in November 1970.

Eric went home, locked the doors and took heroin continually for the next two years. When relatives or friends, both in and out of the music business, tried to visit him at his home, he often hid or refused to answer the door. The only exception, however, was Eric's close friend George Harrison, (at the time he knew nothing about Eric's affair with Pattie), who visited regularly and eventually managed to persuade Eric to break his self-imposed exile to appear at the Concert for Bangla Desh in New York's Madison Square Garden. A forerunner of the star-spangled charity events of today such as Live Aid, the concert was to feature practically every big name in the rock scene of 1971, including Bob Dylan and Ringo Starr.

Eric agreed to do it, providing there was a guarantee that some heroin would be waiting for him when he got to New York. Everything was organized but the heroin was cut with talcum powder, and Eric collapsed after using it. A doctor was summoned immediately, and prescribed the heroin substitute, methadone linctus for the stricken star. Eric was just about able to stagger on stage and somehow managed to throw in the odd, surprisingly good, lick now and then. The audience, oblivious to their hero's illness, gave Clapton rapturous applause at both performances.

The whole story of LAYLA would make a compelling film. Rock guitar-god falls head over heels in love with the wife of one of the Beatles, but his love is unrequited. He falls into a deep abyss of drugs and depression, which lasts for years. On recovery, she finally falls for his charms and accompanies him on a huge American tour and marries him. But renewed pressures eventually turn him into an alcoholic. Death and madness of fellow musicians along the way followed by the divorce of 'Majnun' and his Layla means there is no happy ending, confirming life on the road to be hard and heartless. De Palma or Scorsese would have a field day directing this epic. But, let us return to 1971.

BELOW Eric makes headlines and front pages as the Dominos split under the pressure of recording their second album.

BELOW RIGHT As Eric went into drug-induced hibernation, refusing to record any new material, the HISTORY OF ERIC CLAPTON double album was issued in July 1972 to try and keep Eric's name in the limelight, but it only managed to hold a UK chart position for six weeks.

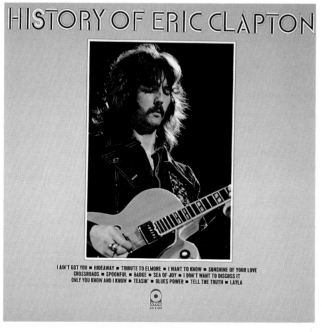

DECEMBER 1968

10–11   Intertel Studios, Wembley
Filming of 'Rock And Roll Circus'

MARCH 1969

18   Staines television studios
Eric plays alongside Jack Bruce, Roland Kirk, Jon Hiesman, Dick Heckstall-Smith, Ron Burton and Vernon Martin for an instrumental called 'Slate 69'. Eric also joins Buddy Guy for the first time for a version of 'Everything Gonna Be Alright'.

BLIND FAITH'S DEBUT

Blind Faith were:

Eric Clapton (guitar, vocals), Stevie Winwood (keyboards, guitar, vocals), Ginger Baker (drums), Rick Grech (bass).

The set was:

'Well All Right', 'Sea Of Joy', 'Sleeping In The Ground', 'Under My Thumb', 'Can't Find My Way Home', 'Do What You Like', 'In The Presence Of The Lord', 'Means To An End' and 'Had To Cry Today'.

JUNE 1969

7   Hyde Park, London
Live recording and filming

A short Scandinavian tour followed. Dates and venues not known

BLIND FAITH US TOUR

The set included:

Cream's 'Sunshine Of Your Love' and 'Crossroads', and Traffic's 'Means To An End' are added to the set.

JULY 1969

12	Madison Square Garden, New York
13	Kennedy Centre, Bridgeport
16	Spectrum, Philadelphia
18	Varsity Stadium, Toronto
20	Civic Centre, Baltimore
26	County Stadium, Milwaukee
27	International Amphitheatre, Chicago

AUGUST 1969

1	Olympia Stadium, Detroit
3	Kiel Stadium, St. Louis
8	Seattle Centre Stadium, Seattle
9	PNE Coliseum, Vancouver
10	Memorial Coliseum, Portland
14	Almeda County Coliseum, Oakland
15	The Forum, Los Angeles
16	Fairgrounds Arena, Santa Barbara
19	Sam Houston Coliseum, Houston
20	Hemisfair Arena, San Antonio
22	Salt Palace, Salt Lake City
23	Memorial Coliseum, Phoenix
24	HIC Arena, Honolulu

RIGHT *Rare poster for Blind Faith's concert at the Arena, Santa Barbara, California.*

THE PLASTIC ONO BAND
The set was:

'Blue Suede Shoes', 'Money', 'Dizzy Miss Lizzy', 'Yer Blues', 'Cold Turkey', 'Give Peace A Chance', 'Don't Worry Kyoto', 'John John'.

SEPTEMBER 1969
13   Varsity Stadium, Toronto

Eric plays with John Lennon (guitar, vocals), Klaus Voorman bass), Alan White (drums), Yoko Ono (vocals).

DELANEY AND BONNIE EUROPEAN TOUR

Delaney And Bonnie And Friends were:

Eric Clapton (guitar, vocals), Delaney Bramlett (guitar, vocals), Bonnie Bramlett (vocals), Jim Gordon (drums), Bobby Whitlock (keyboards, vocals), Carl Radle (bass), Jim Price (trumpet), Bobby Keys (sax), Tex Johnson (percussion), Rita Coolidge (backing vocals).

Dave Mason and George Harrison also joined them on the UK and Scandinavian dates.

NOVEMBER 1969
26   'Beat Club' television programme, Germany

Live recording of 'Comin' Home', 'Poor Elijah' and 'Where There's A Will There's A Way'.

27   Jahrhunderthalle, Frankfurt
28   Congress Halle, Hamburg
29   Sport Palais, Cologne

UK TOUR

Set list for UK tour was taken from:

'Things Get Better', 'Poor Elijah – Tribute to Johnson (medley)', 'Only You Know And I Know', 'I Don't Want To Discuss It', 'That's What My Man Is For', 'Where There's A Will There's A Way', 'Coming Home', 'Long Tall Sally', 'Jenny Jenny', 'Tutti-Frutti' (Little Richard medley), 'Everybody's Trying To Be My Baby'.

DECEMBER 1969
1   Royal Albert Hall, London
2   Colston Hall, Bristol *(2 shows at 6.15pm and 8.45pm)*
3   Town Hall, Birmingham *(2 shows at 6.15pm and 8.45pm)*
4   City Hall, Sheffield *(2 shows at 6.20pm and 8.50pm)*
5   City Hall, Newcastle *(2 shows at 6.15pm and 8.45pm)*
6   Empire Theatre, Liverpool *(2 shows at 6.45pm and 9pm)*
7   Fairfield Hall, Croydon *(2 shows at 6.15pm and 8.35pm)*

Billy Preston joins for the remaining shows.

10–12   Falkoner Theatre, Copenhagen, Denmark

The last show was filmed for Danish television

15   Lyceum, London

Eric joins John and Yoko for their 'Peace For Christmas' concert along with Delaney and Bonnie and Friends. Only two numbers are played, 'Cold Turkey' and 'Don't Worry Kyoko (Mummy's Only Looking For Her Hand In The Snow)'.

DELANEY AND BONNIE US TOUR
FEBRUARY 1970
2   Massey Hall, Toronto, Canada
5   ABC Television Studios, New York

Delaney And Bonnie along with Eric appear on the Dick Cavett Show and play 'Comin' Home', 'Poor Elijah' and 'Where There's A Will There's A Way'.

6–7   Fillmore East, New York
8–9   Tea Party, Boston
11   Electric Factory, Philadelphia

B.B. King jams on the encore

12   Symphony Hall, Minneapolis
14   Chicago Auditorium Theatre, Chicago
15   Memorial Hall, Kansas
19–22   Fillmore West, San Francisco

MARCH 1970
3   Civic Auditorium, Santa Monica

DEREK AND THE DOMINOS UK TOUR
Derek and the Dominos were:

Eric Clapton (guitar, vocals), Jim Gordon (drums), Bobby Whitlock (keyboards, vocals), Carl Radle (bass).

Set list for first part of UK tour:

'Roll It Over', 'Blues Power', 'Have You Ever Loved A Woman', 'Bad Boy', 'Country Life', 'Anyday', 'Bottle Of Red Wine', 'Don't Know Why', 'Tell The Truth'.

JUNE 1970
14   Lyceum, London

World premiere for Derek And The Dominos

AUGUST 1970
1   Roundhouse, London
2   The Place, Hanley, Stoke-on-Trent
7   Mecca Ballroom, Newcastle
8   California Ballroom, Dunstable

Programme for Derek and the Dominos only UK tour.

9	Mothers, Birmingham
11	Marquee, London
12	Speakeasy, London
14	Winter Gardens, Malvern
15	Tofts, Folkestone
16	Black Prince, Bexley
18	The Pavilion, Bournemouth
21	Town Hall, Torquay
22	Van Dyke Club, Plymouth

Laminates for Dominos' road crew.

Set list for second part of UK tour:

'Why Does Love Got To Be So Sad', 'Tell The Truth', 'Blues Power', 'Have You Ever Loved A Woman', 'Keep On Growing', 'Nobody Knows You When You're Down And Out', 'Bottle Of Red Wine', 'Little Wing', 'Roll It Over', 'Bell Bottom Blues', 'Let It Rain'.

SEPTEMBER 1970

20	Fairfield Hall, Croydon
21	De Montfort Hall, Leicester
22	Palais Des Sports, Paris
	Jam with Buddy Guy and Junior Wells, who were supporting the Rolling Stones.
23	Dome, Brighton
24	Philharmonic Hall, Liverpool
25	Greens Playhouse, Glasgow
27	Colston Hall, Bristol
28	Free Trade Hall, Manchester

OCTOBER 1970

2	College Of Technology, Nottingham
4	Coatham Bowl, Redcar
5	Town Hall, Birmingham
7	Winter Gardens, Bournemouth
8	Leeds University, Leeds
9	Penthouse, Scarborough
11	Lyceum, London

DEREK AND THE DOMINOS US TOUR

The set list was taken from:

'Layla', 'Got To Get Better In A Little While', 'Blues Power/Have You Ever Loved A Woman', 'Key To The Highway', 'Tell The Truth', 'Nobody Knows You When You're Down And Out', 'Let It Rain', 'Why Does Love Got To Be So Sad', 'Presence Of The Lord', 'Bottle Of Red Wine', 'Roll It Over', 'Little Wing', 'Crossroads', 'Sweet Little Rock 'N' Roller', 'Stormy Monday', 'Little Queenie'.

15	Rider College, Trenton, New Jersey
16–17	Electric Factory, Philadelphia
21	Lisner Auditorium, Washington
23–24	Fillmore East, New York
	Shows recorded
29	Kleinhalls Music Hall, Buffalo
30	Albany State University Gymnasium, Albany
31	Dome, Virginia Beach

NOVEMBER 1970

1	Civic Auditorium, Jacksonville
5	Johnny Cash TV show, Nashville, Tenn
	Eric plays 'It's Too Late', 'Got To Get Better In A Little While', Blues Power' and is joined by Carl Perkins and Johnny Cash for 'Matchbox'.
6	McFarlin Auditorium, Dallas
7	Community Centre Theatre, San Antonio
13	University Of Nevada, Reno
14	Fairgrounds Coliseum, Salt Lake City
17	Memorial Auditorium, Sacramento
18–19	Community Theatre, Berkley
	Neil Schon joins Eric and is asked to join permanently, but he declines and later joins Santana
20	Civic Auditorium, Santa Monica
	Delaney Bramlett joins Eric on stage. He plays at deafening levels. He isn't asked to join permanently!
21	Civic Auditorium, Pasadena
22	Community Concourse, San Diego
25	Auditorium Theatre, Chicago
26	Music Hall, Cincinatti
	B.B. King joins Eric for 'Everyday I Have The Blues'
27	Kiel Opera House, St Louis
28	Music Hall, Cleveland
29	Painters Mill Music Fair, Owings

DECEMBER 1970

1	Curtis Hixon Hall, Tampa
	Duane Allman joins Eric for the whole concert
2	War Memorial Auditorium, Syracuse
3	East Town Theatre, Detroit
4–5	Capitol Theatre, Portchester
6	Suffolk Community College, Selden
	End of tour.

4 *EC Was Here...*
Or Was He?

opular metaphors for heroin addiction sum it up as simply a slow form of suicide, whereas a more accurate image might be of the Peanuts character Milus hiding under his blanket whenever the going gets too tough. It is in this way that heroin acts as a comforter: anaesthetizing junkies from a capricious, cruel, hard world. Many addicts eke out a miserable, day-to-day existence like this for years, if not decades, sheltering from a world they fear or despise. After nearly ten years of touring around Britain, Europe and the States, Eric Clapton shut himself off and stayed at home taking heroin. He spent his days constructing model aeroplanes and recording endless tunes into his small cassette recorder. He was living in limbo, and according to friends was 'rehearsing for his own funeral'. In a classic act of denial, Eric maintains that he was enjoying himself at the time, and to back him up, there were occasional signs of life in the two years he spent in hiding. In fact, many of the songs that he had recorded at home turned up on his albums in the seventies.

Alice Ormsby-Gore, an ex-girlfriend of Eric's, went back to him in 1971 and they spent two-and-a-half years together in a dark haze of heroin addiction. Alice was very much a substitute for Pattie and as is often the case in such relationships, it was doomed from the start. In fact, Eric met Alice in early 1968 and they lived on and off together, but she left in 1970 when Eric's infatuation with Pattie became apparent to her.

Eric had become a full-time recluse, and apart from his appearance at the Concert for Bangladesh in 1971, he rarely ventured out. His only other exception was to play with his old friend, Leon Russell at the London Rainbow. Not that his presence was noticeable: hardly visible in a dark corner of the stage, Eric played unannounced and largely unrecognized for most of the concert. He had become an enigma to his fans.

FACING PAGE Eric opts for French beret and sunburst Fender Stratocaster on the USA 1975 tour.

RIGHT Innovative typographical cover featuring superstar line-up of Eric Clapton's Rainbow Concert recorded and released in 1973.

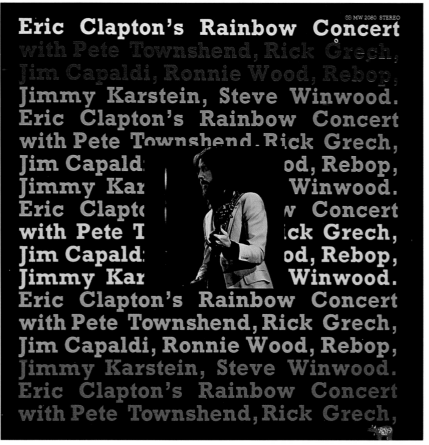

ABOVE Two years out of the limelight guaranteed headlines on Eric's return.

FACING PAGE Eric and Pete Townshend on stage at the Rainbow in Finsbury Park on 13 January 1973. Eric is playing a Gibson Les Paul.

In 1972 Eric did a session for Stevie Wonder's up-coming album. Stevie liked Eric's playing and remarked at the time that his guitar riffs 'were in the same bag as what Ralph Hammer and Ray Parker [regular Stevie guitar collaborators] were doing,' and that they had a 'mutual feeling for each other.' The session turned out to be abortive, and the general public have still to hear the results of these sessions.

Lord Harlech (president of the British Board of Film Censors), who as it happens, was also Alice's father, was organizing a series of charity concerts in London and enlisted Pete Townshend's help in a bid to bring Eric back to the concert stage and, he hoped, off heroin. This was as much a surprise for Eric as it was for his daughter and he was keen to play the concerts. Eric recalled, 'I just don't know why he picked on me to do the Rainbow concert. It could've been anybody but I'm grateful he chose me.'

So, it was announced that Eric Clapton would be making his long-awaited comeback at the Rainbow in the New Year. He was to be backed with a supergroup of celebrity friends; Pete Townshend, Stevie Winwood, Jim Capaldi and Ronnie Wood. The two Clapton concerts were part of the Fanfare for Europe celebrating Britain's entry into the Common Market. Tickets for both shows were sold out within hours and anticipation ran high. Rehearsals initially took place at Ronnie Wood's house on Richmond Hill, and then moved to Guildford's Civic Hall. According to Pete Townshend most of the material they used was drawn from songs that Eric

wrote for his solo album such as 'Let It Rain', and classics such as 'Layla' and 'Little Wing', as well as older songs such as 'Badge' and 'Crossroads' from the Cream period, and 'Presence Of The Lord' from the Blind Faith era.

But no one could rely on Clapton to turn up. In the event, he was excruciatingly late and arrived carrying a suit that did not fit him any more, it had to be let out before he went on stage. Much to everyone's relief he was in relatively good shape and the show went well, though sadly, the live album of the event, released as ERIC CLAPTON'S RAINBOW CONCERT, was recorded notoriously badly and did them little justice. Eric was back and to his overjoyed fans it could only be good news. The truth, however, was quite different.

Eric Clapton had a miserable year in 1973. He was still dependent on heroin; he didn't do any further live appearances after the 13 January Fanfare show, and nor did he do any new recordings, even though he thought about finishing some of the unissued material, with Pete Townshend's help, from the second Dominos album. Nothing came of it, and his hungry public had to make do with a stodgy diet of so-so compilation albums, and a poor live album taken from concerts at the Rainbow. Not a great deal from the 'world's greatest guitarist'.

Inevitably rumours abounded about Clapton's health, and there were genuine fears that he would become just another statistic on the rock 'n' roll casualty list. So, it was an anxious crowd of journalists that gathered in London's Soho on 10 April 1974 for a press conference, at which Slowhand would face his public for the first time in over a year. Clapton came clean about his heroin addiction, and told the press how he was cured using Dr Meg Patterson's controversial 'black box' treatment. (Still not accepted by the British Medical establishment, this cure uses controlled levels of electricity, generated inside a small black, metal box to which the patient is

BELOW The real comeback in 1974 made the front page of all the British music papers. The photographs were all taken at the China Garden Restaurant in Soho, London.

BELOW RIGHT European pic sleeve for 'I Shot The Sheriff'. The single released in July 1974 was a massive hit on both sides of the Atlantic. In the UK it reached number nine and stayed in the charts for nine weeks, and it was Eric's first number one in the States.

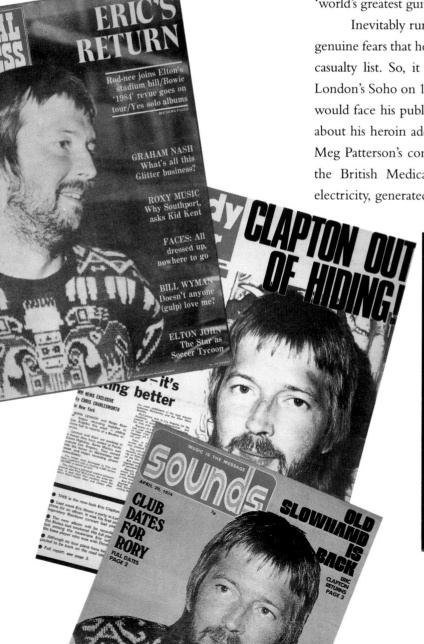

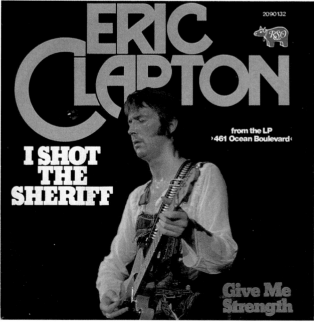

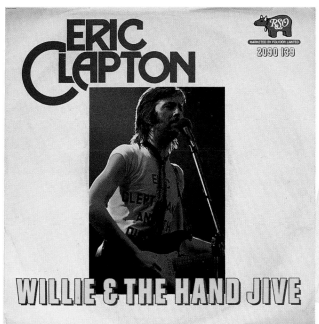

connected via leads clipped to the ear lobe.) 'It was an electric current running through my head that made me want to stop wanting to take heroin,' Eric explained. 'It was so painful that it couldn't be worse than coming down.' This was followed by a recuperation period, which included a stint of manual work on a farm in Wales which belonged to Alice's brother, Frank Ormsby-Gore. (A picture of him there can be found on the original gatefold sleeve of the 461 OCEAN BOULEVARD album.)

Alice had also undergone treatment, not only for heroin addiction but also for alcoholism and she later joined Eric at Frank's farm. As part of their recuperation programme, they were advised not to form an emotional relationship together again. But this only confirmed what Eric already knew, he was still very much in love with Pattie. Alice was aware of this and

ABOVE Rare UK pic sleeve for 'Willie And The Hand Jive' released in October 1974. The back of the sleeve (above right) features authentic instructions on how to do the hand jive.

BELOW European editions of 'Willie And The Hand Jive' with different picture sleeves.

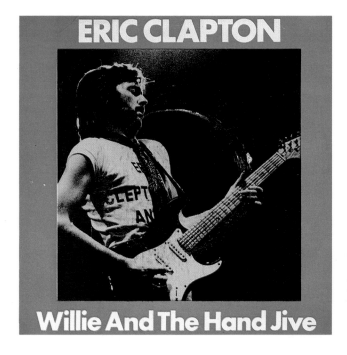

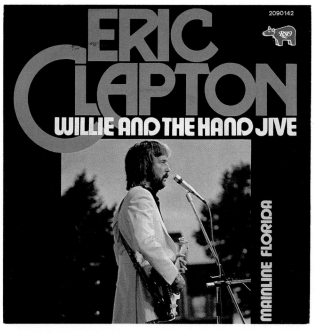

TOP Idyllic cover to 461 OCEAN BOULEVARD, released August 1974. The inside sleeve (above) featured Polaroids, bits of cine film and other mementoes of the recording of the album.

LEFT Fake US car registration plate used by RSO in shop displays in the States.

it was a painful end to a sad relationship. Soon after, Eric started seeing Pattie again, who by this time was feeling neglected by her husband.

Once cured, he wanted to get straight back to work. He was going to record a new album in Miami using Carl Radle from the Dominos on bass, which he hoped would be followed by a tour and, no, he replied patiently for the millionth time, Cream would not be reforming.

By the end of May Clapton had recorded approximately thirty songs with Carl and a new band, which featured Jamie Oldaker on drums, Dick Sims on keyboards, George Terry on guitar and Yvonne Elliman on backing vocals. Among the many recordings was a song written by the then largely unknown Bob Marley. 'George Terry played me this album, BURNIN', and 'I Shot the Sheriff' was on there. I loved it and we did it. But at the time I didn't think it should go on the album, let alone be a single. I didn't think it was fair to Bob Marley. I thought we'd done it with too much of a white feel or something. Shows what I know.' Lifted off the resulting album, 461 OCEAN BOULEVARD, Clapton's lilting, laid-back version of 'I Shot the Sheriff' introduced a new sound, reggae, and a new name, Bob Marley, to the pop audience. It was a smash hit worldwide and Eric's first number one in the United States.

Eric had made a conscious decision to make the album as different as possible to its predecessors. He was tired of being labelled with the 'guitar god' tag and consequently left the extended solos off the album, concentrating more on the relaxed vibes of the songs. There was no clear indication of Eric's lunatic fringe on the album. This became more apparent on the road, although the album's alternate titles 'Feed The Cook' and 'When Pinky Get's The Blues' give a fair indication of his state of mind at the time.

A tour was arranged to promote 461 OCEAN BOULEVARD, but, still recovering from heroin addiction, Eric was not in the best condition to take on the same exhausting round of stadium gigs that had eventually broken Cream. The reality was that in his fragile state, a smaller tour of medium-sized venues might have been better advised. To cope with the pressure of playing to such huge audiences Clapton began to drink heavily, substituting one addiction for another, though at the time he refused to see it as a problem. 'I've been drinking hard since I was fifteen,' he bragged.

The colossal tour began with two disastrous warm-ups in Scandinavia. Stockholm went okay, but Clapton appeared in Copenhagen, in half-buttoned-up dungarees, barely able to stand. The tour started officially a week later, on 28 June at the Yale Bowl, Newhaven, Connecticut, and, fortunately, Eric delighted his audience by wearing a natty see-through plastic mac adorned with a hotel's 'Do Not Disturb' sign. Eric's behaviour was eccentric at times both on and off stage. He is reported to have taken his clothes off and run naked down the aisles on a commercial flight, and, on another occasion, to have blown on a duck whistle at the

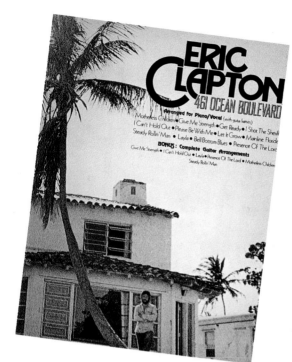

TOP 461 OCEAN BOULEVARD song book.

ABOVE Eric through the years on the cover of this song book.

FACING PAGE Eric sports a see-through plastic mac, complemented by a fetching 'Do Not Disturb' sign on the opening date of his US tour in 1974. He is playing his favourite Fender Strat, 'Blackie'.

ABOVE Eric retreats behind sunglasses to ease conjunctivitis at Madison Square Garden on 13 July 1974.

RIGHT Eric in the spotlight at the Nassau Coliseum, 30 June 1974.

RIGHT Eric solos on a rare and beautiful
Gibson Explorer during the European tour
in November 1974.

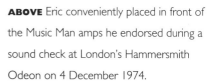

ABOVE Eric conveniently placed in front of
the Music Man amps he endorsed during a
sound check at London's Hammersmith
Odeon on 4 December 1974.

opening of his manager, Robert Stigwood's, production of *Manhattan
Follies*, which resulted in his forcible removal from the theatre. Bonzo Dog
Band's 'Legs' Larry Smith was on tour with him, and acted as compere and
general court jester. Thereafter the concerts would normally conclude with
an outrageous version of Chuck Berry's 'Little Queenie' featuring Legs in a
tap dance routine! And to their eternal chagrin, Eric and Yvonne Elliman
would bump and grind their way through 'Willie and the Hand Jive' and
'Get Ready', climaxing with them taking off each other's tops.

As the tour gathered pace, Eric and the band really started to cook.
Pete Townshend and Keith Moon joined them for some of the American
shows, jamming on stage and staying in the same hotels with the rest of the
entourage. Things descended to madness with the arrival of these infamous
hotel wreckers from The Who. Moon, ever the clown, created mayhem
wherever he went; matched deed for infantile deed by Townshend who, in
one spectacular debauch, put a hole in the wall of Clapton's room. The lads

and lasses were having a great time; at the finale of a show in Greensboro, Townshend smashed Legs' ukelele over Clapton's head. Photographic evidence was regularly printed in the 'Random Notes' pages of *Rolling Stone* magazine and read with great amusement by fans around the world.

As the tour picked up momentum, so did Eric's playing. The musicians were so relaxed that last minute changes would be made to previously arranged songs just to keep things challenging. Eric was supremely happy with his all-American band. 'It's what I always wanted,' he affirmed. 'These guys were steeped in the blues, and steeped in R & B, and if you just let 'em jam, they'd be playing exactly what you want to hear.'

More dates in the United States, Europe and Japan, were added to the 461 OCEAN BOULEVARD tour, which, incidentally, was managed by Roger Forrester on behalf of Robert Stigwood, who was becoming increasingly involved in film and theatre productions. The tour was broken into two legs, thereby giving the band a chance to record a new album in the break. Just before they headed down to Jamaica they were joined by singer/songwriter, Marcy Levy, now better known as one half of Shakespear's Sister. Peter Tosh, founder member of the Wailers, was invited down to the studio one day to help record a few reggae tunes. 'He was weird. He would just be sitting in a chair – asleep, or comatose,' remembers Eric. 'Then someone would count it off, and he'd wake up and play with that weird wah-wah reggae chop.'

THERE'S ONE IN EVERY CROWD followed on directly from 461 OCEAN BOULEVARD. Half the songs were written by Marcy Levy, and it featured a lot of reggae, as well as the odd snatch of gospel and the ever-present blues, but once again, no guitar solos. Although excellently produced by Tom Dowd, who had been around since the Cream days, it

BELOW LEFT Eric looks relaxed on the European pic sleeve of 'Swing Low Sweet Chariot'. The single reached number nineteen in the UK charts.
BELOW RIGHT Eric on the cover of *Rolling Stone* 18 July 1974.

LEFT Eric in one of his Esso jump suits drives along another solo in 1975.

BELOW LEFT Left to right: Yvonne Elliman, Eric and Marcy Levy at play during a break in the 1975 US tour.

BELOW RIGHT Eric poses in his hotel suite during a break in the 1975 US tour.

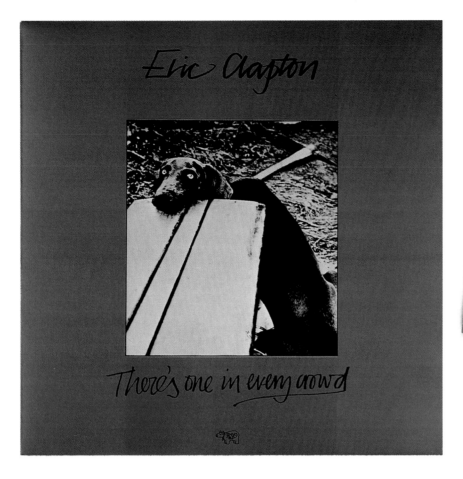

was a fairly uninspired album that has perhaps gained favour over the years. It did not, however, repeat the commercial success of 461 OCEAN BOULEVARD. Eric was quite philosophical about it. 'It's the kind of record that if you didn't like it after maybe the third or fourth time, you wouldn't play it again. But if you did like it, and you carried on listening to it, you'd hear things that were really fine, just little things in the background, little touches.'

The second part of the tour was intended to promote the new album, but Eric and the band rarely played any material from it, perhaps in response to the audience's lack of enthusiasm for THERE'S ONE IN EVERY CROWD, or possibly the band's own dissatisfaction with it. Soundboard tapes of the various gigs reveal that, on some nights, Eric's playing was out of this world, but on others – as has always been, and continues to be, the way – he was content to cruise on auto-pilot. Each performance is like a roll of the dice...you never know when you get a double six. It is not just Eric's mood that effects his playing, but also the audience's response and the other musicians with whom he is playing. RSO took advantage of the many good nights to compile a live album of songs, which restored the fans' confidence in Eric's reluctant deity status.

The tour arrived in Japan for the first time in November 1974, to play five shows. Japan loved Eric and Eric loved Japan. It was a warm and wonderful experience and Japan became a favourite place to play. Eric was

ABOVE LEFT THERE'S ONE IN EVERY CROWD released in April 1975 featured Eric's dog, Jeep, on the cover.

ABOVE Song book for THERE'S ONE IN EVERY CROWD.

BELOW Eric endorses 'Boy Howdy!' beer in 1975.

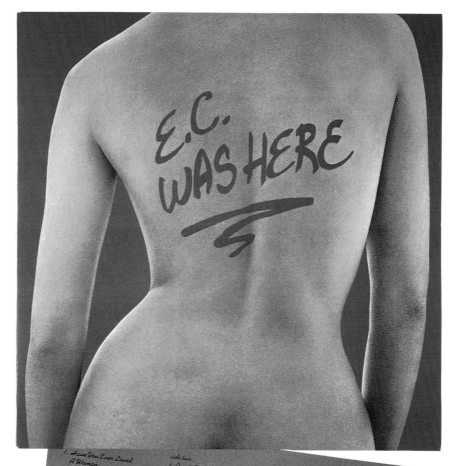

RIGHT The live blues album, EC WAS HERE, released in August 1975. Not an album cover we might expect to see today. The back cover features a rather large pair of breasts over-printed with the song titles and recording details. EC WAS HERE stayed in the UK charts for six weeks, peaking at number fourteen.

BELOW Comic strip used to promote EC WAS HERE.

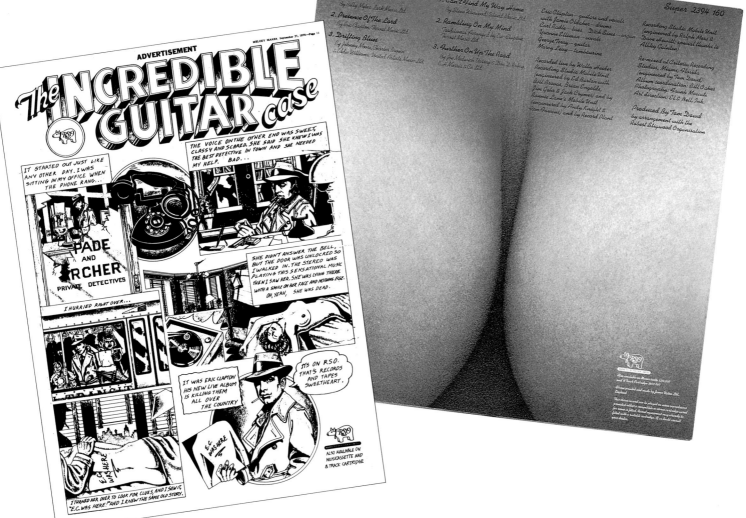

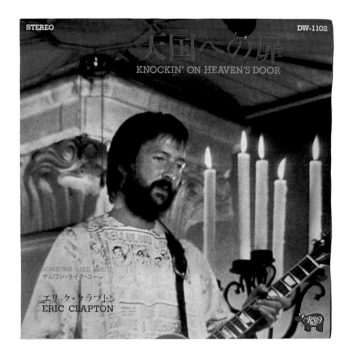

particularly thrilled since he had always had a fascination for Japanese art and film. He was bowled over by the hospitality, it is a Japanese custom to exchange gifts at every opportunity, and lo, Eric was flooded with presents by his fans. But Japan is one of the most controlled of developed societies and the shows reflected that; quiet, polite affairs with the audience staying in their seats, clapping sedately.

After Japan, the band came back to Europe and finished their mammoth expedition in England, at London's Hammersmith Odeon. The reviews were estimable, everyone was on form both nights, and Eric had made a special effort not to drink before going on stage. The record company rush-released the aforementioned live album at the end of the tour. A mix-and-match of songs taken from various venues and concerts during the tour, EC WAS HERE is an unsatisfactory affair. Eric commented at the time of it's release, 'I didn't really want it out now, but the record company was worried about the sales of THERE'S ONE IN EVERY CROWD.'

Eric took a well-deserved break and spent a lot of time with Pattie Boyd. They appeared together at the film premiere of *Tommy* in London and in all the national papers the following morning. They were very much the couple of the moment. Pattie had finally left George Harrison and had joined Eric during the American leg of the 1974 tour in a blaze of publicity. George was fairly generous about the situation, announcing to the world that, 'better she's with some drunken Yardbird than some old dope.'

A Labour government came to power in Britain in 1974, promising to tax the rich 'till the pips squeak'. To avoid the newly imposed high tax bands, some wealthy people, and prominent members of the rock aristocracy, Eric and Pattie among them, took their earnings out of the country. To qualify as a tax exile one had to establish residency in another

ABOVE LEFT Rare Japanese pic sleeve for the single 'Knockin' on Heaven's Door'.
ABOVE 'Knockin' On Heaven's Door', released in August 1975 on RSO. The single only made it to number thirty eight in the UK charts and held a chart position for four weeks.

RIGHT Rare 10 inch sampler, 'Prime Cuts', released by RSO in 1975. It features an unreleased version of 'Smile' which had been left off EC WAS HERE.

BELOW CLOCKWISE 'Hello Old Friend', released in October 1976. Typical RSO single cover in the US. A rare promotional US version of 'Carnival'. The UK version of 'Carnival', released in February 1977.

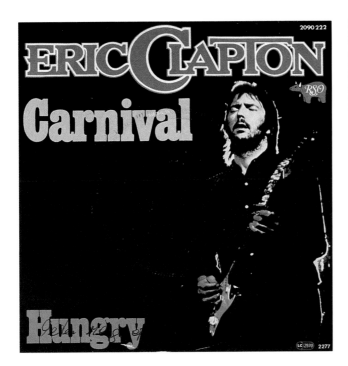

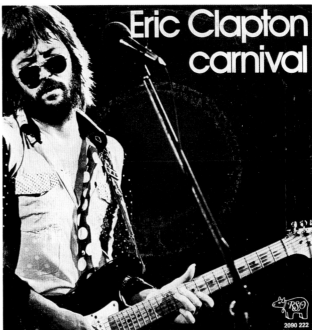

country for a period of no less than two years, during which time the exile is not allowed to spend a period of longer than thirty days in the UK in any one year. Nor is the exile allowed to do any work at all in his or her native country. Eric and Pattie settled in Paradise Island in the Bahamas, a quarter of a mile north of Nassau.

It was during one of his infrequent visits home, while driving his Ferrari, that Eric had a near-fatal accident with a juggernaut. 'I don't know what he did, but he hit me on the door and I just stood on the brakes and stopped the fucking car. The car was still there...it was where I stopped it but the lorry bounced off the car and was in the bushes across the road. It was too quick to know what happened to me or how close to death I'd come.' Eric suffered a temporary loss of hearing in one ear, but there was no permanent damage. After only a few days in hospital and three weeks rest in Nassau, he commenced rehearsals in Miami for another extensive two-legged trip around the States.

The band picked up where they had left off. Rehearsal tapes reveal them having fun with cover versions, and several takes of a smoochy love song, 'Too Lovely To Leave Alone', which sadly, because of time constraints, was destined never to appear as an official release.

The tour began on 16 June 1975 at Tampa Stadium, Florida. The set normally consisted of a mixture of blues standards; bits and pieces from the LAYLA album and a selection of songs from the last two albums. They also played their new single, recorded just prior to the tour's start, a reggaefied version of Dylan's, 'Knockin' On Heaven's Door'. Santana were the main support on the first leg, and Carlos Santana and Eric formed a close friendship based on mutual respect. The two would often encore together giving fans ample opportunity to witness some fine interplay between these

TOP LEFT AND RIGHT European pic sleeves for 'Carnival'.
ABOVE Music press advert for 'Carnival'.

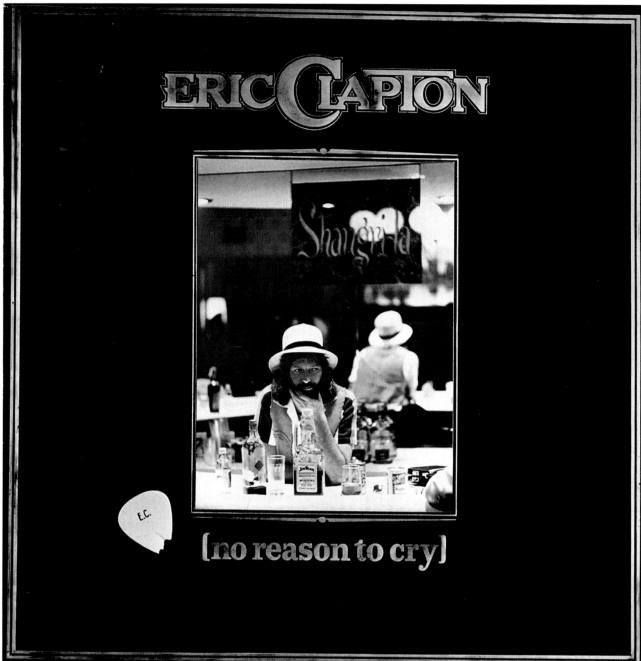

No Reason To Cry album released in August 1976. Recorded at The Band's Shangri-La studios in Malibu with many guests including Bob Dylan, Ronnie Wood, Georgie Fame and Robbie Robertson. No Reason To Cry peaked at number eight in the UK album charts. The back cover (right) featured an unusual typographic display of song titles.

two guitar giants. During a short break in the tour, Eric appeared, disguised and unannounced, at a Rolling Stones gig in Madison Square Garden. Dressed in a full-length denim overcoat, french beret and a massive amount of make-up, which made him look somewhat clown-like, he joined them for the encore of 'Sympathy for the Devil'. Initially the audience didn't recognize the guitar hero, but as soon as Eric broke into a solo, a great cheer went up, and he left the stage to a standing ovation from the ecstatic crowd. After the gig it was straight into the limos and off to the Stones' hotel for some late-night jamming and partying.

The Stones later joined Eric and his band at Electric Lady Studios in New York's Greenwich Village for a new song Eric had been working on called 'Carnival to Rio'. Eric recalls the session fondly, 'Ron Wood, Keith and I all played lead...the best takes were very early on, when nobody knew what they were doing.' He added, somewhat surprisingly, 'later on, when everyone worked out what part to play, it got too sophisticated.' The song was eventually re-recorded as 'Carnival' for the NO REASON TO CRY album. This was probably due to the contractual difficulties of getting all the names on the credits.

Eric was also invited to take part in the sessions for Bob Dylan's new album DESIRE. Little survives of the sessions, and although he played on several songs, only one, 'Romance in Durango', made it on to the album. It was a case of too many indians and no chief. 'He [Dylan] was trying to find a situation where he could make music with new people. It ended up with, like, twenty-four musicians in the studio all playing these incredibly

ABOVE LEFT TO RIGHT Tour programmes for the 1976 tours of the UK and US, and a special commemorative book for the Crystal Palace Garden Party.
BELOW Badge for 1976 UK tour.

MICHAEL ALFANDARY & HARVEY GOLDSMITH
BY ARRANGEMENT WITH THE ROBERT STIGWOOD ORGANISATION
PRESENTS

**GARDEN PARTY IX
AT THE
CRYSTAL PALACE
BOWL
ERIC
CLAPTON**
AND HIS BAND
**FREDDIE KING
THE JESS RODEN BAND
BARBARA   DICK AND THE
DIXON   FIREMEN**
Special Guest Stars
**THE CHIEFTAINS
Saturday 31st July**
TICKETS   Free Car Park
£4·00 INC. VAT   Travel

Announcement for the Crystal Palace Bowl
Garden Party on Saturday 31 July 1976

incongruous instruments, accordion, violin – and it didn't really work. He was after a large sound, but the songs were so personal that he wasn't comfortable with all the people around.' Eric is pictured at one of the sessions in the booklet that accompanies Bob's anthology, *Biograph*.

The tour ended on 30 August with a memorable show at the Scope in Norfolk, Virginia. Eric was moved to comment, 'you won't catch me saying this is my best band. But I'd go see us.' Tony Palmer captured one of the concerts on film and portions were used in the rock documentary *All You Need Is Love*. Unable to tour at home, because of the ever-vigilant tax man, the film gave many of Eric's British fans a tantalizing glimpse of what they were missing. Admittedly, Eric didn't look too clever; he was quite obviously drunk, but his playing stood up remarkably well. He seemed to be having fun, and sometimes it was good enough just to be back.

He returned to England briefly in September on his way to Ireland, and appeared on stage at the Hammersmith Odeon during a Santana concert. But he did not play a single note as the tax man would have interpreted it as promotion for his albums. In Ireland, Eric stayed in County Kildare and took part in the filming of *Circasia*, a very strange charity event. A thirty-minute short in aid of the Central Remedial Clinic and Variety Club of Ireland, *Circasia* also features Sean Connery, Shirley MacLaine and music by the Chieftans. Once again, Clapton appears almost unrecognizable as a clown. The film is rarely shown and is perhaps a curiosity of interest only to film buffs. In all truth, it is best kept out of the public domain.

At year's end there was a short Japanese tour before Eric headed back to Paradise Island with the intention of writing material for his next album. Possibly exhausted by the long tours, Eric was uninspired, and more inclined to relax and play in his tropical idyll than work. Ron Wood visited with some new songs and tried encouraging Eric to write some of his own. 'He was pushing me around trying to get me to write songs and we finally wrote a couple that we didn't use. One was called 'You're Too Good To Die You Should Be Buried Alive', can you believe that?!' Ronnie did, in fact, record this song and released it on one of his solo albums, but shortened the title to 'Buried Alive'.

This meant the album would have to be a compilation of cover versions or collaborations because, as Eric confessed, 'I had nothing'. To that end, he called on several of his well-known friends to help him out, including Ron Wood, Bob Dylan, Billy Preston and The Band. The sessions took place at The Band's picturesque Shangri-La Studios in Malibu, with Eric hoping that he could soak up some of The Band's influence.

The sessions got under way with Richard Manuel's, 'Beautiful Thing' and grew organically from that point on. Bob Dylan was a frequent visitor contributing the haunting 'Sign Language', which he sung as a duet with Clapton. Dylan was as erratic as ever, and unable to 'restrict himself to one way of doing a song. We did 'Sign Language' three ways. In the end I thought fuck it, I'll just go loose as he is,' Eric remembers. Robbie Robertson, Ronnie Wood and Jesse Ed Davis played most of the guitar solos, leaving Eric to concentrate on his vocals and to play acoustic and Dobro guitars.

Regular producer Tom Dowd was absent due to a dispute between Eric's label, RSO and his boss at Warners. With no producer at the helm, the informal nature of the sessions and general lack of discipline could have resulted in disaster. But Rob Fabroni, The Band's producer, was brought in to tidy everything up, and by the time they finished recording there was enough usable material to fill a double album. In the event, RSO released the single album, NO REASON TO CRY taking a line from Marcy Levy's song, 'Innocent Times' and a studio in-joke for the title. NO REASON was generally believed to be a return to form after the disappointment of THERE'S ONE IN EVERY CROWD. It went top twenty in the US and top ten in Britain and still stands as one of the gems in Clapton's back catalogue.

Eric's birthday fell halfway through recording and was celebrated with an amazing party held in the studios. On the unofficial tapes Van Morrison can be heard crooning through 'Stormy Monday', Billy Preston doing several Ray Charles tunes and The Band playing some drunken-blues tracks led by a raucous Rick Danko. Other highlights of the night were the rare sound of Bob Dylan joining in a medley of Beatles songs, and the whole ensemble gathering together for a rock 'n' roll 'Happy Birthday'. Only one of these songs, recorded for private amusement, has been exposed to the public – 'Last Night' available as the bonus cut on the NO REASON TO CRY CD.

As surely as summer follows spring, a new album is followed by another tour. Instead of dragging the new songs around the same old venues, Eric and The Band decided to embark on a tour of British seaside resorts. It was a fun excursion, which wound up at a Warner's Holiday Camp with a show exclusively for patrons. Van Morrison, who was also managed by Harvey Goldsmith, was wont to turn up for encores as did Ronnie Wood, Freddie King and Larry Coryell at the London's Crystal Palace show.

The only sour note came with the racist outburst Clapton made from the stage of the Birmingham Odeon.

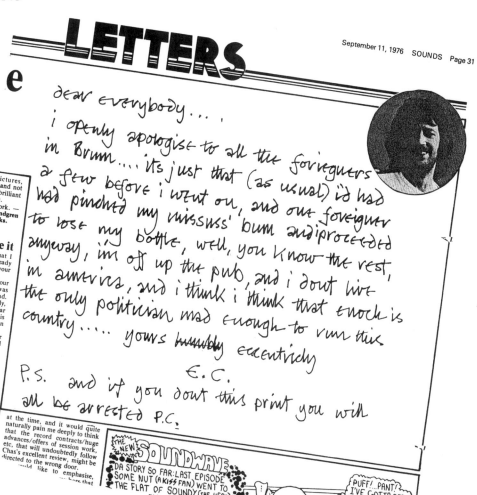

BELOW Infamous written apology from Eric after his drunken racist outburst at Birmingham's Odeon on 5 August 1976. *Sounds* printed the letter in the 11 September issue.

dear everybody...,
i openly apologise to all the foriegners in Brum.... its just that (as usual) id had a few before i went on, and one foreigner had pinched my misssss' bum andiproceeded to lose my bottle, well, you know the rest, anyway, im off up the pub, and i dont live in amurica, and i think i think that enoch is the only politician mad enough to run this country..... yours humbly eccentricly
E.C.
P.S. and if you dont this print you will all be arrested P.C.

RIGHT A beautiful poster advertising The Band's last concert which featured Eric and myriad superstars at the Winterland Ballroom on 26 November 1976.

FACING PAGE Eric and band pictured at London's Hammersmith Odeon, 27 April 1977. In some shots he is playing a rare gold top Gibson Les Paul.

Quoting from an extreme Tory, Enoch Powell, Clapton called for an end to immigration. Labour's attempts to reduce the balance of payments deficit had foundered; the economy was in crisis as the government went to the IMF for a loan; tensions were rising in the ethnic communities, which erupted in sporadic rioting throughout the summer; and the openly racist National Front was recruiting increasing numbers of young people. Clapton's speech not only boasted flagrant prejudice but was also considered virulently inflammatory. The incident received blanket coverage in the music press, with Clapton being roundly condemned. His outburst, and similar statements made by such stars as Rod Stewart around the same time, led directly to the formation of 'Rock Against Racism', an anti-fascist movement, that was soon able to mobilize over 100,000 to benefit concerts up and down the country. In reply, all a

RIGHT Cover of the classic SLOWHAND, which was released in November 1977 and spawned such hits as 'Cocaine' and 'Lay Down Sally'. SLOWHAND held a chart position for thirteen weeks, peaking at number twenty three.

BELOW RIGHT The inside sleeve of the album SLOWHAND contained a pin board montage of photographs featuring Eric in different situations.

FAR RIGHT US music press advert for SLOWHAND.

shame-faced Eric could say was, 'I was drunk. And a drunk will blab off about anything to as many people as he can. You cannot believe anything a drunk says.' As a white man who had made, and still makes, his career from playing what is basically black music, and who instantly connected to grizzled old men raised in shacks a stone's throw from cotton fields, Clapton had stood for the healing power of music. Many regarded drunkenness as a thin excuse, and for some people there will always be a question mark over Eric Clapton. But nothing in his behaviour before or since seems to indicate these beliefs were seriously held.

Country and western singer, Don Williams and the spare sounds of Scottish folk singer, John Martyn began to influence Clapton at this point; pushing his music even further in the laid-back direction it had been going since he split with the Dominos. In September he even guested at Williams' London shows. November 1976 saw the band on the road once more, for a short one-month trip around the States as part of the ongoing promotion for NO REASON TO CRY. At the tour's end, Eric was asked to appear at the Band's farewell concert alongside many other illustrious rock superstars that had been associated with them over the years, including Neil Young,

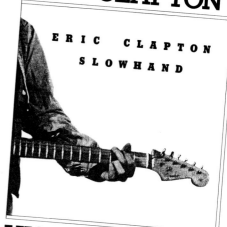

Eric with rare gold top Gibson Les Paul on stage at London's Hammersmith Odeon, 27 April 1977. The show was recorded by RSO but never released. A bootleg, however, did surface in the early nineties. Note the exclusive 'Old Grey Whistle Test' badge; it was only given out to people who had performed on the seminal seventies UK television music show. Eric and his band had filmed a special for them the day before this Hammersmith Odeon concert.

Ronnie Wood, Bob Dylan, Neil Diamond, Joni Mitchell, Muddy Waters and Dr John. Filmed by Martin Scorcese, and recorded as an album, THE LAST WALTZ, the concert and movie marked the end of an era. A more aggressive sound, punk rock, was waiting round the corner. It would scream for the rock–dinosaur's extinction.

Eric spent early 1977 at home in Surrey with Pattie. The next tour would act as a short warm–up to recording the next album at Olympic Studios. They played four memorable shows in London, one of which was broadcast on the BBC's *Old Grey Whistle Test*. Two further shows were recorded for possible release as a double album for the Christmas market. World-famous producer, Glyn Johns occupied the chair behind the studio mixing-desk, and he ruled his charges with an iron hand. Clapton, still drinking heavily, was easily distracted and unreliable throughout this period,

provoking several volatile arguments with Johns who took his job seriously. This is reflected in the final result, SLOWHAND, a superb album, which features 'Wonderful Tonight', written by Eric for his sweetheart.

SLOWHAND and the accompanying tour were a huge success in the States. The album reached number two, but the band was drawing a curtain over itself. Yvonne Elliman had left the previous September to pursue a solo career and George Terry was due to leave as soon as recording was finished on the next album. What remained of the band acted as support for Dylan on a short festival-tour, before going into the studio with Glyn Johns again.

After four albums in three years, and countless tours the band was jaded. There was not much enthusiasm in the studio and recording did not

ABOVE Tour programme for the 1978 US tour which featured a colour version of the black and white cover to SLOWHAND.

BELOW LEFT 'Lay Down Sally', released in November 1977, backed with 'Cocaine'. The single charted for six weeks and reached number thirty nine.

BELOW European pic sleeve of 'Wonderful Tonight' featuring a live shot of Eric on his 1977 European tour.

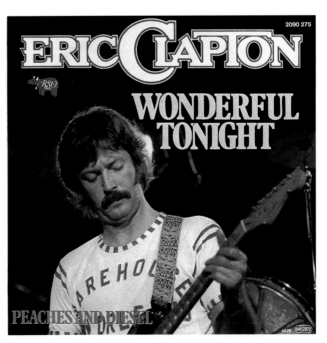

The outer and inner sleeve of Eric's
BACKLESS album.

go well. Eventually, Eric was forced to give orders. 'I was fed up with the
general apathy of everyone involved. So I just thought I'll take a song in
there, and whether they like it or not, we'll do it; record it and we'll put it
out.' The song was 'Golden Ring'. Two songs, 'If I Don't Be There By
Morning' and 'Walk Out in the Rain' came from a cassette Dylan had given
Eric, and Dylan provided the inspiration for the album title, BACKLESS.
'[Dylan] knew exactly what was going on around him all the time. You had
to focus all your attention on him, and if you didn't he knew it. And he'd
turn around and look at you with daggers in his eyes.'

Once the album was finished Eric also lost his song-writing partner and vocalist, Marcy Levy. The band was now down to a four piece, so Clapton had to undertake all the guitar duties, which was great as far as the fans were concerned. BACKLESS was released in November, and the four piece embarked on a European tour, with Muddy Waters as support. This was the first opportunity many Clapton fans had of seeing the blues giant in concert. Despite his age, Waters still came over as a formidable character with a tremendous presence and he was rapturously received, occasionally joining Eric on his encores.

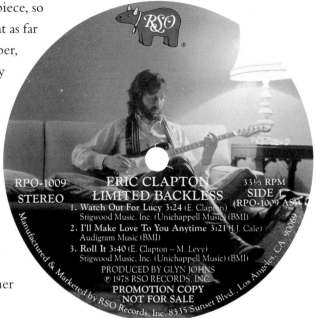

The band sounded a little empty, they missed a second guitarist. At tour manager, Roger Forrester's suggestion, Albert Lee, who had played with Chris Farlone, was recruited, immediately going into rehearsals for yet another huge American tour.

Eric finally married his 'Layla', Pattie, the girl he had fallen in love with all those years ago, in an intimate ceremony at Tuscon's Apostolic Assembly of Faith in Jesus Christ in Arizona, on the eve of the tour's start. They were married by a Mexican preacher and they were flanked during the ceremony by roadies in powder-blue tuxedos. The next night, Eric brought Pattie onstage during his performance of 'Wonderful Tonight' to the crowd's obvious delight. A wedding party was held during a break in the tour at their home in Ewhurst. It made the front pages, mainly because three of the Beatles went up on to the marquee stage and played together for the first time since they had split. Other notable musicians present included Jack Bruce, Ginger Baker, Jeff Beck, Mick Jagger, Lonnie Donnegan and Bill Wyman, all joining in for some rock 'n' roll classics.

The tour resumed, but Clapton could finally see that the band was

ABOVE Rare US white vinyl picture label featuring several tracks from BACKLESS.

BELOW LEFT European pic sleeve for 'Promises' single.

BELOW RIGHT UK pic sleeve for 'If I Don't Be There By Morning'.

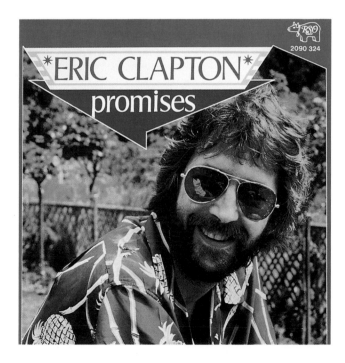

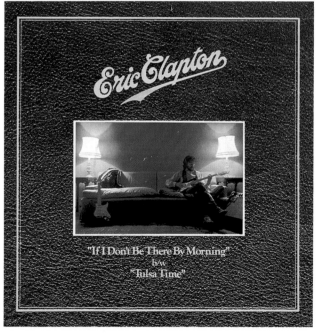

Eric and Pattie 'Layla' Boyd attend the
premiere of *Tommy*.

over. On his return to England, he sent telegrams to everyone, except
Albert Lee, informing them their services were no longer required. By
September an all-British band had been recruited with Henri Spinetti on
drums, Dave Markee on bass and Chris Stainton on keyboards. The sound
had changed but Eric's drinking continued.

Another massive trek around the world was organized taking in new
countries that were unfamiliar with rock tours, such as Poland, Thailand,
Israel and many others. In Poland there was trouble with the security, who,
unused to the frenzy of a rock concert, weighed into the audience with
totalitarian zeal. Eric was distraught. 'How can I play when I see kids right
in front of the stage underneath me, being pushed about by the men from
Sainsbury's [Eric's nickname for the security]. I felt so powerless.'

However, everything ended well in Japan, where two shows were
recorded at Tokyo's Budokan and released as the live double-album, JUST
ONE NIGHT. The breathtaking acoustics of the Budokan makes it one of
best live albums in Clapton's catalogue. Eric looks out from the cover ready
to take on the world. The truth was altogether different.

AUGUST 1971

1	Madison Square Garden, New York

Eric joins George Harrison for the Bangla Desh charity concert.

DECEMBER 1971

4	Rainbow, London

Eric joins Leon Russell for a few numbers.

JANUARY 1973

13	Rainbow, London

Two shows, 6.30pm and 8.30pm

ERIC CLAPTON'S 'COMEBACK'

Eric Clapton and his band were:

Eric Clapton (guitar, vocals), Carl Radle (bass), Jamie Oldaker (drums), Dick Sims (keyboards), George Terry (guitar), Yvonne Elliman (vocals), Marcy Levy (vocals, from November 1974 onwards).

The set was taken from:

'Smile', 'Easy Now', 'Let It Grow', 'Can't Find My Way Home', 'I Shot The Sheriff', 'Willie And The Hand Jive', 'Get Ready', 'Presence Of The Lord', 'Steady Rollin' Man', 'Mainline Florida', 'Have You Ever Loved A Woman', 'Blues Power', 'Can't Hold Out', 'Let It Rain', 'Tell The Truth', 'Mean Old World', 'Bright Lights, Big City', 'Matchbox', 'Badge', 'Key To The Highway', 'Little Wing', 'Layla', 'Crossroads', 'Little Queenie'.

SCANDINAVIAN WARM-UP TOUR

JUNE 1974

20	Tivoli Gardens, Stockholm
21	KB Halle, Copenhagen

US TOUR

28	Yale Bowl, Newhaven, Ct.
29	Spectrum, Philadelphia, Pa.
30	Nassau Coliseum, Uniondale, Ny.

JULY 1974

2–3	International Amphitheatre, Chicago, Il.
4	Music Park, Columbus, Oh.
5	Three Rivers Stadium, Pittsburgh, Pa.
6	War Memorial Stadium, Buffalo, Ny.

Eric joins support The Band for 'Stage Fright'. Freddie King joins Eric for 'Have You Ever Loved A Woman' and 'Hideaway'

7	Roosevelt Stadium, Jersey City, Ny.

Freddie King joins Eric for 'Have You Ever Loved A Woman'.

9	The Forum, Montreal, Canada
10	Civic Centre, Providence, Ri.
12	Boston Garden, Boston, Ms.
13	Madison Square Garden, New York, Ny.

Todd Rundgren, Dickie Betts join Eric for 'Little Queenie'.

14	Capitol Centre, Largo, Md.
18	Diablo Stadium, Tempe, Arizona
19–20	Long Beach Arena, Long Beach, Ca.

John Mayall joins Eric for an instrumental blues shuffle on 19th.

21	Cow Palace, San Francisco, Ca.

(2 shows – afternoon and evening)

23–24	Coliseum, Denver, Co.
25	Kiel Auditorium, St. Louis, Mi.

(2 shows – afternoon and evening)

27	Mississippi Valley Fair Grounds, Davenport, Mi.
28	Memorial Stadium, Memphis, Tn.
29	Legion Field, Birmingham, Al.
31	City Park Stadium, New Orleans, Lo.

AUGUST 1974

1	Omni, Atlanta, Ga.

Pete Townshend joins Eric for 'Layla', 'Baby Don't You Do It' and 'Little Queenie' along with Keith Moon

2	Coliseum, Greensboro, N.C.

Pete Townshend joins Eric for 'Willie And The Hand Jive', 'Get Ready', 'Layla', 'Badge' and 'Little Queenie'. Keith Moon joins from 'Layla' onwards.

4	West Palm Beach International Raceway, Palm Beach, Fl.

Pete Townshend, Keith Moon and Joe Walsh join Eric at various intervals during this closing concert from the first part of their US tour.

SEPTEMBER 1974

Set for second part of US tour was taken from:

'Smile', 'Let It Grow', 'Better Make It Through Today', 'Can't Find My Way Home', 'Let It Rain', 'Little Wing', 'Singing The Blues', 'I Shot The Sheriff', 'Tell The Truth', 'The Sky Is Crying', 'Badge', 'Little Rachel', 'Willie And The Hand Jive', 'Get Ready', 'Blues Power', 'Layla', 'All I Have To Do Is Dream', 'Steady Rollin' Man', 'Little Queenie'

28	Hampton Roads Coliseum, Hampton Roads, Va.
29	Nassau Coliseum, N.Y.
	2 shows at 3pm & 9pm
30	Boston Gardens, Boston, Ma.

OCTOBER 1974

1	The Forum, Montreal, Canada
2	Maple Leaf Garden, Toronto, Canada
4–5	Capitol Center, Largo, Maryland.
6	Spectrum, Philadelphia, Pa.

1974 JAPANESE TOUR

31	Budokan, Tokyo

NOVEMBER 1974

1, 2	Budokan, Tokyo
5, 6	Koseinenkin Hall, Osaka

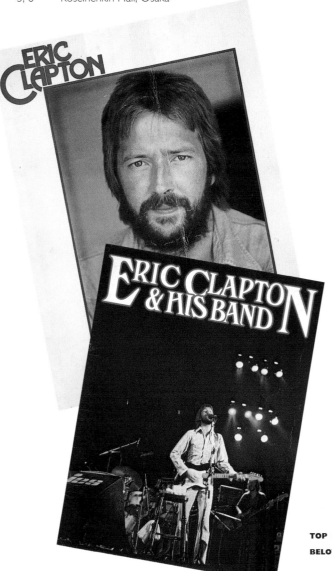

1974 EUROPEAN TOUR

26	Congress Centrum, Hamburg
27	Olympic Hall, Munich.
28	Friedrich Ebert Halle, Ludwigshaven
29	Grugahalle, Essen
30	Ahoy Halle, Rotterdam

DECEMBER 1974

1	Palais Des Sports, Anvers
2	Parc Des Expositions, Paris
4, 5	Hammersmith Odeon, London
	Both shows are recorded. Ron Wood joins Eric on 5th for 'Steady Rollin' Man', and 'Little Queenie'.

1975 NZ/AUSTRALIAN TOUR

The set was taken from:

'Badge', 'Steady Rollin' Man', 'Key To The Highway', 'Milk Cow Blues', 'Can't Find My Way Home', 'Teach Me To Be Your Woman', 'Nobody Knows You When Your Down And Out', 'I Shot The Sheriff', 'Layla', 'Little Wing', 'Tell The Truth', 'Let It Grow'.

APRIL 1975

11	Western Springs, Auckland, New Zealand
13–16	Festival Hall, Brisbane, Australia
17	Horden Pavillion, Sydney, Australia
19–21	Horden Pavillion, Sydney, Australia
23–24	Festival Hall, Brisbane, Australia
26	Memorial Park Drive, Adelaide, Australia
28	Entertainment Center, Perth, Australia

US TOUR

The set for the US 1975 tour was from:

'Layla', 'Bell Bottom Blues', 'Key To The Highway', 'Mainline Florida', 'Keep On Growing', 'Can't Find My Way Home', 'Carnival', 'Stormy Monday', 'Little Wing', 'Tell The Truth', 'Why Does Love Got To Be So Sad', 'Sunshine Of Your Love', 'Motherless Children', 'Mean Old World', 'Driftin' Blues', 'Teach Me To Be Your Woman', Badge', 'Let It Rain', 'Blues Power', 'Knockin' On Heaven's Door', 'Further On Up The Road' 'Crossroads', 'I Shot The Sheriff', 'Better Make It Through Today' and 'Eyesight To The Blind'.

Santana were the support band on most of the tour and Carlos Santana would often join Eric for the encores.

JUNE 1975

14	Tampa Stadium, Tampa, Fla.
15	Jacksonville Coliseum, Jacksonville, Fla.
17	Mobile Municipal Auditorium, Mobile, Ala.
18	Mid-South Coliseum, Memphis, Tenn.
19	Knoxville Coliseum, Knoxville, Tenn.
20	Charlotte Coliseum, Charlotte, N.C.
21	Cincinatti Gardens, Cincinatti, Ohio
22	Madison Square Gardens, New York, N.Y.
	Eric jams with the Rolling Stones on their encore of 'Sympathy For The Devil'

TOP *1974 US Tour programme.*

BELOW *1975 Australian and New Zealand Tour programme.*

23	Niagra Convention Center, Niagra, N.Y.
24	Civic Center, Springfield, Mass.
25	Providence Civic Center, Providence, R.I.
	Live recording
26	Saratoga Performing Arts Center, Saratoga, N.Y.
28	Nassau Coliseum, Uniondale, N.Y.
	Live recording. Carlos Santana, John McLaughlin and Alphonze Mouzon join Eric for 'Stormy Monday' and 'Eyesight To The Blind'
29	New Haven Civic Center, New Haven, N.Y.
30	Pittsburgh Civic Center, Pittsburgh, Pa.

JULY 1975

1	Olympia Stadium, Detroit, Mich.
3	Baltimore Stadiun, Baltimore, Md.
4	Cleveland Coliseum, Cleveland, Ohio
5	Chicago Stadium, Chicago, Ill.
7	Met Sports Center, Minneapolis, Minn.
8	Dane County Coliseum, Madison, Wi.
10	Kansas Municipal Auditorium, Kansas, Mo.
11	Kiel Auditorium, St. Louis, Mo.

AUGUST 1975

3	P&E Coliseum, Vancouver, B.C.
4	Portland Coliseum, Portland, Oregon
5	Seattle Coliseum, Seattle, Wash.
6	Spokane Coliseum, Spokane, Wash.
9	Stanford University, Stanford, Cal.
11	Salt Palace, Salt Lake City, Utah
12	Denver Coliseum, Denver, Colo.
14	The Forum, Los Angeles, Cal.
	Keith Moon, Joe Cocker and Carlos Santana join Eric on stage at various times.
15	Swing Auditorium, San Bernadino, Cal.
	Jerry McGhee joins Eric on 'Further On Up The Road' and 'Stormy Monday'.
16	Sports Arena, San Diego, Cal.
17	Community Center, Tuscon, Arizona
18	Civic Center, El Paso, Tx.
20	Sam Houston Coliseum, Houston, Tx.
21	Tarrant County Convention Center, Fort Worth, Tx.
22	Myriad Coliseum, Oklahoma, Ok.
23	Assembly Center, Tulsa, Ok.
24	Hirsh Coliseum, Shreveport, La.
27	Market Square Arena, Indianapolis, In.
28	Municipal Auditorium, Charleston, W. Va.
29	Greensboro Coliseum, Greensboro, N.C.
30	The Scope, Norfolk, Va.
	Poco join Eric on 'Let It Rain'.

1975 JAPANESE TOUR

OCTOBER 1975

22–23	Festival Hall, Osaka
24	Kyoto Kaikan Hall, Kyoto
27	Kitu-Kyushu Shi Ritsu Sogo Taiiku-Kan, Kokura
29	Shizuoka Sumpu Kaikan, Shizuoka

NOVEMBER 1975

1–2	Budokan, Tokyo

MAY 1976

15	Granby Halls, Leicester
	Eric joins the Rolling Stones on 'Brown Sugar' and 'Key To The Highway'

UK TOUR

Sergio Pastora joins the band on percussion.

The set for the UK tour was taken from:
'Hello Old Friend', 'All Our Pastimes', 'I Shot The Sheriff', 'Nobody Knows You When You're Down And Out', 'Can't Find My Way Home', 'Tell The Truth', 'Kansas City', 'Innocent Times', 'Stormy Monday', 'Going Down Slow', 'Double Trouble', 'Blues Power', 'Layla', 'Key To The Highway', 'Knockin' On Heaven's Door', 'Further On Up The Road'.

JULY 1976

29	Pavilion, Hemel Hempstead
31	Crystal Palace Bowl, London
	Larry Coryell, Ron Wood, Freddie King join Eric on 'Further On Up The Road'

AUGUST 1976

1	Gaumont, Southampton
2	Town Hall, Torquay
3	ABC Theatre, Plymouth
5	Odeon, Birmingham
	Van Morrison joins Eric on 'Kansas City' and 'Stormy Monday'.
6	Belle Vue Kings Hall, Manchester
7	Lancaster University, Lancaster
9, 10	Apollo, Glasgow
12	City Hall, Newcastle
13	Spa Pavilion, Bridlington
15	ABC Theatre, Liverpool
17	Warner Holiday Camp, Hayling Island

FAR RIGHT *1975 US Tour programme.*

1976 US TOUR

The set for the US tour was taken from:

'Hello Old Friend', 'Sign Language', 'Tell The Truth', 'Little Queenie', 'All Our Pastimes', 'Double Trouble', 'Knocking On Heaven's Door', 'Blues Power', 'Can't Find My Way Home', 'Key To The Highway', ' Keep Love On The Move', 'I Shot The Sheriff', 'One Night', 'Have You Ever Loved A Wowan', 'Badge', 'Layla', 'Further On Up The Road'.

NOVEMBER 1976

5	Bayfront Centre, St. Petersburg, Fl.
6	Sportatorium, Miami, Fl.
7	Coliseum, Jacksonville, Fl.
9	Omni, Atlanta, Ga.
10	Municipal Auditorium, Mobile, Al.
11	LSU Asembly Center, Baton Rouge, Lo.
13	Hofeinz Pavilion, Houston, Tx.
15	Convention Center, Dallas, Tx.

Freddie King joins Eric for 'Further On Up The Road'. The majority of the show is broadcast on radio at a later date

16	The Lloyd Noble Center, Norman, Oklahoma
18	Pan Am Center, Las Cruces, New Mexico
19	The Coliseum, Phoenix, Arizona
20	Sports Arena, San Diego, Ca.
22	The Forum, Los Angeles, Ca.
26	Winterland, San Francisco

Eric joins The Band at their historic farewell concert, which is recorded and later released as 'The Last Waltz'

FEBRUARY 1977

14	Cranleigh Village Hall, Cranleigh, Surrey

Eric plays a special 'Round Table' charity concert with Ronnie Lane.

UK TOUR

Sergio Pastora left the band.

The set was taken from:

'Hello Old Friend', 'Sign Language', 'Alberta, Alberta', 'All Our Past Times', 'Tell The Truth', 'Knockin' On Heaven's Door', 'Steady Rollin' Man', 'Can't Find My Way Home', 'Further On Up The Road', 'Stormy Monday', 'Badge', 'Nobody Knows You When You're Down And Out', 'I Shot The Sheriff', 'Double Trouble', 'Key To The Highway', 'Crossroads', 'Layla' and 'Willie And The Hand Jive'.

Eric and his band spend a few days at Pinewood Studios rehearsing.

APRIL 1977

20	De Montfort Hall, Leicester
21	Belle Vue, Manchester
22	Victoria Hall, Stoke
23	Apollo Center, Glasgow
24	City Hall, Newcastle
26	BBC Theatre, Shepherds Bush, London.

Eric and his band are filmed for 'The Old Grey Whistle Test'.

27–28	Hammersmith Odeon, London

Live recording taken on both dates. On the 28th Ronnie Lane and Pattie Boyd join Eric for 'Willie And The Hand Jive'

29	Rainbow Theatre, London.

Pete Townshend joins Eric for 'Layla' and 'Crossroads'.

IRISH AND EUROPEAN TOUR

JUNE 1977

4, 6	National Stadium, Dublin
9	Falkoner Theatre, Copenhagen
10	Stadthalle, Bremen
11	Groenoordhalle, Leiden
13	Forest National, Brussels
14	Le Pavilion, Paris

Ringo Starr joins Eric on tambourine for 'Badge'

15	Philipshalle, Dusseldorf
17	Rhein-Neckar-Halle, Heidelberg
19	Mehrzweckhalle, Wetzikon
20	Olympic Halle, Munich

AUGUST 1977

5	The Bull Ring, Ibiza
11	Nouveau Pabellon Club, Barcelona

1977 JAPANESE TOUR

Yvonne Elliman left the band.

The set for the Japanese tour was taken from:

'The Core', 'Badge', 'Double Trouble', 'Knockin' On Heaven's Door', 'Bottle Of Red Wine', 'Nobody Knows You When You're Down And Out', 'Alberta, Alberta', 'We're All The Way', 'Sign Language', 'Tell The Truth', 'Stormy Monday', 'Layla', 'Key To The Highway'.

SEPTEMBER 1977

26	Festival Hall, Osaka
27	Ken Taiiku-Kan, Yokahama
29	Kaikan Hall, Kyoto
30	Shi Kokaido, Nagoya

OCTOBER 1977

1	Festival Hall, Osaka
4	Makima-Nai Ice Arena, Sapporo
6–7	Budokan, Tokyo
9–10	International Center, Honolulu

1978 US TOUR

The set for the US tour was taken from:

'Peaches And Diesel', 'Wonderful Tonight', 'Lay Down Sally', 'Next Time You See Her', 'The Core', 'We're All The Way', 'Rodeo Man', 'Fools Paradise', 'Cocaine', 'Badge', 'Let It Rain', 'Knockin' On Heaven's Door', 'Key To The Highway', 'Going Down Slow', 'Layla', 'Bottle Of Red Wine'.

FEBRUARY 1978

1	Coliseum, Vancouver, Canada
3	Exhibition Coliseum, Edmonton, Canada
5	Paramount Theatre, Seattle, Wa.
6	WSU Coliseum, Pullman, Wa.
8	Paramount Theatre, Portland, Or.

10	Coliseum, Oakland, Ca.
11–12	Civic Auditorium, Santa Monica, Ca.
	Live recording
13	Aladdin Theatre, Las Vegas, Ne.
15	McNichols Arena, Denver, Co.
18	Metropolitan Centre, Minneapolis, Mi.
19	University Of Iowa Hilton Coliseum, Ames, Io.
20	Convention Centre, Kansas City, Ka.
21	Kiel Auditorium, St. Louis, Mo.
23	Stadium, Chicago, Il.
24	Louisville Gardens, Louisville, Ky.
26	Civic Centre Arena, Huntington, Ind.
28	Municipal Auditorium, Nashville, Tn.

MARCH 1978

1	Mid-South Coliseum, Memphis, Tn.
2	Boutwell Auditorium, Birmingham, Al.
19	Jai-Alai Frontun, Miami, Fl. *Live recording*
20	Civic Center Coliseum, Lakeland, Fl. *Live recording*
21	Civic Center, Savannah, Ga.
22	Coliseum, Macon, Ga.
24	Memorial Coliseum, Charlotte, Va.
25	Carolina Coliseum, Columbia, S.Cal.
26	Von Braun Civic Center, Huntsville, Ala.
28	Cobo Hall, Detroit, Mich.
29	Convention Center, Cleveland, Ohio
31	Civic Center Arena, Baltimore, Md.

APRIL 1978

1	Spectrum, Philadelphia, Pa.
2, 3	Radio City Music Hall, New York, Ny.
5	Civic Center, Springfield, Mass.
7	The Forum, Montreal, Canada
9	Maple Leaf Gardens, Toronto, Canada

1978 FESTIVAL TOUR

JUNE 1978

23	Feijenoord Stadium, Rotterdam
	Supporting Bob Dylan

JULY 1978

1	Zeppelinfield, Nuremburg
	Supporting Bob Dylan
7–8	National Stadium, Dublin
15	Blackbushe Aerodrome, Camberley, Surrey
	Supporting Bob Dylan

1978 EUROPEAN AND UK TOUR

Marcy Levy is no longer with the band.

The set for the European tour was taken from:

'Loving You (Is Sweeter Than Ever)', 'Kindheated Woman Blues', 'Golden Ring', 'Someone Like You', 'Layla', 'Worried Life Blues', 'Tulsa Time', 'Early In The Morning', 'I'll Make Love To You Anytime', 'Double Trouble', 'Badge', 'Wonderful Tonight', 'If I Don't Be There By Morning', 'Key To The Highway', 'Cocaine', 'Crossroads', 'Further On Up The Road'.

NOVEMBER 1978

5	Pabellon Deportivo Del Real Madrid, Madrid
6	Club Juventus, Barcelona
8	Palais Des Sports, Lyon
10	Saarlandhalle, Saarbrucken
11	Festhalle, Frankfurt
12	Olympia Halle, Munich
14	Phillipshalle, Dusseldorf
15–16	Congresscentrum, Hamburg
18	Le Pavilion, Paris
19	Forest National, Brussels
20	Jaap Edenhal, Amsterdam
24	Apollo Theatre, Glasgow *Live recording*
25	City Hall, Newcastle *Live recording*
26	Apollo Theatre, Manchester
28	Victoria Hall, Hanley
29	Gala Ballroom, West Bromwich

DECEMBER 1978

1	Gaumont, Southampton
2	Conference Centre, Brighton
5, 6	Hammersmith Odeon, London
7	Civic Hall, Guildford
	Live recording. George Harrison and Elton John join Eric on 'Further On Up The Road"

1978 European Tour programme.

1979 US Tour programme.

1979 IRISH TOUR

The band:

Eric (guitar, vocals), Albert Lee (guitar, keyboards, vocals), Dick Sims (keyboards), Carl Radle (bass), Jamie Oldaker (drums).

The set was:

'Loving You', 'Worried Life Blues', 'Badge', 'Wonderful Tonight', 'Crossroads', 'If I Don't Be There By Morning', 'Double Trouble', 'Tulsa Time', 'Early In The Morning', 'Cocaine', 'Key To The Highway', 'Carnival', 'Layla' and 'Further On Up The Road'.

MARCH 1979

8	City Hall, Cork
9	St. John's Lyn's, Tralee
11	Leisureland, Galway
12	Savoy Theatre, Limerick
13	Stand Hill, Sligo
15	Downtown Club, Dundalk
16	Army Camp Drill Hall, Dublin
17	National Stadium, Dublin

1979 US TOUR

The set list for the US tour was:

'Badge', 'If I Don't Be There By Morning', 'Worried Life Blues', 'Crossroads', 'Knockin' On Heaven's Door', 'Tulsa Time', Early In The Morning', 'Watch Out For Lucy', 'Setting Me Up', 'Double Trouble', 'Lay Down Sally', 'Wonderful Tonight', 'Cocaine', 'Layla' and 'Further On Up The Road'.

28	Community Center, Tuscon, Az.
29	Civic Center, Albuquerque, NM.
31	University Of Texas Special Events Center, El Paso, Tx.

APRIL 1979

1	Chaparral Center, Midland, Tx.
3	Lloyd Noble Center, Norman, Ok.
4	Hammons Center, Springfield, Mis.
6	Assembly Center, Tulsa, Ok.
7	Convention Center, Pine Bluff, Ark.
9	Summit, Houston, Tx.
10	Tarrant Country Convention Center, Fort Worth, Tx.
11	Municipal Auditorium, Austin, Tx.
12	Convention Center, San Antonio, Tx.
14	Civic Center, Monroe, Lo.
17	Freedom Hall, Johnson City, Tenn.
18	Coliseum, Knoxville, Tenn.
20	University of Alabama Coliseum, Tuscaloosa, Ga.
21	Omni, Atlanta, Ga.
22	Municipal Auditorium, Mobile, Ala.
24	William And Mary University, Williamsburg, Va.
25	The Mosque, Richmond, Va.
26	Capitol Center, Washington, Dc.
28	Civic Center, Providence, RI.
29	Veterans Memorial Coliseum, New Haven.
30	Spectrum, Philadelphia, Pa.

MAY 1979

25	Civic Center, Augusta, Maine
26	Cumberland County Civic Center, Portland, Maine
28	Civic Center, Binghampton, NY.
29	War Memorial Arena, Syracuse, NY.
30	War Memorial, Rochester, NY.

JUNE 1979

1	Memorial Auditorium, Buffalo, NY.
2	Richfield Coliseum, Cleveland, Oh.
4	Sports Arena, Toledo, Oh.
5	Civic Center, Saginaw, Mich.
7	Riverfront Coliseum, Cincinnati, Oh.
8	Market Square Arena, Indianapolis, Ind.
9	Dane County Exposition Center, Madison, Wi.
10	Civic Center, St. Paul, Minn.
12	Stadium, Chicago, Il.
13	Wings Stadium, Kalamazoo, Mich.
15	Notre Dame University, South Bend, Ind.
16	Brown County Veterans Memorial Coliseum, Green Bay, Wisc.
18	Civic Auditorium, Omaha, Ne.
19	Kansas Coliseum, Wichita, Ka.
21	Salt Palace, Salt Lake City, Ut.
23	Coliseum, Spokane, Wa.
24	Coliseum, Seattle, Wa.

1979 WORLD TOUR

Eric Clapton and his Band now consists of:

Eric Clapton (guitar, vocals), Albert Lee (guitar, keyboards),
Dave Markee (bass), Henry Spinetti (drums).

The set was taken from:

'Badge', 'Worried Life Blues', 'If I Don't Be There By Morning', 'Tulsa Time',
'Early In The Morning', 'Watch Out For Lucy', 'Wonderful Tonight', 'Lay Down
Sally', 'All Our Pastimes', 'Double Trouble', 'After Midnight', 'Knocking On
Heaven's Door', 'Country Boy', 'Key To The Highway',
'Cocaine', 'Blues Power', 'Further On Up The Road'.

SEPTEMBER 1979

30	Victoria Hall, Hanley

OCTOBER 1979

6	Stadhalle, Vienna, Austria
7	Sporthalle, Linz, Austria
8	Messehalle, Nurenberg, Germany
10	Palata Pioneer Hall, Belgrade, Yugoslavia
11–12	Dom Sportover, Zagreb, Yugoslavia
15–16	Salo Kongresso, Warsaw, Poland
17–18	Halo Sportowo, Katowice, Poland
	Second concert cancelled due to riot
21–23	Heichal Hatarbut, Tel Aviv, Israel
25	Heichal Hatarbut, Tel Aviv, Israel
27	Binyanei Ha'Ooma, Jerusalem, Israel

The set for the second part of the tour was:

'Tulsa Time', 'Early In The Morning', 'Lay Down Sally', 'Wonderful Tonight', 'If I
Don't Be There By Morning', 'Worried Life Blues', 'Country Boy', 'All Our
Pastimes', Blues Power', 'Knockin' On Heaven's Door', 'Settin' Me Up', Ramblin'
On My Mind', 'After Midnight', 'Cocaine', 'Layla' and 'Further On Up The Road'.

NOVEMBER 1979

16	National Theatre, Bangkok, Thailand
18	Araneta Coliseum Cinema, Manila, Phillipines
20	Academic Hall, Hong Kong,
23	Kemin Bunka Center, Ibaragi, Japan
25	Shi Kokaido, Nagoya, Japan
26	Kaikan Hall, Kyoto, Japan
27	Koseinenkin Hall, Osaka, Japan
28	Yubin Chokin Hall, Hiroshima, Japan
30	Shin-Nittetsu, Taiiku-Kan, Kokura, Japan

DECEMBER 1979

1	Furitsu Taiiku-Kan, Osaka, Japan
2, 3	Budokan, Tokyo, Japan
	Live recording for Just One Night double album.
6	Kyoshin Kaijo, Sapporo, Japan

TOP *Pages from the 1979 Japanese Tour programme.*
ABOVE *1979 Israeli Tour programme.*   **ABOVE** *1979 Japanese Tour programme.*

5 *Another Ticket, Another Ride*

he early eighties were not the best years for Eric. Seven years of alcoholism had taken its toll on his ravaged and ulcer-ridden body. He began to rely more and more heavily on the band to come up with new songs, his playing had suffered and his fans had given up hope of ever hearing his fiery guitar solos again. In short, Eric was coasting on auto-pilot, and to make things worse, he refused to accept that he had a drinking problem.

Eric recorded an album in March 1980 with Gary Brooker at Surrey Sound Studios, but the final result was less than had been hoped for. Turn Up Down, as it was called, was rejected by the record company and shelved on the advice of all concerned. It wasn't that Eric's playing was particularly bad on the album, though his voice was distressed by the drink, the real problem was his dependence on the band for new ideas and songs, which meant that Turn Up Down was not really an Eric Clapton album at all. Gary had contributed some fine material, as had Albert Lee, and they even played some of their songs on the UK tour in 1980. However, Eric's record label, RSO, felt it would be wiser to have more emphasis on material written, or at least, chosen by him.

RSO decided to have a second attempt at recording an album. This time recording took place in the sunnier climes of the Bahamas. The environment proved to be conducive in producing some good sounds, while Eric, spurred on by the first, humiliating rejection of his career, threw himself into his work wholeheartedly, though he did not cut down on his alcohol intake. He turned back to his blues roots. 'I was totally fed up writing ditties with pleasant melodies. I thought it was time for me to re-connect myself to what I know best.'

FACING PAGE Eric glides on auto-pilot at London's Hammersmith Odeon in 1980.

FACING PAGE TOP The superbly recorded, live double album, JUST ONE NIGHT was a huge chart success reaching number three in the UK charts and holding a chart position for twelve weeks. Recorded in December 1979 at Tokyo's Budokan JUST ONE NIGHT was released in May 1980 to coincide with Eric's UK tour.

FACING PAGE BOTTOM Handwritten message to Japanese fans on the inside sleeve.

ABOVE EC and Strat on the cover of the UK 1980 tour programme.

RIGHT Rare, numbered promotional 12 inch single of the live version of 'Wonderful Tonight' and 'Further On Up The Road' recorded at the Budokan, Tokyo in December 1979. Both tracks were taken from the JUST ONE NIGHT double album.

The second attempt, ANOTHER TICKET is a great, bluesy collection, and includes a gut-wrenching version of Muddy Waters' 'Blow Wind Blow'. The whole album improves with age, though it remains generally underrated and deserving of much more than the scant attention that has been paid to it thus far. Sadly, Eric was unable to promote ANOTHER TICKET properly. After a gig in Minneapolis in March 1981, only a few dates into yet another massive American sold-out tour, Eric collapsed and the promotional tour was cut short. He was rushed to hospital with an ulcer the size of a golf ball on the verge of rupturing. The news made 'Clapton Close to Death' headlines all over the world. And for once, the tabloids were not exaggerating. But, incredibly, Clapton continued to drink. 'I was still happy drinking and actually quite terrified of not drinking. I had to go further down that road to complete insanity before I stopped.' The cancellation of the tour was almost certainly the main reason for the relative failure of ANOTHER TICKET. By the time he had recuperated the album was already a dead duck.

Eric is an obsessive. He will push things to the limit; sometimes constructively, sometimes not. In the early eighties his urges were destructive, and the energy that should have been used to fuel his work was being wasted. 'I think what happens to an artist is – when he feels the mood swings that we all suffer from if we're creative – instead of facing the reality that this is an opportunity to create, he will turn to something that will stop that mood, that

ERIC CLAPTON · JUST ONE NIGHT

a tour of japan is something
which i always approach with
mixed feelings. the audiences are
invariably generous and almost
over appreciative, but the pitfalls
still exist: ill health, the feeling
of being somewhat of a freak
in the rightly closed society they
are so proud of, but all in all it
never fails to work out sweetly
for all involved ~ many thanks
to mr. udo, tats and tak ~
see you again soon
Eric clapton
12. march. 1980

irritant. And that could be drink, or heroin, or whatever.'

Only a few days after coming out of hospital, Eric was involved in a car accident while being driven by a record company employee and was taken straight back to hospital. The doctors, once again, recommended that he take an extended break and stay off the booze, and for once, Eric took heed of the medical advice. He returned home to his beloved Surrey mansion and rested, finding relaxation in his new passion, fishing. Pattie would sometimes accompany him on his fishing trips. Eric did not reappear on stage again until September, when he played alongside Jeff Beck at a few concerts in aid of Amnesty

ABOVE ANOTHER TICKET was released in February 1981.

LEFT Rare Canadian 12 inch single.

FACING PAGE TOP Insert to the ANOTHER TICKET album.

MIDDLE Original artwork for inside sleeve.

BOTTOM LEFT Picture sleeve for 'Another Ticket' single released April 1981.

BOTTOM RIGHT 'I Can't Stand It'/'Black Rose' as released in February 1981.

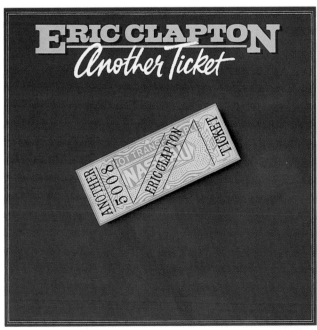

CIVIC HALL, Wolverhampton

The John Wile Testimonial

Eric Clapton

IN CONCERT

Wed., 18th November 1981

Evenings 7-30

STALLS

£5.50

E 21

A. B. Cooper (Printers) Ltd. MANCHESTER

To be retained.

No Ticket exchanged nor money refunded.
No Cameras or Recording Equipment.
Official Programmes sold only in the Theatre.

ABOVE TOP Ticket for the John Wile Testimonial in 1981

ABOVE 1980 UK tour programme.

BELOW Rare deleted 1982 box set which contained three albums, BACKLESS, 461 OCEAN BOULEVARD and SLOWHAND.

International. These were followed by a quick hike around Scandinavia before returning to England and Wolverhampton for football player, John Wile's testimonial. (At the time Eric was a big fan of the once-mighty football team, West Bromwich Albion and Wile was one of the team's heroes. Eric's support for West Brom turned out, in the end, to be nothing more than another temporary obsession; a passing phase.)

Eric had begun to slow up visibly. He ended 1981 with a short tour in Japan, and did not tour again until June 1982. In December 1981, Eric finally admitted to his tour manager, Roger Forrester, that he had an alcohol problem and he wanted to get better. This admission was the first true sign that he was indeed ready to confront the hellhound that had been trailing him for years. In January 1982, Eric and Roger flew out to Minneapolis, where Eric entered the Hazelden Foundation, a rehabilitation clinic for alcoholics. Eric learnt to get his self respect back by attending group-therapy sessions, and accepting responsibilities that he never had to face in the outside world before due to his privileged 'rock star' status, and because his manager and personal assistant did everything for him. In addition, Eric had to face the truth about himself and it was a very painful experience, especially when he realized, in the cold light of day, what he had done to people close to him over the years of alcoholic haze. Pattie, in particular, had been hurt but she stayed loyal to Eric. In fact, she, too, attended a short course in Hazelden, which taught her how to react to the new dry Eric.

Eric took advantage of his rest period in 1982 to break away from the Robert Stigwood Organisation and change management. Roger Forrester, a former tour manager who over time had become a personal friend, took over as Eric's manager, and Eric formed his own record company, Duck Records (known for a short time as Great Records). Eric, like many superstar's who

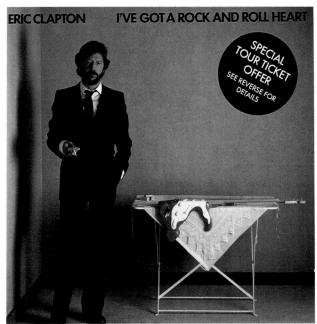

TOP LEFT The 12 inch single 'I've Got A Rock And Roll Heart'.

TOP RIGHT The 7 inch single featured an exclusive advance ticket offer for Eric's upcoming UK tour.

ABOVE The 12 inch of 'The Shape You're In'.

ABOVE RIGHT 7 inch picture single 'The Shape You're In'.

RIGHT 7 inch version with pic sleeve.

FAR RIGHT Poster for MONEY AND CIGARETTES album.

ERIC CLAPTON   MONEY AND CIGARETTES

Eric's MONEY AND CIGARETTES aLBUM, released in February 1983, featured a memorable photo of him standing next to a melting Fender Stratocaster on the cover. The album made a seventeen-week impression in the UK charts and reached number thirteen.

form their own labels, hoped to sign other acts. However, more than a decade later, the world is still waiting for the first signing to Duck.

When he came out, Eric was eager to start work immediately, so Roger Forrester arranged a short one-month US jaunt. It was a visibly healthier Eric that played on this tour. He played a fairly sedate set in sold-out, medium-sized venues rather than the half-empty stadiums he had played at in previous years. It did not matter about the size of the venue, he was back and working again, and what is more, he was getting good reviews.

Leaving RSO was a big step for Eric and a sure sign of his new-found confidence. As soon as the management changes were complete, Eric and the band flew out to Compass Point Studios in the Bahamas to record Eric's first album for his own label. Things, however, did not go well at first, and

after due deliberation, Eric found courage to fire his band. He felt that he wasn't being stretched enough by them, and consequently his playing was becoming lack-lustre. 'I started on that album with the English rhythm section, but I couldn't get any kick out of them. The thrill was gone, and there was a feeling of paranoia in the studio because they sensed it too.'

Producer Tom Dowd brought in a crack session team as replacements; 'Duck' Dunn on bass; Roger Hawkins on drums and the legendary Ry Cooder on slide guitar. Albert Lee was kept on and the prospect of the three guitar giants on one album had the music press in a froth. Eric was like a new man at the sessions and they bore rich fruit in the glorious return to form of MONEY AND CIGARETTES. The album was released in February 1983 to enthusiastic notices: Albert King's 'Crosscut Saw' being a particular highlight, with Eric coping once again with those familiar string bends of King's.

Back to full strength, and with a hot new record to promote, Eric set off on his first comprehensive world tour in two years with Chris Stainton back on keyboards. Chris had written to Eric saying he understood why Eric had sacked the band, thought it had been the right thing to do, and had no ill feelings about it. Eric was so touched by this genuine letter that he invited Chris back to promote the new album. The band obviously enjoyed playing together and getting to know each other in a live setting. Sadly, because he was unused to touring, Roger Hawkins threw in the towel after only a few dates. He was replaced by Clapton-veteran, Jamie Oldaker, who is regarded by many as the best drummer Eric has ever had. The tour came to England in April and May and included a four-night stint at London's Hammersmith Odeon, but the most memorable show was the homecoming concert at Guildford's Civic Hall. Eric's family and numerous

ABOVE LEFT Roger Waters's PROS AND CONS OF HITCH HICKING UK tour programme.

ABOVE Extremely rare Australian 7 inch of 'You Don't Know Like I Know', released in November 1984. Featuring Eric and Phil Collins it is the only release available of this recording and because it was deleted soon after release it is one of the most sought after items amongst collectors.

ABOVE Left to right: Jimmy Page, Eric and Jeff Beck duel it out during the US ARMS tour in December 1983.

BELOW A clean shaven Eric strums his Martin acoustic on 21 September 1983, during the second of two charity concerts at London's Royal Albert Hall.

FACING PAGE May 1983 at the Hammersmith Odeon during Eric's UK tour to promote the MONEY AND CIGARETTES album. The beard is back to full length before being clipped to its eighties stubble.

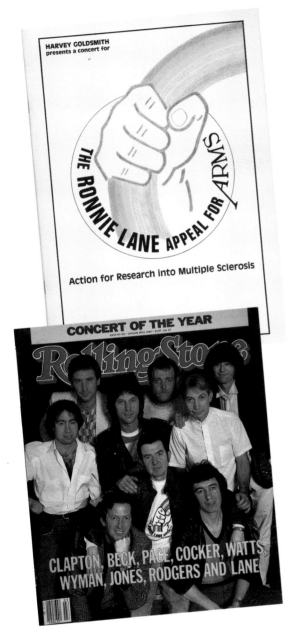

TOP ARMS tour programme for the 20 September 1983 concert at London's Royal Albert Hall.

ABOVE The ARMS US band make the cover of *Rolling Stone*.

friends were invited to witness the fabulous concert, which featured an eclectic series of guest appearances by stars such as Phil Collins, Jimmy Page, Paul Brady and English pub-rock troubadours, Chas and Dave on the encores. Eric was ecstatic, 'I feel much more confident. I know what I can do, yet I know my limits. When I'm playing well it knocks me out.' The tour took in Europe and returned to the States for a second leg, where it ended at the atmospheric Red Rocks Amphitheatre in July. Most of the shows, particularly those in the US, were recorded on an experimental digital recording system, the forerunner to DAT, which Sony was testing on the tour, but not one has ever seen official release.

Eric spent August helping Roger Waters record his first solo album since leaving Pink Floyd. THE PROS AND CONS OF HITCHIKING, was a typical Waters' project and drew the inevitable Floydian comparisons. Surprisingly, and against management advice, Eric agreed to join Waters' promotional touring band when the album was released in 1984. But before that, Eric was due to celebrate his twenty years in the business with a special charity concert at the Royal Albert Hall in September 1983.

Demand was such that the celebration concert sold out quickly and another date was added. The first concert was dedicated to former Faces' bass player, Ronnie Lane who was fighting a heroic battle against multiple sclerosis and proceeds went to the MS charity, ARMS. Proceeds from the second concert went to the Prince's Trust. Both concerts featured a veritable who's who of sixties British rock, and stars included Jimmy Page, Jeff Beck, Stevie Winwood, Bill Wyman, Charlie Watts, Andy Fairweather Low and Kenny Jones. Ronnie Lane had the audience in tears when he strolled on stage, but the musical highlight was the encore, which featured all three Yardbird guitarists playing on stage together for the first time since their demise in the mid sixties. Everyone enjoyed the event so much – Eric described the shows as a 'delight' – that it was decided to take this ad-hoc band to the United States. Stevie Winwood had other commitments so was replaced by Joe Cocker, but the rest of the line up were the same, and they rocked out to a series of classics including a duelling version of the Led Zep classic, 'Stairway to Heaven'.

After the ARMS tour Eric rented a small isolated cottage in Wales and took the opportunity to lock himself away and write some new songs. Having written a collection, he decided to test them out on live audiences before recording them. One of the songs, 'Same Old Blues' was a lengthy blues piece that gave Eric plenty of opportunity to show off his raucous fretwork. He playing a varied and unusual set away from the gaze of the established music industry. Eric purposely avoided the usual circuit and his New Year 1984 tour was a relatively low-key European affair, taking in Switzerland, Italy, Greece and Egypt. The tour ended in February, and immediately after, Eric and the band flew off to record their next album in Monserrat, with Phil Collins at the helm.

TOUR DATES 1980-1984

1980 UK TOUR

Gary Brooker (keyboards, vocals) joins the band.

The set for UK and Scandinavian tour was taken from: 'Tulsa Time', 'Early In The Morning', 'Lay Down Sally', 'Wonderful Tonight', 'Country Boy', 'Thunder And Lightning', 'Blues Power', 'All Our Pastimes', 'Setting Me Up', 'Leave The Candle', 'If I Don't Be There By Morning', 'Ramblin' On My Mind', 'Have You Ever Loved A Woman', 'After Midnight', 'Cocaine', 'Layla', 'Further On Up The Road'.

MAY 1980

2	New Theatre, Oxford
3	Brighton Centre, Brighton
4	Bingley Hall, Stafford
7	City Hall, Newcastle
8	Odeon, Edinburgh
9	Apollo, Glasgow
11	Leisure Centre, Deeside
12	Coventry Theatre, Coventry
13	Hippodrome, Bristol
15–17	Hammersmith Odeon, London
18	Civic Hall, Guildford

Jeff Beck joins Eric for 'Ramblin' On My Mind'

SCANDINAVIAN TOUR

SEPTEMBER 1980

19	Aalborghall, Allborg
20	Broendbyhall, Copenhagen
21	Vejlbyrisskovhall, Aarhus
23	Olympen, Lund
24	Scandinavium, Gothenburg
25	Drammenshall, Oslo
27	Isstadion, Stockholm
29	Icehall, Helsinki

1981 IRISH TOUR

JANUARY 1981

31	Simmonscourt, Dublin

FEBRUARY 1981

1	Leisureland, Galway
2	City Hall, Cork
3	Youree Youth Center, Carlow
5	Rainbow Theatre, London

One-off date in London

1981 US TOUR

MARCH 1981

2	Memorial Coliseum, Porland, Or.
3	Coliseum, Spokane, Wa.
5–7	Paramount Theatre, Seattle, Wa.
9	Yellowstone Metra, Bilings, Mont.
10	The Four Seasons Arena, Great Falls, Mont.
13	Dane County Exposition Center, Madison, Wi.

Remainder of the tour is cancelled due to Eric's hospitalization for serious ulcer troubles

SEPTEMBER 1981

9–10, 12	Theatre Royal, Drury Lane

Eric plays alongside Jeff Beck at the 'Secret Policeman's Other Ball' charity concerts in aid of Amnesty International.

BELOW *1984 Australian Tour Programme.*

1981 SCANDINAVIAN TOUR

The set was:

'Tulsa Time', 'Lay Down Sally', 'Wonderful Tonight', 'Worried Life Blues', 'After Midnight', 'Whiter Shade Of Pale', 'Country Boy', 'Double Trouble', 'Rita Mae', 'Knockin' On Heaven's Door', 'Blues Power', 'Ramblin' On My Mind', 'Have You Ever Loved A Woman', 'Cocaine', 'Layla', 'Further On Up The Road'.

LEFT AND BELOW
1981 Scandinavian Tour handbill.

OCTOBER 1981

7	Icehall, Helsinki
9	Isstadion, Stockholm
10	Scandinavium, Gothenburg
12	Drammenshall, Oslo
13	Olympen, Lund
15	Forum, Copenhagen
16	Vejlbyrissnovhall, Aarhus
17	Randers Hallen, Randers

NOVEMBER 1981

16	Civic Hall, Wolverhampton.

Eric plays one-off gig for the John Wile (West Bromwich Albion football player) testimonial

RIGHT *UK music press advertisement for a one-off show in Wolverhampton.*

John Wile Testimonial
CHANGE OF DATE
Eric Clapton + SUPPORT
IN CONCERT
Wolverhampton Civic Hall
NOW MONDAY, 16TH NOV 1981 7.30PM
Tickets for Wed, 18th Nov are valid for Mon, 16th Nov.
Refunds will be available ONLY UNTIL MON, 9th NOV from place of purchase.

1981 JAPANESE TOUR

The set for the Japanese tour was taken from:

'Tulsa Time', 'Lay Down Sally', 'Wonderful Tonight', 'After Midnight', 'I Shot The Sheriff', 'Whiter Shade Of Pale', 'Setting Me Up', 'Another Ticket', 'Blues Power', 'Badge', 'Motherless Children', 'Ramblin' On My Mind', 'Have You Ever Loved A Woman', 'Cocaine', 'Layla' and 'Further On Up The Road'.

27	Kenmin Hall, Niigata, Japan
30	Dichi Koseinenkin Hall, Nagoya, Japan

DECEMBER 1981

1	Festival Hall, Osaka, Japan
3	Sun Palace, Fukuoka, Japan
4	Kaikan Dai-Ichi Hall, Kyoto, Japan
7	Budokan, Tokyo, Japan
8	Bunka Taiiku-Kan, Yokohama, Japan
9	Budokan, Tokyo, Japan

1982 US TOUR

The set was taken from:

'Tulsa Time', 'Lay Down Sally', 'I Shot The Sheriff', 'Blow Wind Blow', 'Wonderful Tonight', 'Pink Bedroom', 'Whiter Shade Of Pale', 'Key To The Highway', 'Double Trouble', 'Blues Power', 'Cocaine', 'Layla', 'Further On Up The Road'.

JUNE 1982

5	Paramount Theatre, Cedar Rapids, Mich.
6	Civic Auditorium, Omaha, Ne.
10–11	Pine Knob Pavilion, Detroit, Mich.
12	Memorial Auditorium, Buffalo, NY.
13	Blossom Music Center, Cleveland, Oh.
17	Cumberland County Civic Center, Portland, Maine
18	Broome County Coliseum, Binghampton, NY.
19	Performing Arts Center, Saratoga, NY.
22	Hampton Roads Coliseum, Hampton, NY.
23	Coliseum, Charlotte, N.Ca.
24	Vicking Hall, Bristol, Tenn.
27	Civic Center, Augusta, Ga.

1981 Japanese Tour programme.

28   Coliseum, Jacksonville, Fl.

29   Civic Center, Lakeland, Fl.

30   Sportatorium, Miami, Fl.

Muddy Waters joins Eric on 'Blow Wind Blow'

DECEMBER 1982

22   The Royal, Guildford

Eric plays one-off charity show in this Guildford pub.

1983 US TOUR

Eric Clapton and his Band now consists of:

Eric Clapton (guitars, vocals), Jamie Oldaker (drums), Duck Dunn (bass), Albert Lee (guitar, vocals), Chris Stainton (keyboards).

The set was:

'After Midnight', 'I Shot The Sheriff', 'Worried Life Blues', 'Crazy Country Hop', 'Crosscut Saw', 'Slow Down Linda', 'Sweet Little Lisa', 'Key To The Highway', 'Tulsa Time', 'Rock 'N' Roll Heart', 'Wonderful Tonight', 'Blues Power', 'Long Distance Call', 'Have You Ever Loved A Woman', 'Ramblin' On My Mind', 'Let It Rain', 'Cocaine', 'Layla', 'Further On Up The Road'.

FEBRUARY 1983

1–2   Paramount Theatre, Seattle, Wa.

3   Cumberland County Civic Center, Portland, Ore.

6   Convention Center, Sacramento, Ca.

7   Cow Palace, San Francisco, Ca.

8   Universal Amphitheatre, Los Angeles, Ca.

9   Long Beach Arena, Long Beach, Ca.

11   Veterans Memorial Coliseum, Phoenix, Ar.

13   Erwin Events Center, Austin, Tx

14   The Summit, Houston, Tx.

15   Reunion Arena, Dallas, Tx.

17   Mid-South Coliseum, Memphis, Tenn.

18   Kiel Auditorium, St. Louis, Mo.

19   Hara Arena, Dayton, Ill.

21   Spectrum, Philadelphia, Pa.

Ry Cooder joins Eric on 'Crossroads'

22   Brendan Byrne Arena, East Rutherford, N.J.

25   Omni, Atlanta, Ga.

26   The Gardens, Louisville, Ky.

MARCH 1983

1   Centrum, Worcester, Mass.

2   Hershey Park Arena, Hershey, Pa.

3   Civic Arena, Pittsburgh, Pa.

1983 UK AND EUROPEAN TOUR

The set was taken from:

'Tulsa Time', 'I Shot The Sheriff', 'Worried Life Blues', 'Lay Down Sally', 'Let It Rain', 'Double Trouble', 'Sweet Little Lisa', 'Key To The Highway', I've Got A Rock 'N' Roll Heart', 'Ain't Going Down', 'After Midnight', 'The Shape You're In', 'Wonderful Tonight', 'Blues Power', 'Ramblin' On My Mind', 'Have You Ever Loved A Wowan', 'Cocaine', 'Layla', 'Further On Up The Road'.

APRIL 1983

8, 9   Playhouse, Edinburgh

11   City Hall, Newcastle

12   Empire, Liverpool

14–16   National Stadium, Dublin

20   Stadhalle, Bremen

21   Grugahalle, Essen

23   Ahoy Halle, Rotterdam

24   Chapitau De Pantin, Paris

26   Sportshalle, Cologne

27   Festhalle, Frankfurt

29   Rhein Neckar Halle, Eppelheim

30   St. Jakobshalle, Basle

ABOVE *Ticket for Frankfurt concert 27 April 1983.*

TOP *Tickets for Edinburgh and Newcastle-upon Tyne concerts April 1983.*

ABOVE *Advertisement for Köln and Essen concerts April 1983*

MAY 1983

2   Palaeur, Rome

3   Palazzo Dello Sport, Genoa

5   Palais De Sports, Toulouse

7   Sports Palace, Barcelona

8   Velodromo Anoeta, San Sebastian

13   Cornwall Coliseum, St. Austell

14   Arts Centre, Poole

16–19   Hammersmith Odeon, London

21   Apollo, Manchester

22   De Montfort Hall, Leicester

23   Civic Hall, Guildford

      Paul Brady, Phil Collins, Jimmy Page, Chas and Dave join Eric

      on the encores

JUNE 1983

5   New Victoria Theatre, London

      Eric plays a special charity concert for 'Save The Children'.

US TOUR

25   Kingswood Music Theatre, Toronto, Canada

27–29   Pine Knob Pavilion, Detroit, Mich.

JULY 1983

1   Performing Arts Center, Saratoga, NY.

2–3   Jones Beach, Long Island, NY.

5   Merriweather Post Pavilion, Columbia

7   Blossom Music Theatre, Cleveland, Oh.

9   Civic Center Arena, St. Paul, Minn.

10   Milwaukee Summerfest, Milwaukee, Wi.

11   Poplar Creek, Chicago, Il.

13   Kings Island Timberwolf Theatre, Cincinnati, Oh.

14   Wings Stadium, Kalamazoo,

16–17   Red Rocks Amphitheatre, Denver, Co.

      The Blasters join Eric on 17th for

      'Further On Up The Road'

UK ARMS TOUR

SEPTEMBER 1983

20   Royal Albert Hall, London

      ARMS concert

21   Royal Albert Hall, London

      The Prince's Trust concert

US ARMS TOUR

NOVEMBER 1983

28–29   Reunion Arena, Dallas, Tx.

DECEMBER 1983

1–3   Cow Palace, San Francisco, Ca.

5–6   Forum, Los Angeles, Ca.

8–9   Madison Square Garden, New York, NY.

RIGHT *Programme and ticket for Prince's Trust concert on 21 September 1983.*

RIGHT *Programme*
for UK tour.

BELOW *Programme for*
US ARMS Tour and
ticket for UK ARMS
concert on 20
September 1983.

EUROPEAN/MIDDLE EAST TOUR

JANUARY 1984

20–21	Hallenstadion, Zurich
23–24	Teatrotenda, Milan
26	Beogradski-Sajam Hala, Belgrade
28, 29	Sporting Of Athens, Athens

FEBRUARY 1984

2	American University, Cairo
5–6	Binyanei Ha'Ooma, Jerusalem

RIGHT AND BELOW RIGHT
Press advertisements for the Australian Tour 1984.

ROGER WATERS 'PROS AND CONS OF HITCHIKING' TOUR

JUNE 1984

16–17	Isstadion, Stockholm
19	Ahoy Halle, Rotterdam
21–22	Earls Court, London
	Live recording
26, 27	NEC, Birmingham

JULY 1984

3	Hallenstadion, Zurich
6	Palais Des Sports, Paris
17–18	Civic Center, Hartford, Ct.
20–22	Meadowlands Arena, New Jersey, NJ.
24	Spectrum, Philadelphia, Pa.
28–29	Maple Leaf Gardens, Toronto, Canada
31	The Forum, Montreal, Canada

1984 AUSTRALIA & HONG KONG TOUR

The band consists of:

Eric Clapton (guitar, vocals), Jamie Oldaker (drums), Peter Robinson (synthesizer), Marcy Levy (vocals), Duck Dunn (bass), Chris Stainton (keyboards).

The set was:

'Everybody Oughta Make A Change', 'Motherless Children', 'I Shot The Sheriff', 'Same Old Blues', 'Tangled In Love', 'She's Waiting', 'Stepping Out', 'Tulsa Time', 'Badge', 'Love Sign', 'Wonderful Tonight', 'Let It Rain', 'Long Distance Call', 'Have You Ever Loved A Woman', 'Ramblin' On My Mind', 'Cocaine', 'Layla', 'Knock On Wood', 'You Don't Know Like I Know'.

NOVEMBER 1984

13–14	Hodern Pavilion, Sydney
17	Festival Hall, Brisbane
20–21	Hodern Pavilion, Sydney
23–25	Sports And Entertainment Centre, Melbourne
28	Entertainments Centre, Perth

DECEMBER 1984

2	The Coliseum, Hong Kong

6 Plugged in: The Albert Hall Years

ric finally surged back into view at Live Aid in 1985. One of the biggest media events of the century, Live Aid was broadcast simultaneously to almost every nation on earth. The pop industry fed the world and gained exposure such as it could never have dreamed possible. The concert made U2, and elevated Queen and Eric Clapton to heights even those megastars had never before reached. Eric gave one of the performances of his career to one of the largest audiences ever assembled. In a short, twenty-minute set featuring the classics 'White Room', 'She's Waiting' and 'Layla' he re-established himself as one of rock's most important and influential artists.

Clapton had clearly enjoyed a return to form during the recording of his last album, BEHIND THE SUN. Produced by Phil Collins it featured some of his best guitar playing in quite some time, particularly on 'Just Like a Prisoner' and his vocals were delivered with new force. However, all had not gone smoothly prior to release. When Warner Brothers received delivery of the final product, they could not hear anything that sounded to them like a hit single. Not to worry, Eric Clapton has always sold plenty of albums. But in the eighties, singles came to be seen more and more as a trailer for the album and record companies wanted chart hits. Consequently, the company refused to release the album.

Eric was understandably upset. 'I never considered that to be a priority in my life, and still don't. But I suppose I had to bend with it, and I wanted to know what they thought hit single material was.' So Eric agreed to listen to some songs by Texan songwriter, Jerry Williams, which Warners sent to him. 'I liked them a great deal. So I said yeah, sure, I'll do them, and we'll see how it works out.'

FACING PAGE Eric wearing spectacles during his short three-date stint at Birmingham's NEC. All three concerts were in aid of the chemical dependency centre projects.

ABOVE Joyous cover for BEHIND THE SUN that was released in March 1985. The album was a top ten hit for Eric, reaching number eight, and it spent fourteen weeks in the UK charts.

Things worked out fine. Four songs were recorded with a group of top LA session musicians, known locally as the 'A Team'. Three of the songs made it on to the album, one becoming the new single, 'Forever Man'. To promote it, Clapton agreed to another first, the making of a video. As much as albums needed singles, singles needed videos, since so many American households were receiving MTV. 'It was fun, but it goes against the grain for me. The video thing's a bit obnoxious. The mystery is being taken out of music, which for me has always been something to close your eyes to and have your own picture.'

Suddenly, in the mid and late eighties, EC was everywhere. There was a video of a gig from the 1985 tour, recorded at the Civic Centre, Hartford, on 1 May, during which he demonstrates that he has recaptured

FOREVER MAN

TOO BAD
N IS ONE STEP AWAY

JAPAN TOUR 1985

U.S. TOUR 1985

Behind the Sun
TOUR 1985

the fierce intensity of the early seventies. A haunting soundtrack for the BBC thriller *Edge of Darkness* won him an award and much acclaim. And everyone wanted to be seen with 'The World's Greatest Guitarist'. He guested with Lionel Richie, Dire Straits, Buddy Guy and Junior Wells, while Mark Knopfler returned the favour when he joined Eric on a UK and European tour in 1987, though Eric was surprised to find out that, when Mark called him to ask if it would be okay to come to the gigs, he'd meant as a member of the band.

His career was back on course, but his personal life was in tatters. By the end of 1985, Eric's fairy-tale romance with Pattie was almost at an end.

TOP LEFT 12 inch single cover for 'Forever Man' as released in March 1985.

TOP RIGHT 12 inch square 1985 Japanese tour programme.

ABOVE LEFT 1985 US tour programme.

ABOVE MIDDLE 1985 tour badge.

ABOVE 1985 US tour sweatshirt.

ABOVE Eric solos in Richmond, Virginia during the Behind The Sun tour in 1985.
LEFT EC, George Harrison, Ringo Starr, Dave Edmunds, Rosanne Cash, Earl Slick, and Stray Cats Slim Jim Phantom and Lee Rocker pose with rockabilly legend Carl Perkins at the *Blue Suede Shoes* television recording.
FACING PAGE EC and band backstage at Live Aid. Back row: Duck Dunn, Chris Stainton, Jamie Oldaker. Middle Row: Shaun Murphy, Marcy Levy, and Eric centre.

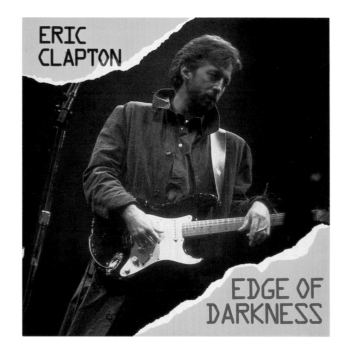

ABOVE 7 inch single from the award-winning soundtrack to the BBC thriller, *Edge Of Darkness*. The single, released in October 1985, reached number sixty five and stayed in the UK charts for three weeks.

ABOVE RIGHT Award-winning EDGE OF DARKNESS six-track album as released in November 1985.

BELOW Pic sleeve for 'She's Waiting' which was released in June 1985. The B side includes a rare track, 'Jailbait', which is unavailable elsewhere.

The constant touring contradicted his desire to start a family and Pattie was unable to have children. So, when his latest model girlfriend became pregnant, a split was inevitable. In a blaze of tabloid headlines they divorced. 'It was best, with the birth of my son Conor it was impossible for Pattie.' They do, however, still remain close friends, 'there's a real thread that holds us together'.

In early 1986, Eric made another break when he ditched his band and made a conscious decision to record a commercial album. Long-time friend Phil Collins was again asked to occupy the producer's chair and the drummer's stool, as well as contribute backing vocals. Bass and keyboards were handled by two members of the 'A Team', Nathan East and Greg Phillinganes. Something of a dream team, the quartet enjoyed recording together so much that they were determined to tour when the album was completed, that is, if Phil Collins could fit it into his hectic schedule.

Eric's new band weren't the only new aspect to his sound, he also had a new guitar, custom built to his exact specifications by Fender. 'It's the best guitar ever made. Of all the ones I've ever tried, Gibson, Fender, Gretch – all of them – this is the most satisfying for me to play.' The 'Eric Clapton Fender Stratocaster Signature Series' guitar was later made commercially available and proved popular with many pros including Edge and Pete Townshend. As for his faithful sixteen-year-old guitar, 'Blackie', 'It's off the road completely. I play it at home occasionally, but it's too precious for me to take out for fear of loss or breakage or something like that.'

The new axe was heard for the first time on the new

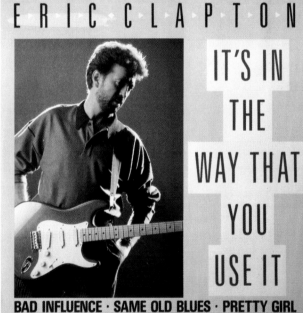

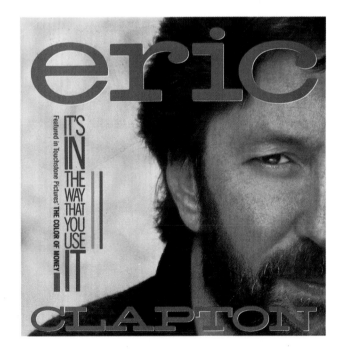

TOP LEFT Moody sleeve to his then biggest selling album, AUGUST.

TOP RIGHT The 12 inch of 'Behind The Mask' which included the rare 'Wanna Make Love To You'.

ABOVE The 12 inch of 'It's In The Way That You Use It'.

ABOVE RIGHT The 12 inch sleeve for 'Holy Mother'.

RIGHT US 7 inch single of 'It's In The Way That You Use It'.

Mark Knopfler joins Eric at the Royal Albert Hall in January 1987.

album, originally called ONE MORE CAR, ONE MORE RIDER, but later retitled, AUGUST, in celebration of the birth of Eric's son Conor that month. Clapton had produced the commercial record he wanted. It was a huge success worldwide, as was the single 'Behind The Mask', which once again confirmed the unlikely figure of Eric Clapton as a superstar. 'I think I sold myself a long time ago. I made some kind of deal with myself to get along, to please people, just to make life easy'.

To promote AUGUST, Phil Collins managed to shake off the demands of Genesis and his solo career to join the rest of the boys for a summer tour of festivals that began in Scandinavia and ended at Birmingham's NEC Arena.

After the tour, Eric kept up his high profile by popping up all over town at various functions, concerts and radio interviews. Eric-mania was back. But the superstar's dignity was almost scuppered by the hilarious events surrounding the filming of his next video at Ronnie Scotts in London. 'Tearing Us Apart' is sung as a duet with Tina Turner, but she was unavailable for the shoot so, ludicrously, it was decided to hire a look-alike instead. It never stood a chance of working, the amateurish filming and split second flashes of a pair of black legs and glossed lips ensured the embarrassing video was never shown.

The birth of his son and the subsequent responsibility of fatherhood was a challenge for Eric. He had always craved stability, yet heretofore he had always found a means of running away. 'It seems impossible for me to find myself in a relationship without wanting to get away at some point; to go and be a little boy again; play the guitar and misbehave.' Eric's relationship with Conor's mother, Lory Del Santo was always unstable and although Eric had strong feelings for her, they never really lived together for any great length of time. He recorded a raunchy number about her called 'Lady Of Verona', but it remains unreleased. Conor and his mother spent most of their time in Lory's native Italy, so Eric became a regular commuter between London and Milan, fitting family visits into his busy schedule.

Extra-curricular activity in 1986 saw him play on sessions for Bob Dylan, Robert Cray and Chuck Berry amongst others, and record the soundtrack for the *Lethal Weapon* film starring Mel Gibson and Danny Glover. Soundtracks were beginning to provide Eric with a fruitful avenue for his talents.

In early 1987, Eric took up his annual residency at London's majestic Royal Albert Hall in what has become a legendary ritual, eagerly participated in by both artist and fans. Though not the largest indoor venue in London, for Eric it is preferable to the cold atmosphere of the Arena at Wembley, because in it he finds an intimacy that the bigger hall lacks. 'You come off stage at Wembley, and you don't ever want to go back there. Cream's farewell concert was at the Albert Hall, and I always liked it.' So the Albert Hall it is, though it's limited capacity means longer and longer

ABOVE Soundtrack to the massively successful cop movie *Lethal Weapon* starring Mel Gibson and Danny Glover.

BELOW LEFT Duet with Tina Turner on the single 'Tearing Us Apart'. It spent three weeks in the charts and reached number fifty-six. It was released in June 1987.
BELOW US picture disc of 'Tearing Us Apart'.

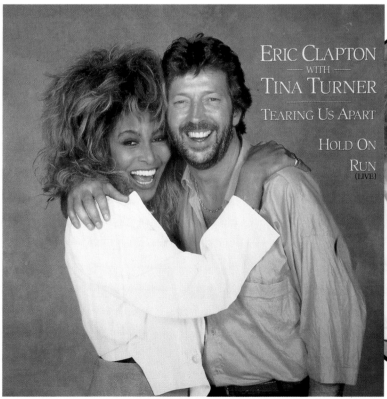

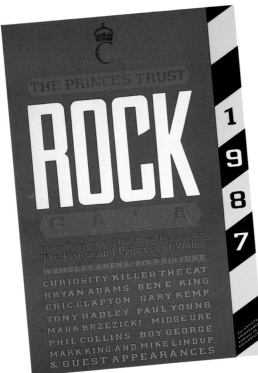

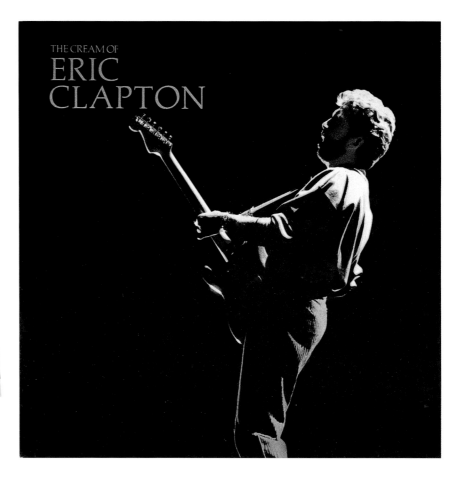

TOP LEFT Programme for the 1987 Prince's Trust Concert at Wembley Arena.

TOP RIGHT The successful 1987 compilation, THE CREAM OF ERIC CLAPTON.

ABOVE EC whips up a storm at The Ritz, New York in 1986 as pictured on the front cover of the UK 1987 tour programme.

residencies each year. In the United States, however, it is impossible, and unfair to ask audiences to converge on one, central arena. So in April, he and his four-piece band did a short thirteen-date tour of the States. Some of the shows were recorded for a double, live album, which Eric was contractually obliged to deliver to Warner's.

Eric Clapton was now, perhaps for the first time, a household name. It seemed a day did not go by when he was not seen on television or heard on the radio. The prestigious British TV arts programme, *The South Bank Show*, profiled him in a film, which intercut a lengthy and revealing interview with rare and archive footage. In it Eric comes over as a vulnerable, sad man who has difficulty in coming to terms with his fame.

BBC Radio One also broadcast their version of Eric's life story as a series of six, one-hour shows called *Behind the Mask*, which included new interviews with him and his associates, as well as a musical retrospective. His profile could not be higher and his work schedule increased even more. His old record label, Polydor, decided it was the ideal time to release a new greatest-hits compilation. The album, aptly titled THE CREAM OF ERIC CLAPTON, was released in September 1987 and sold massively to fans – new and old alike. It was so successful that Polygram instigated a larger, more comprehensive retrospective, planned to include unreleased material.

As the pressure mounted, so did his desire for alcohol. He had been drinking again, on and off, since 1983, but not in the same life-threatening quantities that he had consumed in the seventies. However, the occasional glass soon became the occasional bottle. The final irony came at the end of 1987 when Eric agreed to perform in a series of television and press advertisements for Michelob beer in the United States. As a practising alcoholic this had to be seen as a bad joke, although he was only shown playing and chatting to people and not drinking beer. 'By the time it came out in December of 1987, I was actually in treatment in Minnesota. I was in a room full of recovering alcoholics, myself one of them, and everybody went, "Is that you?" I said, "Yep." What was I going to say? It was me when I was drinking.'

His work schedule was even heavier this year than the last: probably organized in such a way to keep his mind on work rather than alcohol. Eric has loved film since early childhood, and soundtracks allowed him to work without having to step into the full glare of the media spotlight . Yet this seemingly natural progression to musical involvement in film came late in his career.

It wasn't until 1985 that he scored his first full soundtrack, for the BBC's nuclear thriller, *Edge of Darkness*. A successful first foray, it earned Eric an award and led to further movie work. Soon after, he wrote soundtracks for the phenomenally successful *Lethal Weapon* films.

After the success of the *Edge of Darkness* and *Lethal Weapon* soundtracks, Eric launched himself into other similar projects in between tour dates. He recorded an instrumental guitar track for the film *Buster* based on the life of the 'Great Train Robber' and featuring Phil Collins in the title role; the majority of the soundtrack for Mickey Rourke's *Homeboy,* and the title and incidental music for a stark, black and white documentary about World War II called *Peace In Our Time*. As well as writing full soundtracks, Eric has also contributed to *The Hit, Communion, Back To The Future, The Color Of Money* and *Water*, to name but a few. He also played alongside Bob Dylan on the soundtrack to *Hearts Of Fire*.

Soundtracks are hard and repetitious work for the musician, necessitating as they do, looking at sequences over and over again whilst playing along to get the right mood and phrasing. The musician really has to involve himself deeply in the scene, to convey the right atmosphere. This can be very draining, particularly when the picture is violent.

CROSSROADS was the lavish, four-CD boxed set that Polygram had prepared to celebrate Eric's twenty-five years as a working musician. Released in April 1988, it contained a massive seventy-three songs and comprised all the major hits; rare, deleted early numbers; B sides and several unreleased outtakes. It was a superb package that sold in bucket loads and, justly, the project's co-ordinator, Bill Levenson was awarded a Grammy for it. The highlight for many fans was the inclusion of several numbers from the legendary, aborted sessions for the second Derek and the Dominos album and a new version of 'After Midnight'. It set an

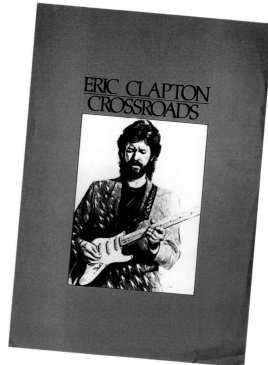

TOP Press release for 4 CD box set, CROSSROADS, which featured all the hits as well as a generous quantity of rare and unreleased material. One of the first and best-selling box sets of its kind.

ABOVE Eric provided the soundtrack to Mickey Rourke's flop boxing movie, *Homeboy.*

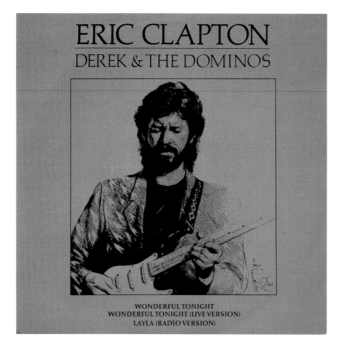

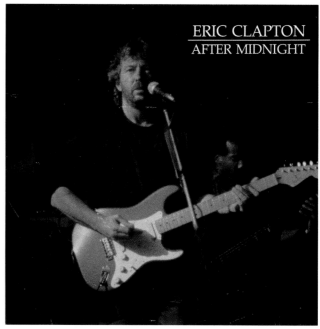

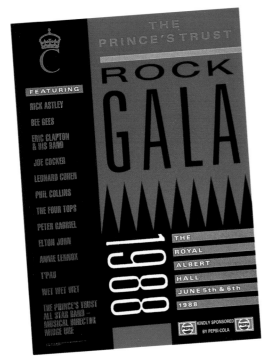

TOP LEFT CD single released on the back of the CROSSROADS set.

TOP RIGHT Eric recorded J.J. Cale's 'After Midnight' in September 1987 for a Michelob beer commercial.

ABOVE The programme for the 1988 Prince's Trust Concert, held at the Royal Albert Hall in London, features a similar constructivist-influenced design to the previous years.

industry standard, and many subsequent box sets on other artists are based on this release, which included something for everyone – from the casual fan to the obsessive train-spotter type.

In celebration of his twenty-five years in the business, Eric embarked on a world tour that began in England, took in the States and culminated in Japan. He had stopped drinking, looked good and played enthusiastically. Mark Knopfler, on sabbatical from Dire Straits, joined him for most of the concerts. The highlight in the UK was perhaps the traditional, small show they played at Guildford's Civic Hall for friends and family. Eric had played at this venue many times, mainly for local charities and with many guest stars including Phil Collins, Jimmy Page, George Harrison, Jeff Beck and Muddy Waters. This year saw Elton John on stage with Eric and afterwards he joined the rest of the gang for the aprés-gig party at Eric's place.

It was, overall, a successful year culminating in Japan with an exclusive four-date tour billed as 'Rock Legends – Eric Clapton, Mark Knopfler and Elton John'. As well as performing their own mini-sets, of which Eric had the lion's share, this one-off featured all three friends on stage together. The concert, held in the huge Tokyo Dome, known locally as 'The Egg' because of it's shape, was televised in Japan for fans who were unable to get tickets for these sold-out shows.

Eric, however, felt trapped by the expectations of his audience – the show was basically the same as that played on the previous two tours. This was Eric's 25th Anniversary Tour, and considering the wealth of material at his disposal, Eric should have been prepared to risk some of the more unfamiliar material rather than churning out endless versions of 'Wonderful Tonight', 'Cocaine' and 'Layla'. However, it was to be several years before Eric had the strength of conviction to do something more adventurous.

TOP LEFT Wonderful programme for the 25th anniversary world tour of 1988. It features pictures of Eric through the years.

TOP RIGHT Jacket and sweatshirt for the 25th anniversary tour.

ABOVE Silver poster for the Clapton/John/Knopfler Japan tour.

RIGHT Ticket for 4th November 1988.

The recording of a new album and a first-time tour in Africa made 1989 an exciting year. It had been three years since the last long player and he could no longer put off recording a new album. Eric, it seemed, had dried up when it came to writing new songs, which was one of the reasons for the long time-lapse between this album and the last one. He was forced to look elsewhere for material and eventually, covered songs by Jerry Williams, George Harrison and Robert Cray, as well as doing classics such as 'Hound Dog' and 'Before You Accuse Me'. 'In Jerry Williams' case, I tend to think his material is so malleable, so easily adjusted, that I can put myself into that and really be me, singing his words with his chord changes. I don't feel that I'm hiding behind him in any way.' This may well have been the case, but the fact remains he was feeling uninspired.

The best number was a collaboration with Robert Cray on 'Old Love', a poignant song about being haunted by the memories of a past lover. 'Robert took 50 per cent of the guitar playing. The only thing we didn't share was the singing. I wanted to keep that for me. I thought that was one of the best marriages on record that I've done.' George Harrison also gave Eric a hand on his song, 'Run So Far'. 'That was the only one of all his songs that didn't have his augmented chord in it, which drives me crazy.'

At the end of the album sessions, Warners proclaimed, once again, that there was no obvious hit single. They were looking for another 'Layla'. Eric once more bowed to the company's wishes, and on his return to London recorded 'Bad Love' in collaboration with Mick Jones from Foreigner. 'I thought, well, if you sit down and write a song in a formulated way, it's not so hard. You think, "What was Layla comprised of? A fiery intro modulated into the first verse, and a chorus with a riff around it." I had

BELOW Eric and the band take their places with Elton John on 7 February, 1988, before taking a bow after another successful show at Guildford's Civic Hall .

BELOW RIGHT Eric looking dapper at the Prince's Trust Concert at London's Royal Albert Hall in June 1988.

FACING PAGE Eric shows off his new boots, and huge pleated trousers on the 1988 US tour when he floors the wah-wah pedal during 'White Room'.

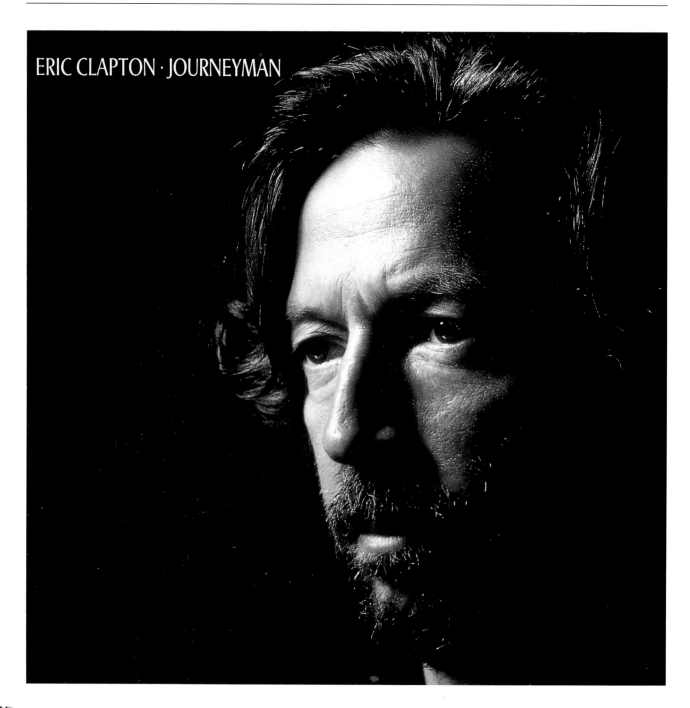

this stuff in my head, so I just juggled it around, and Mick Jones came in to help tidy up. He was the one who said, "you should put a Badge middle in there." So we did that. Although it sounds like a cold way of doing it, it actually took on it's own life.'

JOURNEYMAN was released in November 1989 and was a hit worldwide, as was the single, 'Bad Love'. Eric even performed on the prime-time BBC chat show, *Wogan*. The album saw the welcome return of his guitar solos, which had been missing from studio recordings for so long. It also marked the return of the wah-wah pedal. 'I've always liked wah-wah, but I was scared of it for a while because it became very fashionable in the Philadelphia sound and then sort of burned out.'

The African tour was a joyous affair. The highpoint being a show in

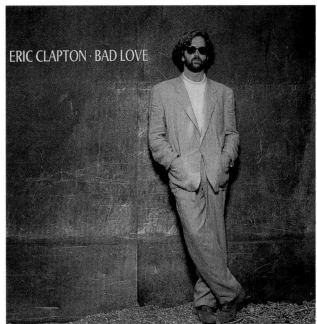

FACING PAGE The cover to JOURNEYMAN and 1990 UK tour sweatshirt.

ABOVE The 7 inch of 'No Alibis'.

ABOVE RIGHT Mean and moody cover to the 12 inch of 'Bad Love'. Backed with 'Before You Accuse Me' the single featured live bonus tracks 'Badge' and 'Let It Rain' from the 15 July 1986 NEC show.

RIGHT Limited-edition box set for 'No Alibis' included a guitar pin.

BELOW Limited-edition box set of 'Bad Love' which included two photos and a family tree by Pete Frame.

ABOVE Mike Rutherford and Eric wait for their cue during rehearsals for the Wintershall concert on 1 July 1989.

BELOW Wintershall poster and ticket. The tickets cost a mere £55 each!

Mozambique before an ecstatic, though mostly impoverished, audience of 100,000. The entry fee was the equivalent of one English pound, and all proceeds went towards funding social and cultural programmes for the war-torn country. 'It was a great honour to do something that I'd sort of touched on at Live Aid and the Mandela concert. To do it on the spot was what really made you choke up. You were actually playing to these people.' During 'Same Old Blues' the 100,000-strong audience mesmerized the performers by singing the riff like an African chorus. 'The black guys in the band were moved to tears. It really choked me up. There was a banner in the front of the audience saying, "Mr Clapton, Thank you for bringing us some paradise."' Eric has always done a lot for charity, both publicly and a great deal more in private, which he continues to do to this day, but this was obviously a very special event for Eric and his band.

Eric spent the remainder of 1989 playing on various sessions and

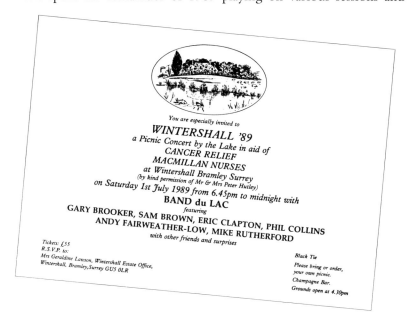

dropping in to jam with friends such as Elton John and the Rolling Stones. He was also interviewed on Sue Lawley's *Saturday Matters* with Pete Townshend, and together they played an acoustic version of Muddy Waters' 'Standin' Around Crying'. Eric has never really been a spokesman for his generation, and although he has always been candid in relation to his private life, he prefers to let his fingers do the talking. So it came as no surprise that Pete Townshend came over as the most loquacious of the two.

Eric ended the year on a high, playing with the Rolling Stones in Atlantic City, the show being broadcast all over the States on pay-per-view television. His execution of 'Little Red Rooster' was stunning, almost arrogant. Eric had, it seemed, fallen in love with his guitar again and was not afraid to show it. 'It's something that has taken a long time to come to terms with. Two years ago, or even a year ago, it would have been a lot harder to deal with. Now I sat and enjoyed the show. At the time when I was supposed to get up, someone came and told me, and I walked up and played, and it was just like water off a duck's back.'

The regular Albert Hall concerts were extended to new record lengths: eighteen and twenty-four nights in 1990 and 1991, and their scope was broadened. In unique style the shows were divided into four separate, and different, categories; a basic two guitar, four-piece band, a thirteen-piece with horn section, and a blues band, rounding off with a series of orchestral nights featuring the National Philharmonic.

On the blues nights Eric was joined by some of his favourite musicians; Buddy Guy, Robert Cray, Albert Collins and Jimmie Vaughan. For many longtime fans these shows were the highlight as they heard Eric play pure blues, without irksome interruptions from the over-familiar hits. The shows were also broadcast on Radio One to the grateful appreciation of those who were unable to attend the concerts.

BELOW 1989 Royal Albert Hall ticket with advance notice of the concerts.
BOTTOM Rare programme for the cricket team tour of 1989 and (right) the UK 1989 tour programme.

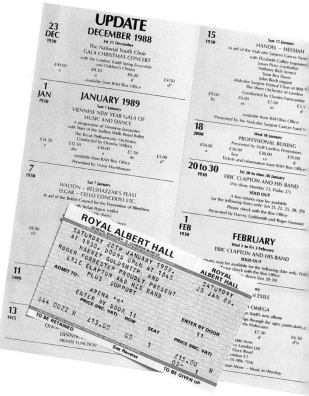

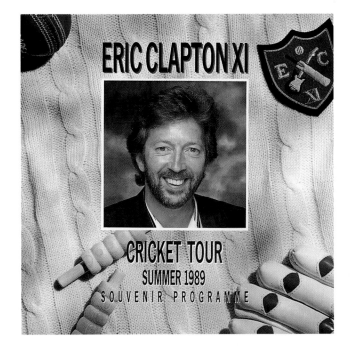

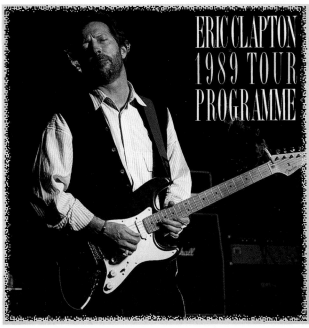

ABOVE Lapping up the applause at the last Albert Hall show in February 1989.

LEFT The Band on Blues night at the Albert Hall in February 1990. Left to right, Johnnie Johnson, Eric and Robert Cray.

FACING PAGE Eric with hair gelled down on the set of the video shoot for Phil Collins's 'I Wish It Would Rain'.

ABOVE Press ad for the 1991 Royal Albert Hall season.

BELOW Original and final programme for the 1991 Albert Hall shows. The sad looking programme on the right was the original design, but it was withdrawn after a few days.

Eric also enjoyed the orchestral nights, even if results were mixed. 'It's a selfish thrill to play with an orchestra. It's very hit-or-miss because they play in a different time scale. Orchestras hit the beat just slightly after the conductor's baton comes down; behind the beat, in effect. I play right on the beat or sometimes in front of it. I like pushing the beat, and so the marriage is very difficult. It's a challenge to get it right. But more often than not, it's a very painful disappointment.' The audiences loved it though, and the orchestral run was extended to six nights in 1991, as were the blues nights.

Eric and his band then took off on another triumphant world tour. They were joined in Knebworth by Mark Knopfler and Elton John for a wonderful concert that was beamed around the world. Eric was looking forward to a rest after the American leg, when disaster struck on 28 August. Stevie Ray Vaughan, Buddy Guy and Jimmie Vaughan had joined Eric for the encore of 'Sweet Home Chicago' and were all due to fly to the windy city by helicopter after the show. 'Bobby Brooks, my agent, was in the helicopter with Stevie Ray (Vaughan), as were Nigel Browne and Colin Smythe of my crew. There was a convoy of about five helicopters, and they had to fly back through this thick fog up to about 100 feet (91 metres) above the ground. Once we came out of that, we just took off for Chicago. When I got back, I went straight to bed and was woken about seven in the morning by my manager, Roger Forrester, saying that the helicopter with Stevie Ray and our chaps hadn't come back. Then a bit later, someone discovered the wreckage. That was it.'

All four were lost. Eric, the band and the crew were traumatized, but decided to play the last five dates of the tour. Otherwise, as Eric explained, 'it would have been unbearable. I don't know how we got through it. But it was the best tribute I thought we could make – to carry on and let

RIGHT Eric concentrates hard at the Albert Hall in March 1991.

BELOW Eric receives the applause of the crowd during the final bows at the Albert Hall in February 1991. Left to right, Buddy Guy, Johnnie Johnson, Robert Cray, Jerry Portnoy, Joey Spampinato.

Lavish limited-edition of the 24 NIGHTS double album. The box contained a laminated backstage pass, a guitar string, guitar picks, the 24 NIGHTS double CD set together with extra tracks not featured on the regular release, and two books. One was a photographic journey through rehearsals right to the shows themselves. The other was a diary of the events. The set is autographed by Eric and artist Peter Blake.

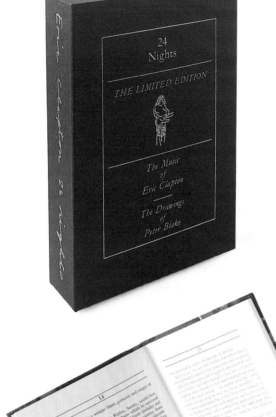

everybody who was coming to see us know it was in honour of their memory.' He further reflected, 'that awful helicopter crash marred what had been until then an incredibly happy and productive year.'

After a one-month break the tour continued on to South America, Hong Kong, Singapore, Japan, New Zealand and Australia. It ended in March 1991 at London's Royal Albert Hall, where it started. The Royal Albert Hall shows were the finale to an exhaustive world tour. (The largest Eric had ever undertaken, it made even the band-breaking American tours endured by Cream seem small.) He went all out at the Royal Albert Hall, playing twenty-four nights, and again, performing with four different line-ups; quartet, big band, blues band and orchestra. It was a herculean effort that entailed four sets of rehearsals, with four different sets of musicians, switching between styles and genres as he went. Every night was magical. All were recorded and four filmed, and edited highlights were released as a double live album and full-length video, aptly titled 24 NIGHTS.

When the shows were over Eric worked on the track selection and planned to take the rest of the year off to spend some time with his son. He headed off to America to join Conor, and the pair spent time doing the ordinary things fathers and sons do together, such as going to the circus and cinema. 'I think I was as close as I have ever been to anybody. It was probably the closest relationship I have ever had because I invested so much hope into it. This was the year that I would stop working altogether for a while so that we could spend more time together.'

Conor was staying with his mother and her boyfriend in a high-rise apartment block, while Eric took up residency in a nearby hotel. Then fate played its cruellest hand: Conor fell from an open window to his death. The tragedy made international headlines, and the world grieved with Eric and his family. Even the newspapers treated the incident with due respect, although, sadly, the funeral was marred by the despicable tactics employed by some photographers.

Eric abandoned track selection of the live album, leaving it in the hands of his producer, Russ Titelman. Devastated, he flew to Antigua with Roger Forrester. Once there he grieved, dividing his time between his house and a hire boat. He healed and comforted himself on the only instrument he had with him; a basic acoustic strung with gut. Ironically, mourning provided the spur he needed. 'I started writing right after he died but I couldn't really put into words what I was feeling because I didn't want it to be trite. I didn't really want anyone to know and I didn't want to know myself. I didn't want to hear what I had to say and it took a long time.'

At the end of August an ideal opportunity to get back to work presented itself when Eric was asked to write the soundtrack to Lili Zanuck's tale of undercover narcotic cops, *Rush*. Eric's spare and brooding guitar work provides a perfect accompaniment to the harrowing scenes of addiction as the undercover cops become further and further involved in the squalid lives of the drugs gang they are tracking.

The soundtrack also gave Eric another worldwide smash with the moving single, 'Tears In Heaven'. 'Tears' was written in Antigua along with several others that were not intended for the film, and although clearly it springs from the death of his son, it also fits rather appropriately with the film. Some of the other songs Eric wrote while in Antigua were given their first public airing during the concert filmed for MTV's *Unplugged* series in which musicians and groups are asked to abandon their traditional electrical and digital equipment and use only acoustic instruments.

The concert took place on Stage 1 at Bray Studios in front of a lucky clutch of 300 who had won tickets in a competition run by BBC Radio One. After some words of wisdom from the floor manager, Eric and his

BELOW LEFT Arty cover to 24 NIGHTS double album, which was released in December 1991. The album spent seven weeks in the UK charts and reached number seventeen.

BELOW 'Wonderful Tonight' single taken from the 24 NIGHTS double album. The single released in October 1991 was a live version and reached number thirty and spent seven weeks in the UK charts.

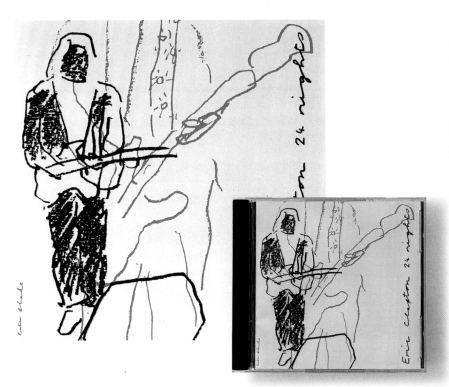

ABOVE 1993 tour programme.

BELOW LEFT Eric's haunting 'Tears in Heaven' was written for his son Conor who had tragically died months before.

BELOW RIGHT Eric's most successful album to date UNPLUGGED.

band took to the small, club-sized stage to tumultuous applause. Eric sat down with bassist Nathan East on his left and guitarist Andy Fairweather Low to his right. To the rear left was Steve Ferrone on drums, immediately behind was percussionist Ray Cooper, and to his right were pianist Chuck Leavell and backing singers Tessa Niles and Katie Kissoon. They began with a new instrumental, 'Signe', which was the name of the boat Eric had charted in Antigua, and on board which the piece had been written. This was followed by two blues numbers, 'Before You Accuse Me' and 'Hey Hey'. The confined, club-like atmosphere must have reminded Eric of his early days trolling up and down the country with the Yardbirds and John Mayall. Intimate new songs, 'Circus has Left Town', 'My Father's Eyes' and 'Lonely Stranger' were given their first airing in front of an audience, as was 'Tears In Heaven'. All were warmly received, leaving not a dry eye in the house.

The majority of the set was made up of a selection of his favourite blues tracks and when Eric played unaccompanied, his vocals sounded eerily like Robert Johnson. New recruit, Andy Fairweather Low played rhythm guitar and mandolin on several numbers, despite running away when a make-up girl approached him halfway through. Eric was evidently relaxed, swapping jokes at intervals with both the audience and the crew. The whole band performed like seasoned troopers, and when Eric unexpectedly tore into an impromptu version of 'Rollin' And Tumblin' during a short technical break, they effortlessly followed him. The crowd were on their feet, clapping and stomping at this Cream classic, but the

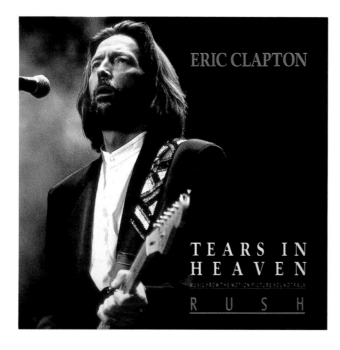

ABOVE Shea Stadium August 1992.
ABOVE RIGHT Birmingham Arena February 1992.
BELOW RIGHT Steve Cropper and Eric at New York's Madison Square Garden for Bob Dylan's 30th anniversary concert.
BELOW 1992 world tour badge.

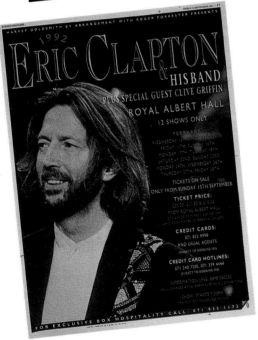

TOP Japanese brochure for Honda cars featuring Eric on the cover.

BELOW Press advertisement for 1992 Royal Albert Hall shows..

producer was caught on the hop and only managed to record half of it, which is why it fades in on the CD.

Eric was not too keen to release UNPLUGGED at first, thinking it could only appeal to a niche market of Clapton obsessives. He could not have been more wrong. UNPLUGGED has become one of the biggest albums of his career, selling over 12 million copies, and winning several Grammys on the way. Taken by surprise, Eric discovered that his audience were prepared to be challenged. The music business also learnt something new, and an 'Unplugged album' is fast becoming almost obligatory for every act of any decent stature.

Frequently during his tour of 1990, Eric was badgered by people asking about George Harrison's plans, or lack of them. So on his return Eric started talking to George, and eventually convinced him to play live once again. So in December 1991, Eric and the band backed the ex-Beatle on a tour of Japan. They decided on Japan because it provided a large, sympathetic audience unswayed by the expectations that would have been thrust on them in Europe or the United States. The cast blew up a storm on songs taken from the Beatles' albums and George's solo albums, as well as several numbers from Eric and his band. An album, LIVE IN JAPAN was released and is a must for fans of Eric's guitar playing.

In 1992 Eric toured England, Europe and the United States once more, and did several double-headline stadium shows with Elton John, including three memorable shows at Wembley Stadium. He also joined Elton John in the studio for a version of 'Runaway Train', which was released as a single but failed to make any impact on the charts.

In September he was invited to attend the MTV Awards in Los Angeles where he received the bauble for Best Video for 'Tears In Heaven'. This was followed by a stunning performance at Madison Square Garden for Bob Dylan's 30th Anniversary tribute concert. The show gathered a mass of stars from differing musical backgrounds including Lou Reed, Johnny Winter, Ronnie Wood, Neil Young, George Harrison and Tom Petty. Each artist was asked to perform one or two numbers of Bob's in their own style. Eric charged through electrifying versions of 'Love Minus Zero' and 'Don't Think Twice', with impressive backing from the legendary Booker T & the MGs. The whole event was broadcast live around the world and edited highlights were later released as a double CD.

The Royal Albert Hall shows in 1993 were again something special, exclusively dedicated to the blues. Most of the audience were thrilled to be given a history lesson in the roots of rock 'n' roll by an acknowledged master, but a handful did walk out disappointed at not hearing the hits. Afterwards, Eric took a well-deserved break and did not reappear until June, when he played a charity concert for New York's Apollo Theatre at B.B. King's request, alongside Albert Collins, Jeff Beck and Buddy Guy.

After a well-deserved holiday, Eric returned to England and played some very special charity concerts. The first was at Cowdray Park in Sussex where he played alongside Phil Collins, Tony Banks, Mike Rutherford, Tim Renwick, David Gilmore, John Deacon and Roger Taylor amongst others. He only played on four numbers, but nevertheless, was, for many of the £80 to £140 a head ticket holders, the highlight of the night.

In early October, he also played three unique concerts for the Chemical Dependency Centre Projects. These shows were held in Birmingham and Sheffield and featured special guests Nine Below Zero, ZZ Top and Joe Cocker. Eric played a varied set, which comprised all aspects of his career, blues, unplugged and the hits. Joe Cocker joined him for several numbers during the set and ZZ Top joined the whole ensemble for the encore of the perennial 'Sweet Home Chicago'. However, the highlight for many were the stirring versions of Jimi Hendrix's 'Stone Free' and 'The Burning of the Midnight Lamp', which he had recorded a few weeks before on a tribute album of Jimi's songs. In fact, only 'Stone Free' was used.

ABOVE 1993 blues show programme..

BELOW Eric at the Albert Hall 1993.

As soon as he finished the shows, Eric flew out to Japan for a large tou, and on his immediate return, started recording tracks for his long-awaited new studio album, and preparing for a twelve-night stint at the Royal Albert Hall in February and March 1994.

Eric clutches his six Grammy Awards.

Eric Clapton is now bigger than at any other point in his long and illustrious career. The nineties have been, so far, an endless series of successes, prompted by the virtuoso playing of a man who has truly etched his place in the rock history books. He has finally reached artistic maturity after years of false starts and half-hearted albums.

After cheating the Grim Reaper he has gained the same legendary status and mythical aura of other great musicians such as Jimi Hendrix and Robert Johnson, who unfortunately both died early in their artistic life. In 1993 his stature was confirmed with the award of an armful of Grammies for UNPLUGGED and the election of Cream to the Rock 'n' Roll Hall of Fame.

UK AND SCANDINAVIAN TOUR

The band now consists of:

Eric Clapton (guitar, vocals), Jamie Oldaker (drums), Shaun Murphy (vocals) Marcy Levy (vocals), Duck Dunn (bass), Chris Stainton (keyboards), Tim Renwick (guitar).

The set was taken from:

'Everybody Oughta Make A Change', 'Motherless Children', 'I Shot The Sheriff', 'Same Old Blues', 'Blues Power', 'Tangled In Love', 'Stepping Out', 'Just Like A Prisoner', 'Lay Down Sally', 'Tulsa Time', 'Something Is Wrong With My Baby', 'Badge', 'Behind The Sun', 'Wonderful Tonight', 'Long Distance Call', 'Have You Ever Loved A Woman', 'Ramblin' On My Mind', 'Cocaine', 'Layla', 'Knock On Wood', 'You Don't Know Like I Know', 'Further On Up The Road'.

FEBRUARY 1985

27–28   Playhouse, Edinburgh

MARCH 1985

1–2	NEC, Birmingham
4–5	Wembley Arena, Wembley
9	Icehall, Helsinki
11	Scandinavium, Gothenburg
12	Valbyhallen, Copenhagen
14	Drammenshallen, Oslo
15	Isstadion, Stockholm

US TOUR

The set was taken from:

'Tulsa Time', 'Motherless Children', 'I Shot The Sheriff', 'Same Old Blues', 'Blues Power', 'Tangled In Love', 'White Room', 'Behind The Sun', 'Wonderful Tonight', 'Stepping Out', 'Never Make You Cry', 'She's Waiting', 'She Loves You', 'Something Is Wrong With My Baby', 'Lay Down Sally', 'Badge', 'Let It Rain', 'Double Trouble', 'Cocaine', 'Layla', 'Forever Man', 'Further On Up The Road'.

APRIL 1985

9	Reunion Arena, Dallas, Tx.
10	The Summit, Houston, Tx.
11	South Park Meadows, Austin, Tx.
13	Civic Center, Pensacola, Fl.
15	Civic Center, Lakeland, Fl.
	George Terry joins Eric for several numbers
16	James L. Knight Center, Miami, Fl.
18	Duke University, Durham, NC.
19	Civic Center, Savannah, Ga.
20	Omni, Atlanta, Ga.
22	Coliseum, Richmond, Va.
	Recorded for radio broadcast
23	Civic Center, Baltimore, Md.
25	Meadowlands Arena, East Rutherford, N.J.
26	Nassau Coliseum, Uniondale, Ny.
28	Civic Center, Providence, R.I.
	Dick Sims joins Eric for a few numbers
29	Spectrum, Philadelphia, Pa.

TOP *Press advertisement for Eric's 1985 UK tour.*
BELOW *1985 guest pass.*

1985 Coca-Cola Summer of Stars at Red Rocks

ERIC CLAPTON
AND HIS BAND

SECOND NIGHT ADDED BY POPULAR DEMAND

THU JUL 7:30 **11**
SUN JUL 7:30 **14**

With Special Guest:
Graham Parker & The Shot

7:30 PM
$13.50, $14.50
A Concerts West Production

All shows are subject to 10% city seat tax, and $1.15 Select-A-Seat service charge. General Admission tickets $1.00 higher Day of Show. For further information call 691-9779 or 778-0700. Charge your tickets by Phone Mon.-Fri. 10am-6pm at 778-6691

KPKE

Coca-Cola

2 KWGN-TV DENVER

ABOVE *UK press advertisement for two dates at Red Rocks.*

MAY 1985

1	Civic Center, Hartford, Ct.
	Filmed for video release
2	Civic Center, Portland, Maine
3	The Forum, Montreal, Canada
8	*Late Night with David Letterman* TV show

JUNE 1985

21	Kingswood Music Theatre, Toronto, Canada
22	Blossom Music Theatre, Cleveland, Oh.
23	Finger Lakes Music Center, Canandiagua, NY.
25	Performing Arts Center, Saratoga, NY.
26	The Centrum, Worcester, Mass.
27	Merriweather Post Pavilion, Columbia, Maryland
28	Garden State Arts Center, Holmdel, NJ.
30	The Summer Festival, Milwaukee, Wi.

JULY 1985

1	The Gardens, Louisville, Kentucky
2–3	Pine Knob Pavilion, Detroit, Mi.
5	Poplar Creek Music Theatre, Chicago, Il.
6	Music Center Amphitheatre, Indianapolis, Ind.
7	Riverbend Music Theatre, Cincinnati, Oh.
9	Sandstone Amphitheatre, Kansas City, Ka.
11	Red Rocks Amphitheatre, Denver, Co.
13	JFK Stadium, Philadelphia, Pa. *Live Aid concert*
14	Red Rocks Amphitheatre, Denver, Co.

17–19	Universal Amphitheatre, Los Angeles, Ca.
21	Compton Terrace, Phoenix, Ar.
22	Pacific Amphitheatre, Costa Mesa, Ca.
23–24	Concord Pavilion, San Francisco, Ca.
	Carlos Santana joins Eric on 23rd for the encore of 'Further On Up The Road'
26	Center Coliseum, Seattle, Wash.
	Lionel Richie joins Eric on stage for 'Knock On Wood' and 'You Don't Know Like I Know'
27	PNE Coliseum, Vancouver, Canada

1985 JAPANESE TOUR

Marcy Levy is replaced by Laura Creamer.

OCTOBER 1985

5, 6	Olympic Pool, Tokyo, Japan
7	Koseinenkin Hall, Osaka, Japan
9	Shimin Kaikan, Nagoya, Japan
10	Festival Hall, Osaka, Japan
11	Sun Palace, Fukuoka, Japan
14	George Sullivan Arena, Anchorage, Alaska

1985 EUROPEAN TOUR

20	Civic Hall, Guildford, Surrey.
	Phil Collins joins Eric. Carl Perkins also joins for 'Matchbox', 'Blue Suede Shoes' and 'Goodnight Irene'.
21	Limehouse Studios, London *TV concert with Carl Perkins*
23	Halle Des Fetes, Lausanne, Switzerland
24	Hallenstadion, Zurich, Switzerland
27–28	Theatro Tenda, Milan, Italy
29	Palasport, Turin, Italy
31	Palasport, Naples, Italy

NOVEMBER 1985

1	Palaeur, Rome, Italy
2	Palasport, Genova, Italy
4	Theatro Tenda, Bologna, Italy
5	Palasport, Florence, Italy
6	Palasport, Padova, Italy

DECEMBER 1985

3	Dingwalls, London
	Jam with Buddy Guy and Junior Wells
6	Theatro Tenda, Milan
	Jam with Sting
12	The Dickens pub, Southend, Essex *Eric joins Gary Brooker and friends for a small charity concert calling themselves The Pier Head Restoration Band.*

presents:

ERIC CLAPTON

Passaia

Halle des FÊTES
Palais de BEAULIEU
Lausanne 23. Okt. 1985 20ºº h

HallensTadion Zürich
24. Okt. 1985 20ºº h

SBS Bankverein

ABOVE *Swiss poster for two shows in Lausanne and Zurich.*

13   The Parrot pub, Forest Green, Surrey
      The Pier Head Restoration Band performance

19, 22   Hammersmith Odeon, London
      Eric plays with Dire Straits for their Xmas season concerts.
      He plays on 'Two Young Lovers', 'Cocaine', 'Solid Rock' and
      'Further On Up The Road'.

23   Village Hall, Dunsfold, Surrey.
      Eric joins Gary Brooker for a special concert which also
      features Mick Fleetwood and Albert Lee.

FEBRUARY 1986

23   100 Club, London

JUNE 1986

20   Wembley Arena

1986 SCANDINAVIAN, EUROPEAN AND UK TOUR

The band now consists of:

Eric Clapton (guitar, vocals), Phil Collins (drums), Greg Phillinganes (keyboards, vocals), Nathan East (bass, vocals).

The set was :

'Crossroads', 'White Room', 'I Shot The Sheriff', 'Wanna Make Love To You', 'Run', 'Miss You', 'Same Old Blues', 'Tearing Us Apart', 'Holy Mother', 'Behind The Mask', 'Badge', 'Let It Rain', 'In The Air Tonight', 'Cocaine', 'Layla', 'Sunshine Of Your Love', 'Further On Up The Road'.

JULY 1986

1   Isle Of Calf Festival, Oslo

4   Roskilde Festival, Copenhagen

10   Montreux Jazz Festival, Montreux
      Live recording

12   Juan Les Pins Festival, Antibes

14–15   NEC, Birmingham
      Live recording

AUGUST 1986

14   The Gardens Club, Kensington

16   Finchley Cricket Club, Finchley

SHORT US CLUB TOUR

OCTOBER 1986

16   Fox Theatre, St. Louis

27   Madison Square Garden, New York

NOVEMBER 1986

8   Mean Fiddler, London

20–21   The Metro, Boston

23–24   The Ritz, New York
      Keith Richards joins Eric on 23rd for 'Cocaine' and 'Layla'

DECEMBER 1986

23   Village Hall, Dunsfold, Surrey

1987 UK AND EUROPEAN TOUR

Mark Knopfler joins band for most dates and Steve Ferrone replaces Phil Collins.

The set was:

'Crossroads', 'White Room', 'I Shot The Sheriff', 'Hung Up On Your Love', 'Wonderful Tonight', 'Miss You', 'Same Old Blues', 'Tearing Us Apart', 'Holy Mother', 'Badge', 'Let It Rain', 'Cocaine', 'Layla', 'Money For Nothing', 'Sunshine Of Your Love'.

JANUARY 1987

3–4   Apollo, Manchester

10–12   Royal Albert Hall, London

16   Ahoy Halle, Rotterdam

17   Forest National, Brussels

18   Le Zenith, Paris

20   Westfalenhalle, Dortmund

21   Sporthalle, Hamburg

22   Festhalle, Frankfurt

23   Olympiahalle, Munich

26   Palatrussardi, Milan

29   Palaeur, Rome

30   Palasport, Florence

MARCH 1987

27   Cranleigh Golf Club, Surrey

1987 US TOUR

Phil Collins replaces Steve Ferrone.

ABOVE *Large format Japanese programme for the 1987 tour.*

APRIL 1987

11   Oakland Coliseum, Oakland, Ca.

13   Pacific Amphitheatre, Costa Mesa, Ca.

14   The Forum, Los Angeles, Ca.

15   Ebony Showcase Theatre, Los Angeles, Ca.
      Filming of a B.B. King special.

16   McNichols Arena, Denver, Co.

18   Civic Center, St Paul, Minn.

21   Market Square Arena, Indianapolis, Ind.

22   Joe Louis Arena, Detroit, Mich.

23   Richfield, Coliseum, Cleveland, Ohio

25   Capitol Center, Largo, Md.

26   Civic Center, Providence

27   Madison Square Garden

MAY 1987

6   Wembley Arena, London

JUNE 1987

5–6   Wembley Arena, London

18   Wembley Arena, London

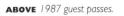

ABOVE *1987 guest passes.*

JULY 1987

4 Pinewood Studios

SEPTEMBER 1987

4 Lonestar Cafe, New York

OCTOBER 1987

6 Ronnie Scott's Club, London

9 Dingwalls, London

AUSTRALIAN AND JAPANESE TOUR

Steve Ferrone returns to replace Phil Collins.

OCTOBER 1987

23 Entertainment Centre, Sydney

24 Entertainment Centre, Brisbane

27 Sports and Entertainment Centre, Melbourne

NOVEMBER 1987

2, 4–5 Budokan, Tokyo

7 Nagoya Gym, Nagoya

9 Castle Hall, Osaka

DECEMBER 1987

19 Dunsfold Village Hall, Surrey

1988 UK TOUR

New band members are: Ray Cooper (percussion), Tessa Niles and Katie Kissoon (backing vocals). Mark Knopfler also joins the band on guitar.

JANUARY 1988

22–23 NEC, Birmingham

25–31 Royal Albert Hall, London

FEBRUARY 1988

2–4 Royal Albert Hall, London

7 Civic Hall, Guildford

UK CHARITY CONCERTS

JUNE 1988

5–6 Royal Albert Hall, London

8–9 Hammersmith Odeon, London

11 Wembley Stadium, Wembley

JULY 1988

2 Wintershall, Surrey

1988 US AND CANADIAN TOUR

Mark Knopfler joins the band again.

The set was taken from:

'Crossroads', 'White Room, 'I Shot The Sheriff', 'Lay Down Sally', 'Wonderful Tonight', 'Tearing Us Apart', 'After Midnight', 'Can't Find My Way Home', 'Motherless Children', 'Badge', 'Same Old Blues', 'Cocaine', 'Layla', 'Money For Nothing', 'Sunshine Of Your Love'.

AUGUST 1988

1 Starplex Amphitheatre, Dallas, Tx.

2 Lakefront Arena, New Orleans, Lo.

4 Civic Arena, Pittsburgh, Penn.

6 Meadowlands Arena, East Rutherford, NJ.

7 Spectrum, Philadelphia, Penn.

8 Capitol Center, Largo, Md.

10 Civic Center, Hartford, Conn.

11 Nassau Coliseum, Uniondale, NY.

13, 14 Great Woods, Boston, Mass.

16 Palace Of Auburn Hill, Detroit, Mich.

17 Alpine Valley, Milwaukee, Wi.

19 Fiddlers Green, Denver, Co.

21 Shoreline Amphitheatre, San Fransico, Ca.

22 Arco Arena, Sacramento, Ca.

23 Irvine Meadows Amphitheatre, Lugana Hills, Ca.

25 Hollywood Bowl, Los Angeles, Ca.

Eric plays with Elton John on 'Saturday Night's Alright'

26 Coliseum, Portland, Or.

27 The Dome, Tacoma, Wa.

28 PNE Coliseum, Vancouver, Canada

29 Pantages Theatre, Los Angeles, Ca.

Eric plays with Little Feat on 'Apolitical Blues'

30 Olympic Saddledome, Calgary, Canada

OCTOBER 1988

1 Saskatchewan Place, Saskatoon, Canada

3 The Arena, Winnipeg, Canada

4 MET Center, Minneapolis, Minn.

6 The Forum, Montreal, Canada

7 Maple Leaf Gardens, Toronto, Canada

8 Copps Coliseum, Hamilton, Canada

11 Bottom Line Club, New York, NY.

Eric plays with Jack Bruce on 'Spoonful' and 'Sunshine Of Your Love'

LEFT *Nelson Mandela programme at which Eric joined Dire Straits.*

ABOVE *Photo pass for the Albert Hall Show on 4 February 1988.*

1988 JAPANESE TOUR

The line up was:

Eric Clapton (guitar, vocals), Mark Knopfler (guitar, vocals), Elton John (piano, vocals), Nathan East (bass, vocals), Alan Clark (keyboards), Steve Ferrone (drums), Ray Cooper (percussion), Tessa Niles (backing vocals), Katie Kissoon (backing vocals).

The set was:

'Crossroads', 'White Room', 'I Shot The Sheriff', 'Lay Down Sally', 'Wonderful Tonight', 'Tearing Us Apart', 'Can't Find My Way Home', 'After Midnight', 'Money For Nothing', 'Candle In The Wind', 'I Guess That's Why They Call It The Blues', 'I Don't Wanna Go On With You Like That', 'I'm Still Standing', 'Daniel', 'Cocaine', 'Layla', 'Solid Rock', 'Saturday Night's Alright For Fighting', 'Sunshine Of Your Love'.

31   Rainbow Hall, Nagoya

NOVEMBER 1988

2   The Dome, Tokyo *Live recording*

4   Budokan, Tokyo *Sting joins Eric on 'Money For Nothing'*

5   The Stadium, Osaka

28   Hard Rock Cafe, London *Charity Gig*

DECEMBER 1988

23   Dunsfold Village Hall, Surrey

1989 UK TOUR

Four-piece line up was:

Eric Clapton (guitar,vocals), Nathan East (bass,vocals), Phil Collins (drums,vocals), Greg Phillinganes (keyboards,vocals).

JANUARY 1989

10   Dingwalls, London

16   Sheffield City Hall, Sheffield

17   City Hall, Newcastle

18   The Playhouse, Edinburgh

20–22,   Royal Albert Hall, London

24–26   Royal Albert Hall, London

Nine-piece line up:

Eric Clapton (guitar, vocals), Nathan East (bass, vocals), Steve Ferrone (drums), Mark Knopfler (guitar, vocals), Greg Phillinganes (keyboards, vocals), Alan Clark (keyboards), Ray Cooper (percussion), Tessa Niles and Katie Kissoon (backing vocals).

The nine-piece set list was:

'Crossroads', 'White Room', 'I Shot The Sheriff', 'Bell Bottom Blues', 'Lay Down Sally', 'Wonderful Tonight', 'Wanna Make Love To You', 'After Midnight', 'Can't Find My Way Home', 'Forever Man', 'Same Old Blues', 'Tearing Us Apart', 'Cocaine', 'Layla', 'Solid Rock', 'Behind The Mask', 'Sunshine Of Your Love'.

28–30   Royal Albert Hall, London

FEBRUARY 1989

1–3   Royal Albert Hall, London

RIGHT AND ABOVE *1989 guest passes*

MAY 1989

9   Bottom Line Club, New York
    Eric joins Carl Perkins for a set.

31   The Armoury, New York
    Eric joins in all-star finale of 'I Hear You Knocking'

JULY 1989

1   Wintershall, Surrey
    Eric plays at a charity concert alongside Gary Brooker, Phil Collins, Mike Rutherford, Stevie Winwood amongst others.

1989 MINI WORLD TOUR

The line up:

Eric Clapton (guitar, vocals), Nathan East (bass, vocals), Steve Ferrone (drums), Phil Palmer (guitar), Alan Clark (keyboards), Ray Cooper (percussion), Tessa Niles and Katie Kissoon (backing vocals).

The set was:

'Crossroads', 'White Room', 'I Shot The Sheriff', 'Bell Bottom Blues', 'Lay Down Sally', 'Wonderful Tonight', 'I Wanna Make Love To You', 'After Midnight', 'Can't Find My Way Home', 'Forever Man', 'Same Old Blues', 'Tearing Us Apart', 'Cocaine', 'Layla', 'Badge', 'Sunshine Of Your Love'.

6–7   Statenhal, The Hague

9–10   Hallenstadion, Zurich

13   Sultan's Pool, Jerusalem

14   Zemach Amphitheatre, Sea Of Galilee

15–17   Caesrea Amphitheatre, Caesrea

22   Somhlolo National Stadium, Swaziland

25–26   Conference Centre, Harare, Zimbabwe

28   Boipuso Hall, Gabarone, Botswana

30   Machava National Stadium, Maputo, Mozambique

SEPTEMBER 1989

28   Da Campo Boario, Rome
    Eric joins Zucchero for 'Wonderful World'

OCTOBER 1989

7   Madison Square Garden, New York
    Eric joins Elton John for 'Rocket Man'

10   Shea Stadium, New York
    Eric joins the Rolling Stones for 'Little Red Rooster'

19   Los Angeles Coliseum, Los Angeles
    Eric joins the Rolling Stones for 'Little Red Rooster'

25   Rockefeller Center, New York *Eric plays 'Hard Times', 'Old Love' and 'Before You Accuse Me'*

28   BBC Theatre, Shepherds Bush, London
    Eric and Pete Townshend play 'Standing Around Crying'

NOVEMBER 1989

18   Royal Albert Hall, London
    Eric plays 'Edge Of Darkness' at this charity show for Parents For Safe Food'

DECEMBER 1989

?   Convention Center, Atlantic City, N.J.
        Eric joins the Rolling Stones for 'Little Red Rooster' and
        'Boogie Chillin''

23   Ex-Serviceman's Club, Chiddingfold
        Eric joins No Stiletto Shoes for a charity show

1990 UK, EUROPEAN AND SCANDINAVIAN TOUR

Four-piece line up:

Eric Clapton (guitar, vocals), Nathan East (bass, vocals), Steve Ferrone (drums), Greg Phillinganes (keyboards, vocals).

The set was taken from:

'Pretending', 'I Shot The Sheriff', 'Running On Faith', 'Breaking Point', 'Can't Find My Way Home', 'Same Old Blues', 'Bad Love', 'Lay Down Sally', 'Hard Times', 'Before You Accuse Me', 'No Alibis', 'Old Love', 'Tearing Us Apart', 'Wonderful Tonight', 'Cocaine', 'Layla', 'Knocking On Heaven's Door', 'Crossroads', 'Sunshine Of Your Love.'

JANUARY 1990

14–16   NEC, Birmingham

17   BBC Theatre, Shepherds Bush, London

18–20   Royal Albert Hall, London

22–24   Royal Albert Hall, London
        Phil Collins joins Eric on 'Knocking On Heaven's Door' on 24th

Thirteen-piece lineup:

Eric Clapton (guitar, vocals), Nathan East (bass, vocals), Steve Ferrone (drums), Phil Palmer (guitar), Greg Phillinganes (keyboards, vocals), Alan Clark (keyboards), Ray Cooper (percussion), Tessa Niles and Katie Kissoon (backing vocals), Ronnie Cuber, Randy Brecker and Alan Rubin (horns).

The set was as above

26–28, Royal Albert Hall, London

30–31   Royal Albert Hall, London

FEBRUARY 1990

1   Royal Albert Hall, London

Blues band line up:

Eric Clapton (guitar, vocals), Buddy Guy (guitar, vocals), Robert Cray (guitar, vocals), Johnnie Johnson (piano, vocals), Jamie Oldaker (drums), Robert Cousins (bass).

The set was taken from:

'Key To The Highway', 'Worried Life Blues', 'Watch Yourself', 'Have You Ever Loved A Woman', 'Standing Around Crying', 'Long Distance Call', 'Johnnie's Boogie', 'Going Down Slow', 'You Belong To Me', 'Cry For Me', 'Howlin' For My Baby', 'Same Thing', 'Money', 'Five Long Years', 'Everything's Gonna Be Alright', 'Something On Your Mind', 'My Time After A While', 'Sweet Home Chicago', 'Hoochie Coochie Man', 'Wee Wee Baby.'

3–5   Royal Albert Hall, London

Orchestra band

As thirteen piece less horn section plus National Philharmonic Orchestra

8–10   Royal Albert Hall, London

Nine-piece band

The set was:

'Pretending', 'No Alibis', 'Running On Faith', 'I Shot The Sheriff', 'White Room', 'Can't Find My Way Home', 'Bad Love', 'Before You Accuse Me', 'Old Love', 'Tearing Us Apart', 'Wonderful Tonight', 'Cocaine', 'Layla', 'Crossroads', 'Sunshine Of Your Love'.

14   Icehall, Helsinki

16   The Globe, Stockholm

17   Skedsmo Hall, Oslo

19   KB Hall, Copenhagen

20   Sporthalle, Hamburg

22   Forest National, Brussels

23   Grugahalle, Essen

24   Statenhal, The Hague

26–7   Palatrussardi, Milan

MARCH 1990

1   Olympic Hall, Munich

3–4   Zenith, Paris

5   Festhalle, Frankfurt

1990 US TOUR

24   Saturday Night Live, New York

28   Omni, Atlanta

30   Coliseum, Charlotte

31   Dean Smith Center, Chapel Hill

APRIL 1990

2   Madison Square Garden, New York
        Daryl Hall joins Eric for 'No Alibis'

3   Meadowlands, East Rutherford

4   Spectrum, Philadelphia

6   Coliseum, Nassau

7   Carrier Dome, Syracuse

9–10   Centrum, Worcester

12–13   Civic Center, Hartford

15   Palace Of Auburn Hills, Detroit
        Stevie Ray Vaughan joins Eric for 'Before You Accuse Me'
        and 'After Midnight'

16   Riverfront Coliseum, Cincinnati

17   Coliseum, Richfield

19   Market Square Arena, Indianapolis

20   Hilton Coliseum, Ames

21   The Arena, St Louis

23   Lakefront Arena, New Orleans

24   The Summit, Houston

25   Reunion Arena, Dallas

27   McNichols Arena, Denver

29   Tingley Coliseum, Albuquerque

30   ASU Pavilion, Phoenix

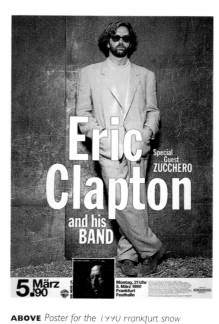

ABOVE *Poster for the 1990 Frankfurt show*

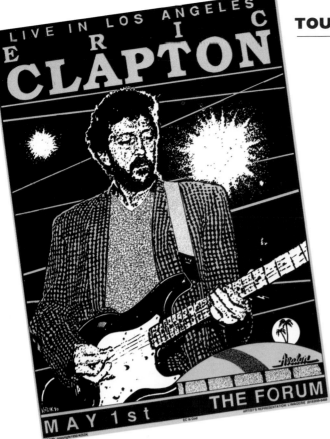

ABOVE *Rare poster for Eric's show at the LA Forum on the 1990 US tour.*

JULY 1990

21–23	The Arena, Miami
25	The Arena, Orlando
27	Suncoast Dome, St. Petersburg
28	Lakewood Amphitheatre, Atlanta
30	Starwood Amphitheatre, Nashville
31	Mid-South Coliseum, Memphis

AUGUST 1990

2	The Coliseum, Greensboro
3–4	Capitol Centre, Washington
6–7	Meadowlands, East Rutherford
9–11	Great Woods, Mansfield
13	Saratoga P.A.C., Saratoga
14–15	The Spectrum, Philadelphia
17–18	Nassau Coliseum, Uniondale
21	Blossom Music Theatre, Cleveland
22	Pine Knob Pavilion, Detroit
23	Riverbend Music Theatre, Cincinnati
25	Alpine Valley Music Theatre, East Troy

Eric is joined by Jeff Healey on 'Crossroads' and 'Sunshine Of Your Love'.

26	Alpine Valley Music Theatre, East Troy

Eric is joined by Buddy Guy, Stevie Ray Vaughan, Jimmie Vaughan and Robert Cray for 'Sweet Home Chicago'.

28	Sandstone Amphitheatre, Kansas
29	The Arena, St. Louis
31	Thompson-Boling Arena, Knoxville

SEPTEMBER 1990

1	Oak Mountain Amphitheatre, Birmingham
2	Coast Coliseum, Biloxi

BELOW *US press advertisement for the Alpine Valley shows.*

MAY 1990

1	The Forum, Los Angeles

George Harrison joins Eric for 'Crossroads' and 'Sunshine Of Your Love'

3	Sports Arena, San Diego
4	Pacific Amphitheatre, Costa Mesa
5	Shoreline Amphitheatre, San Francisco

JUNE 1990

6	The Armoury, New York

Eric plays at the 1990 Elvis Awards. He performs 'Before You Accuse Me' with his band and is then presented with the 'Living Legend Award' by Buddy Guy. Eric and his band plus Buddy Guy, Dave Stewart, Richie Sambora, Neil Schon, Lou Reed, Bo Diddley and Steve Perry then play 'Sweet Home Chicago'.

30	Nordoff-Robins Charity Concert, Knebworth, Hertfordshire.

Eric and his band play 'Pretending', 'Before You Accuse Me', 'Old Love' and 'Tearing Us Apart'. They are then joined by Mark Knopfler for 'Solid Rock', 'I Think I Love You Too Much' and 'Money For Nothing'. Elton John then also joins in the fun for 'Sacrifice', 'Sad Songs' and 'Saturday Night's All Right For Fighting'. They encore with an extended 'Sunshine Of Your Love'. They whole concert is broadcast live on the radio. Part of the show is also released on video.

Eric and his band go back to the US for the second part of their tour.

ABOVE *Silver Clef charity concert programme.*

ABOVE *Poster for the Alpine Valley concerts in August 1990.*

1990 WORLD TOUR

The set was:

'Pretending', 'No Alibis', 'Running On Faith', 'I Shot The Sheriff', 'White Room', 'Can't Find My Way Home', 'Bad Love', 'Before You Accuse Me', 'Old Love', 'Badge', 'Wonderful Tonight', 'Cocaine', 'Layla', 'Crossroads' and 'Sunshine Of Your Love'.

29	Estadio Nacional, Santiago, Chile

OCTOBER 1990

3	Estadio Centenario, Montevideo, Uruguay
5	Estadio River Plate, Buenos Aires, Argentina
7	Praca Da Apoteose, Rio De Janeiro, Brazil
9	Ginasio Nilson Nelson, Brazilia, Brazil
11	Ginasio Mineirinho, Belo Horizonte, Brazil
13	Orlando Scarpelli Stadium, Florianopolis, Brazil
16	Ginasio Gigantinho, Porto Alegre, Brazil
19–21	Olympia, Sao Paulo, Brazil

NOVEMBER 1990

7–8	The Supertop, Auckland, New Zealand
10	Royal Theatre, Canberra, Australia
12–13	Festival Theatre, Adelaide, Australia
15	National Tennis Center, Melbourne, Australia
16–17	Entertainment Center, Sydney, Australia
19	Entertainment Center, Brisbane, Australia
24	The Stadium, Singapore, Singapore
26	Negara Stadium, Kuala Lumpur, Malaysia
29	The Coliseum, Hong Kong

DECEMBER 1990

4–6	Budokan, Tokyo, Japan
9	Olympic Pool, Tokyo, Japan
10	Rainbow Hall, Nagoya, Japan
11	Castle Hall, Osaka, Japan
13	The Arena, Yokohama, Japan

JANUARY 1991

Eric and his band play a couple of warm-up dates in Ireland before starting a mammoth season in London.

31	The Point, Dublin, Ireland

FEBRUARY 1991

2	The Point, Dublin, Ireland

1991 ROYAL ALBERT HALL SHOWS

Four-piece line up:

Eric, Phil Collins, Nathan East, and Greg Phillinganes

The set played by the four-piece was:

'Pretending', 'No Alibis', 'Running On Faith', 'I Shot The Sheriff', 'White Room', 'Can't Find My Way Home', 'Bad Love', 'Before You Accuse Me', 'Old Love', 'Badge', 'Wonderful Tonight', 'Cocaine', 'Layla', 'Crossroads', 'Sunshine Of Your Love'.

5–7	Royal Albert Hall, London
9-11	Royal Albert Hall, London
	Steve Ferrone replaced Phil Collins on drums

Nine-piece line up

The above four piece and Phil Palmer (guitar), Ray Cooper (percussion) Chuck Leavell (keyboards and vocals), Katie Kissoon and, Tessa Niles (vocals).

13–15	Royal Albert Hall, London
17–19	Royal Albert Hall, London

Blues band line up:

Eric, Jamie Oldaker (drums), Jimmie Vaughan (guitar), Jerry Portnoy (harmonica), Joey Spampinato (bass), Chuck Leavell and Greg Phillinganes (keyboards), Johnnie Johnson (piano), Albert Collins, Robert Cray and Buddy Guy (all guitar).

The set played by the Blues band was:

'Watch Yourself', 'Hoodoo Man', 'Hideaway', 'Standing Around Crying', 'All Your Love', 'Have You Ever Loved A Wowan', 'Long Distance Call', 'It's My Life Baby', Key To The Highway', 'Wee Wee Baby'. Then with Johnnie Johnson, 'Tanqueray', 'Johnnie's Boogie'. Then with Albert Collins, 'Tired Man', 'Mother-In-Law Blues', 'Black Cat Bone'. Then with Robert Cray, 'I Feel So Glad', 'Reconsider Baby', 'Stranger Blues'. Then with Buddy Guy, 'Hoochie Coochie Man', 'Little By Little', 'My Time After A While' and an encore of 'Sweet Home Chicago'.

23–25	Royal Albert Hall, London
27–28	Royal Albert Hall, London

MARCH 1991

1	Royal Albert Hall, London

Orchestra line up:

Consisted of nine piece line up plus the National Philharmonic Orchestra conducted by Michael Kamen.

The set played by the Orchestra was:

'Crossroads', 'Bell Bottom Blues', 'Holy Mother', 'I Shot The Sheriff', 'Hard Times', 'Can't Find My Way Home', 'Edge Of Darkness', 'Old Love', 'Wonderful Tonight', 'White Room', 'Concerto For Electric Guitar', 'Layla', 'Sunshine Of Your Love'.

3–5	Royal Albert Hall, London
7–9	Royal Albert Hall, London

SEPTEMBER 1991

4	The Roxy, Los Angeles
	Eric joins Buddy Guy for a jam
29	The Palace, Hollywood
	Eric sits in with Nathan East's house band on the 'Sunday Comics' TV show.

GEORGE HARRISON'S TOUR OF JAPAN

Eric and his band back George Harrison for a Japanese tour. Andy Fairweather Low replaces Phil Palmer who joined Dire Straits for their 'On Every Street' tour.

The set was:

'I Want To Tell You', 'Old Brown Shoe', 'Taxman', 'Give Me Love', 'If I Needed Someone', 'Something', 'Fish On The Sand', 'Love Comes To Everyone', 'What Is Life', 'Dark Horse', 'Piggies', 'Pretending', 'Old Love', 'Badge', 'Wonderful Tonight', 'Got my Mind Set On You', 'Cloud 9', 'Here Comes The Sun', 'My Sweet Lord', 'All Those Years Ago', 'Cheer Down', 'Devil's Radio', 'Isn't It A Pity', 'While My Guitar Gently Weeps', 'Roll Over Beethoven'.

'Fish On The Sand' and 'Love Comes To Everyone' are dropped after a few shows.

DECEMBER 1991

1	Yokohama Arena, Yokohama, Japan
2–3	Castle Hall, Osaka, Japan
5	Kokusai-Tenjijo, Nagoya, Japan
6	Sun Plaza Hall, Hiroshima, Japan
9	Fukuoka Kokusai Center, Fukuoka, Japan
10–12	Castle Hall, Osaka, Japan
14–15, 17	Tokyo Dome, Tokyo, Japan
	George's son, Dhani, joins in for the encore on the 17th

UNPLUGGED CONCERT

JANUARY 1992

16	Bray Studios, Berkshire *Eric and his band play an all acoustic concert which is filmed for MTV's 'Unplugged'*

The set list on the night ran as follows:

'Signe', 'Before You Accuse Me', 'Hey Hey', 'Tears In Heaven', 'Circus Left Town', 'Lonely Stranger', 'Nobody Knows You When You're Down And Out', 'Layla', 'Signe (take 2)', 'My Father's Eyes', 'Running On Faith', 'Walking Blues', 'Alberta', 'San Francisco Bay Blues', 'Malted Milk', 'Signe (take 3), 'Tears In Heaven (take 2)', 'My Father's Eyes (take 2)', 'Rollin' And Tumblin'', 'Running On Faith (take 2), 'Walking Blues (take 2), 'San Francisco Bay Blues (take 2)', 'Malted Milk (take 2), 'Worried Life Blues', 'Old Love'.

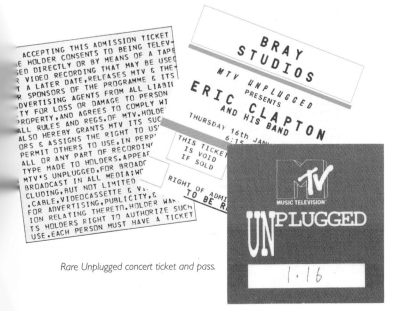

Rare Unplugged concert ticket and pass.

1992 UK TOUR

The set was taken from:

'White Room', 'Pretending', 'Anything For Your Love', 'I Shot The Sheriff', 'Running On Faith', 'My Father's Eyes', 'She's Waiting', 'Circus Left Town', 'Tears In Heaven', 'Signe', 'Malted Milk', 'Nobody Knows You When You're Down And Out', 'Tearing Us Apart', 'Before You Accuse Me', 'Old Love', 'Badge', 'Wonderful Tonight', 'Layla', 'Crossroads' and 'Sunshine Of Your Love'.

FEBRUARY 1992

1	Brighton Center, Brighton
3–5	National Indoor Arena, Birmingham
7–8	Sheffield Arena, Sheffield
12–14	Royal Albert Hall, London
16–18	Royal Albert Hall, London
22–22	Royal Albert Hall, London

MARCH 1992

2–3	SECC, Glasgow

1992 US TOUR

Gina Foster replaces Tessa Niles

1992 guest pass for the Royal Albert Hall.

Set is taken from following:

'White Room', 'Pretending', 'Anything For Your Love', 'I Shot The Sheriff', 'Running On Faith', 'She's Waiting', 'Circus Left Town', 'Tears In Heaven', 'Before You Accuse Me', 'Old Love', 'Badge', 'Wonderful Tonight', 'Layla', 'Crossroads' and 'Sunshine Of Your Love'.

APRIL 1992

17–23	Las Colinas, Dallas
	Eric and his band rehearse for upcoming US tour.
25	Reunion Arena, Dallas, Tx.
27	Lakefront Arena, New Orleans, La.
28	Civic Center, Birmingham, Al.
29	The Pyramid, Memphis, Tn.

MAY 1992

1	Thompson-Boling Arena, Knoxville, Tn.
2	The Coliseum, Charlotte, N.C.
4–5	The Spectrum, Philadelphia
6	Civic Center, Hartford, Ct.
8	Byrne Arena, East Rutherford, NJ.
10	Capitol Center, Washington, D.C.
11	Dean Smith Center, Chapel Hill, N.C.
13–14	Rosemont Horizon, Chicago, Il.
16	Bradley Center, Milwaukee, Wi.
17	Target Centre, Minneapolis, Mi.
19	Market Square Arena, Indianapolis, In.
20	Richfield Coliseum, Cleveland, Oh.
21	Riverfront Coliseum, Cincinnati, Oh.
23	The Omni, Atlanta, Ga.
24	Suncoast Dome, St. Petersburg, Fl.
25	The Arena, Miami, Fl.

1992 EUROPEAN TOUR

Some of the dates are double headliners with Elton John.

JUNE 1992

14–15	Rehearsals in Ghent, Belgium.
16	Flanders Expo., Ghent, Belgium
18	Hippodrome De Vincennes, Paris, France
	Elton John double bill
19	Feyemoord Stadium, Rotterdam, Holland
	Elton John double bill
21	Olympic Riding Stadium, Munich, Germany
22	Waldbuehne, Berlin, Germany
23	Westfalenhalle, Dortmund, Germany
26	Wembley Stadium, Wembley, England
	Elton John double bill, Eric joins Elton John for 'Runaway Train'
27	Wembley Stadium, Wembley, England
	Elton John double bill, and Jimmie Rogers joins Eric for a jam
28	Wembley Stadium, Wembley, England
	Elton John double bill. Bonnie Raitt joins Eric on 'Before You Accuse Me'.and 'Sunshine Of Your Love'. Eric joins Elton for a version of 'The Bitch Is Back' alongside Brian May, Curtis Stigers and Bonnie Raitt.

JULY 1992

3	Pontaise Stadium, Lausanne, Switzerland
	Elton John double bill
4	St. Jakob Stadium, Basle, Switzerland
	Elton John double bill
6	Stadio Communale, Bologna, Italy
	Elton John double bill
10	Stadio Brianteo, Monza, Italy
	Elton John double bill
12	Montreux Jazz Festival, Montreux, Switzerland

ABOVE *UK Press advertisement for Eric and Elton John's double headline shows at Wembley Stadium.*

ABOVE *US advertisement for Eric and Elton John's Dodger Stadium shows.*

1992 US TOUR

AUGUST 1992

11	Civic Arena, Pittsburgh
13	Meadowbrook Music Theater, Rochester.
	Eric joins Little Feat for 'Mellow Down Easy' and 'Apolitical Blues'.
14	The Palace Of Auburn Hills, Detroit
17–18	Great Woods, Mansfield
19	PAC, Saratoga Springs
21–22	Shea Stadium, New York
	Elton John double bill
24	Poplar Creek Music Theatre, Chicago
25	Riverport Amphitheatre, St. Louis
29–30	Dodger Stadium. Los Angeles
	Elton John double bill

SEPTEMBER 1992

3–4	Shoreline Amphitheatre, San Francisco
6	Tacoma Dome, Seattle
9	Pauley Pavilion, Los Angeles
	MTV Awards. Eric and his band perform 'Tears In Heaven'

OCTOBER 1992

16	Madison Square Garden, New York
	Eric joins all-star cast for a concert tribute to Bob Dylan who was celebrating his 30th anniversary in the industry. Eric played 'Love Minus Zero' and 'Don't Think Twice'. Eric later joined in the grand finale with the all star band led by Bob Dylan, playing 'My Back Pages' and 'Knockin' On Heaven's Door'.

DECEMBER 1992

31	Woking Leisure Centre, Surrey

JANUARY 1993

12	Plaza Hotel, Los Angeles
	Cream re-form for the Rock 'n' Roll' hall of Fame awards. They play 'Sunshine Of Your Love', 'Born Under A Bad Sign' and 'Crossroads', The show is filmed and recorded

1993 ALBERT HALL SHOWS

The band now consists of:

Eric Clapton (guitar, vocals), Andy Fairweather Low (guitar), Duck Dunn (bass). Richie Hayward (drums), Chris Stainton (drums), Jerry Portnoy (harmonica), Roddy Lorimer, Tim Sanders and Simon Clarke (horns).

The set was taken from:

'How Long', 'Alabama Women', 'Terraplane Blues', From Four Until Late', 'Kidman Blues', 'County Jail Blues', '32-20', 'Chicago Breakdown', 'Hey Hey', 'Walkin' Blues', 'Long Distance Call', 'Blow Wind Blow', 'Key To The Highway', 'Tell Me Mama', 'Juke', 'Blues Leave Me Alone', 'Going Away Baby', 'Coming Home', 'Meet Me In The Bottom', 'Forty Four', 'It's My Life', 'Love Her With A Feeling', 'Tore Down', 'Born Under A Bad Sign', 'Let Me Love You Baby', 'Groaning The Blues', 'Hear Me Calling', 'Ain't Nobody's Business', 'Sweet Home Chicago'.

Jimmie Vaughan is the support and jams most nights on the encore, 'Sweet Home Chicago'.

FEBRUARY 1993

20–23   Royal Albert Hall, London

26–27   Royal Albert Hall, London

On the 20th Eric played 'Blues With A Feeling' and 'Further On Up The Road'. 'All Your Love' was also played for the first few dates before being dropped in favour of longer guitar solos. Buddy Guy jams on the encore 'Sweet Home Chicago' on the 26th.

MARCH 1993

1–3   Royal Albert Hall, London

5–7   Royal Albert Hall, London

Lou Ann Barton sings on the encore of 'Sweet Home Chicago'.

JUNE 1993

15   Apollo Theatre, Harlem, New York

Eric plays alongside B.B. King, Albert Collins, Jeff Beck, Buddy Guy for a special charity show

CHARITY CONCERTS

FOR THE CHEMICAL DEPENDENCY CENTRE PROJECTS

Maggie Ryder replaces Gina Foster and Nathan East replaces Duck Dunn

OCTOBER 1993

1–2   NEC Birmingham

ZZ Top join Eric for 'Sweet Home Chicago' on 2nd October

3   Sheffield Arena, Sheffield

Joe Cocker, Nine Below Zero join Eric for 'Sweet Home Chicago'.

ABOVE *UK advertisement for Eric's 1993 Royal Albert Hall show.*
RIGHT *UK advertisement for Eric's 1994 Royal Albert Hall show.*

JAPAN TOUR

OCTOBER 1993

12–13   The Budokcan, Tokyo

14   Rainbow Hall, Nagoya

17   Kokusai Centre, Fukuoka

18–19   Castle Hall, Osaka

21–22   The Budokan, Tokyo

23   The Arena, Yokohama

25–27   The Budokan, Tokyo

30   The Arena, Yokohama

31   The Budokan, Tokyo

DECEMBER 1993

31   Woking Leisure Centre, Surrey

JANUARY 1994

19   Waldorf, New York

BELOW *Japanese Tour poster for Eric's 1993 Tour.*

1994 ROYAL ALBERT HALL SHOWS

Dave Bronze replaces Nathan East

FEBRUARY 1994

20–22   Royal Albert Hall, London

24–26   Royal Albert Hall, London

28   Royal Albert Hall, London

MARCH 1994

1–2   Royal Albert Hall, London

4–6   Royal Albert Hall, London

7 *Moonlighting*

hatever claims are made for Eric Clapton – 'World's Greatest Guitarist' or boring, grey muso – one thing cannot be disputed, Eric Clapton qualifies as one of the hardest working men in rock. Take a look back through this book and see how much time he has spent on the road, and how much off it – not much. Then start counting the albums and the singles. It'll take you till the end of the century to finish totting them up. Compare his output to that of the Beatles or Stones. No five-year breaks between records and tours for this hardworking boy from Surrey. Nothing, not heroin addiction, alcoholism, the deaths, first of friends on the road, or that of his son, stopped him working.

Ever since he was given his first cardboard guitar and threw Shadows' poses in the bedroom mirror, Eric has loved his instrument. It is in his blood. It takes him down and it takes him right back up again. He is compulsive, and never stops playing.

As his reputation grew so did the queue of musicians who wanted to play with Eric Clapton and/or wanted the 'World's Greatest Guitarist' to play on their records. Throughout his career he has taken many opportunities to play with fellow musicians whom he respects; carrying on a simultaneous career as the most in-demand session musician in the world.

In December 1963, when Eric was a member of the Yardbirds they were used as a pick-up band by visiting American legend, Sonny Boy Williamson. A frightening character by all accounts, he would play the part of the bluesman to the hilt and was invariably drunk by the time he got on stage. Not too impressed by these young English whitey upstarts, Williamson gave the aspiring blues band a hard time. Eric was in thrall

FACING PAGE Buddy Guy and Eric at the Royal Albert Hall in February 1991.

FROM TOP DOWN

Otis Spann's 'Stirs Me Up' single which also features Jimmy Page. ■ Various artists WHAT'S SHAKIN' album features Eric in The Powerhouse. He played on 'I Want To Know', 'Crossroads' and 'Steppin' Out'. ■ Aretha Franklin's LADY SOUL album features Eric on 'Good To Me As I Am To You'.

nonetheless. 'He made you do things that you probably would have liked to have done and musically would have come around to doing.'

Eric's next guest appearance was, without doubt, one of his major highlights of 1964. The session for Muddy Waters' pianist, Otis Spann, was attended by the great bluesman himself. It was the beginning of a long, close friendship between the founding father of blues, Muddy Waters, and the heir apparent, Eric Clapton, which continued until Muddy's death in 1983.

During his time with John Mayall's Bluesbreakers, Eric played on only two sessions. He played with John Mayall on three tracks for Champion Jack Dupree's album, FROM NEW ORLEANS TO CHICAGO (Decca) in late 1965, and, he was asked to take part in an experimental studio group, the Powerhouse, put together by producer Joe Boyd on behalf of Elektra records. The group consisted of Eric on lead guitar; Stevie Winwood (Spencer Davis Group) on keyboards and vocals; Ben Palmer (Eric's long-time friend from the Rooster days) on piano; Jack Bruce (Manfred Mann) on bass; Paul Jones (Manfred Mann) on harmonica and Pete York (Spencer Davis Group) on drums. The only product of this potentially devastating line-up was a single, 'What's Shaking'.

Eric's reputation grew with the rave revues. By the time he joined Cream he was a superstar with a loyal following. During recordings of Cream's third album in New York, producer Tom Dowd invited him to play a solo on a song for Aretha Franklin. He played on one number 'Good To Me As I Am To You' though the 'First Lady of Soul' was absent. However, a lot of great musicians were present, which made the session a testing time for Eric. 'It was pretty nerve-wracking, but I had one pass at it and they gave me a standing ovation, which really amazed me.'

While on tour with Cream in the States, Eric spent his spare time hanging out in Greenwich Village jamming whenever, wherever and with whomever possible. One night he went to check out B.B. King at the Café A Go Go. 'I went down. We were introduced and he seemed to know of me, which was nice.' It was an amazing night, Eric, sporting an afro, relaxed on his Marshall with his psychedelic Gibson SG, soloing and trading licks with B.B. King. Eric was more comfortable playing in the intimate surroundings of a club than in the cavernous barns were the Cream concerts were staged. The show was recorded, but the tapes have been lost.

Another legendary club Eric dropped into occasionally was the Scene, where he played some incendiary sets with Jimi Hendrix, and on one occasion, with Jeff Beck. Despite the fact that you couldn't put a price on such a meeting today, no one at the time bothered to bring along a tape recorder.

Eric and George Harrison had known each other since 1964, when the Yardbirds supported the Beatles at their Christmas shows. Their friendship grew during the late sixties, so when the Beatles formed their own record label, Apple, it came as no surprise that George invited Eric to provide guitar for some of their artists. Jackie Lomax and Billy Preston were fortunate enough to have Eric play on their records. Ironically, his name did not appear on the album sleeves due to contractual difficulties, but it was not too hard to recognize his distinctive playing on the various tracks.

Eric was also asked to contribute a solo to George's song 'While My Guitar Gently Weeps' for the Beatles' WHITE ALBUM. Again he appeared uncredited. Eric remembers it well, 'it was one of the ones they did completely live in the studio with everyone. I think there was one small bit of overdubbing – just an effect or something – but it was really nice to see them all working live together. To be playing along was a real thrill.' George returned the favour when he co-wrote the Cream classic 'Badge', and played rhythm guitar on the track as L'Angelo Misterioso.

Eric enjoys the diversity and challenge of session work for contradictory reasons: he says they are good for the ego and that they bring him back down to earth. Looking back at his career, it is amazing to see quite how varied his session work has been. Shortly after Cream's demise he played in a one-off supergroup in the Rolling Stones' *Rock 'N' Roll Circus* film, alongside Mitch Mitchell, Keith Richards and John Lennon. They did 'Yer Blues' off the WHITE ALBUM. Mick Jagger joined them at rehearsals for a spirited version of Buddy Holly's 'Peggy Sue'. Although the film was completed, it has yet to see official release due to Mick's dissatisfaction with the Stones' performance. However, persistent rumours of it's imminent release probably mean that it will see the light of day at some stage.

Early in 1969, Eric began rehearsing at home with Stevie Winwood and Ginger Baker before tentatively entering Morgan Studios in London to record. During the same period he appeared in the film *Supersession*, which as the title suggests, threw virtuosos musicians of different musical genres together and filmed the results. Eric played alongside Buddy Guy for the first time, and also with Roland Kirk, Dick Heckstall-Smith, Jack Bruce, and Jon Hiseman. Jimi Hendrix was also due to play, but he missed his plane. Other musicians who did make it were Stephen Stills, Buddy Miles and various members of Led Zeppelin. The film was released on video.

During Blind Faith's American tour, Eric spent more time with the support bands Free and Delaney and Bonnie than he did with his own collapsing unit. In New York's Scene club at the start of the tour, an electric jam session took place, featuring Eric, Paul Kossoff from Free, Stevie Winwood, sundry members of Spooky Tooth and Delaney and Bonnie.

When the tour reached Los Angeles Eric joined Delaney and Bonnie in the studio to record the single they had co-written, 'Comin' Home'. 'Delaney and Bonnie were just such down-home cats and they were getting very little applause, very little money, and the only reason they were on the bill was because I'd asked for them to be the second act. I wanted to be lead guitarist with Delaney and Bonnie because they were singing soul music.'

At the end of the US tour Blind Faith went their separate ways. On his immediate return to England, Eric received a desperate call from John

FROM TOP DOWN

The Beatles' WHITE ALBUM features Eric on 'While My Guitar Gently Weeps'. ■
George Harrison's WONDERWALL MUSIC album features Eric on the track 'Ski-ing'.
■ The ANTHOLOGY OF BRITISH BLUES VOL.I AND 2, a compilation of various artists features Eric on 'Miles Road', 'Tribute To Elmore', 'Freight Loader', 'Snake Drive', 'West Coast Idea', 'Draggin' My Tale' and 'Choker'.

TOP ROW LEFT TO RIGHT

Jackie Lomax's IS THIS WHAT YOU WANT? album features Eric on 'Sour Milk Sea', 'The Eagle Laughs At You', 'You've Got Me Thinking' and 'New Day'. ■ THAT'S THE WAY GOD PLANNED IT by Billy Preston features Eric on the title track 'That's The Way God Planned It' and 'Do What You Want To'. ■ Martha Velez's FIENDS AND ANGELS album features Eric on 'It Takes A Lot To Laugh, It Takes A Train To Cry', 'I'm Gonna Leave You', 'Feel So Bad' and 'In my Girlish Days'.

BOTTOM ROW LEFT TO RIGHT

Eric plays on 'Man Hole Covered Wagon' for Shawn Phillips's CONTRIBUTION album. ■ Leon Russell's self-titled album features Eric on 'Delta Lady', 'Prince Of Peace', 'Roll Away The Stone'.

■ ENCOURAGING WORDS by Billy Preston features Eric on 'Right Now' and the title track 'Encouraging Words'.

Lennon asking him to fly out to Toronto for a last minute Plastic Ono Band concert. Without thinking he accepted and flew out. The band members, John, Eric, Klaus Voorman, Alan White and Yoko, had their only rehearsal on the plane over to Canada. The final concert had mixed results. 'I thought it was excellent. It was a thing that paid off, I don't think that he'd entertained the idea of solo performances much before that'.

On his return home Eric played on an abortive Rick Grech album alongside George Harrison. Two songs survived, finally appearing as bonus tracks on the European CD version of Blind Faith's eponymously titled album. Shortly afterwards, John Lennon requested Eric's services on the Plastic Ono Band's first single, the harrowing 'Cold Turkey'.

In December 1969, Eric along with most of Delaney and Bonnie and Friends, joined John and Yoko at their Peace For Christmas charity concert in London. It was a self-indulgent affair that summed up the late sixties; well-intentioned hippies out of their minds on hard drugs, trying to express their spoiled superstar angst, and confused desire for world peace in interminable 'free-form' jamming. In a brief, forty-minute set they and their pals played just two songs, 'Cold Turkey' and 'Don't Worry Kyoko'. The results were eventually released in 1972 as a freebie gift with John and Yoko's SOMETIME IN NEW YORK CITY.

By January 1970 Eric was ready to record his first solo album with help from Delaney and Bonnie. They flew out to Los Angeles where

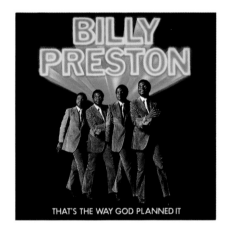

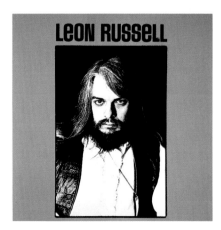

Delaney and Eric were booked for various sessions, including one for King Curtis. The session is still one of Eric's all-time favourites. 'Just the spontaneity of the recording, it was so quick. I played it with him and we did it in about ten minutes and it was great'. 'Teasin' was released as a single on Atlantic and features some tasteful slide playing from Eric, against a background of King's powerful sax.

In the same period, Buddy Holly's Crickets were recording their first new album in a long time and Eric played on a remake of the classic 'That'll Be The Day' for the ROCKIN' 50'S ROCK 'N' ROLL album, which, incidentally, is now deleted and very hard to find.

As soon as he finished his own album, Eric joined Delaney and Bonnie for a short American tour before flying home. On his return, he stepped up the session work while he decided which direction to take his own career. March 1970 was particularly productive; along with George Harrison he contributed to 'I'm Your Spiritual Breadman' for Ashton Gardner and Dyke's THE WORST OF album, and was credited as Sir Cedéric Clayton. He also turned out for Stephen Stills to record two songs, 'Fishes And Scorpions' and 'Go Back Home', on Stills' first two solo albums. In addition, Eric not only provided the guitar work on George Harrison's next solo album, but the backing band as well, Derek and the Dominos.

Next up, was blues legend and childhood hero, Howlin' Wolf, who had just signed with the Rolling Stones label in England. The cream of

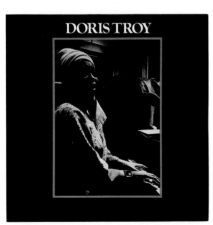

TOP ROW LEFT TO RIGHT

Eric plays on both sides of Vivian Stanshall's 'Labio-Dental Fricative'/'Paper Round' single. ■ Jonathan Kelly's 'Don't You Believe It' single which features Eric.

BOTTOM ROW LEFT TO RIGHT

Doris Troy's self-titled album features Eric on 'Ain't That Cute', 'Give Me Back My Dynamite', 'I've Got To Be Strong', 'You Give Me Joy Joy', 'Don't Call Me No More' and 'Get Back' as a bonus track on the CD version. ■ Stephen Stills' self-titled album features Eric on 'Go Back Home'.

FROM TOP DOWN

Eric plays on one track, 'I'm Your Spiritual Breadman', for Ashton Gardner And Dyke's album THE WORST OF ASHTON GARDNER AND DYKE. ■ The Crickets' ROCKIN' 50's ROCK 'N' ROLL features Eric on 'Rockin' 50's Rock 'N' Roll' and 'That'll Be The Day'.

British musicians paid homage, including Stevie Winwood, Ringo Starr, Bill Wyman, Charlie Watts and Klaus Voorman and Eric felt privileged to be taught the slide part of 'Little Red Rooster' by its creator. But it didn't throw him off his stride; the rehearsal actually appears on the LONDON SESSIONS album, alongside some superlative playing by Eric.

Eric continued to help George out with Apple acts Doris Troy and Billy Preston. He also played on a session for Doctor John with Mick Jagger for the album SUN MOON AND HERBS.

During the recording of Derek and the Dominos' LAYLA AND OTHER ASSORTED LOVE SONGS double album, Eric managed to squeeze in the production of an album by Buddy Guy and Junior Wells, PLAY THE BLUES. He later contributed some slide work in October 1970 and February 1971. In November 1970 he made one of the more unusual appearances of his career on the Johnny Cash Show playing with Johnny and Carl Perkins on a version of 'Matchbox' with the Dominos providing backup.

By April 1971, Derek and the Dominos had just about burned themselves out on cocaine and heroin. Halfway through the recording sessions for their second album, Eric had a huge row with Jim Gordon, and almost inevitably, it marked the end for the band. Clapton picked up his guitar after the argument, walked out and hid from the world until George Harrison begged him to appear at the star-studded Concert for Bangladesh in August. The film and soundtrack pay witness to a dramatic return to form by Bob Dylan, who stole the day. Eric, however, was content to stay in the background throwing in the odd searing lick now and then.

Eric also came out of hiding to play with Stevie Wonder at a session at the Air Studios in London. The pair hit it off and although Stevie was reportedly pleased with the recording, the tracks have never been released. Perhaps the tracks will appear on a comprehensive Stevie Wonder retrospective one day. Eric's only other appearance of the year came unannounced, when he walked on stage to tumultuous applause during a gig by Leon Russell at the London Rainbow in December.

He did not return to the stage until January 1973 for two concerts held in celebration of Britain's entry into the Common Market. Backed by close friends Pete Townshend, Stevie Winwood, Jim Capaldi, Rick Grech and Ronnie Wood the comeback shows were ineptly recorded and produced a poor live album, THE RAINBOW CONCERT. Many regarded the album as a waste and an inaccurate reflection of the concert, and those who actually attended attest to the strength of Eric's playing on both nights.

In early 1973, Pete Townshend tried to revive Eric's interest in his own career, and keep him away from drugs, by helping to re-mix and re-record portions of the Dominos aborted second album. But it was a futile effort, and although they were working from Eric's home, he quickly dropped the idea, despite pleas and offers of assistance from Townshend. Basically, Eric was still addicted to heroin and unable to work. It was several

---

months before he could face the prospect of a real comeback.

In fact, Eric did not feel ready to face the world again until spring 1974. At a press conference in April, he came clean about his drug problems, and announced that he'd be flying to Miami to record a new album and would then set off on a world tour. Before any of this though, he played on the soundtrack to *Tommy* and filmed the role of the *Preacher*.

When Eric hit the road again, he was joined on stage almost every night by his superstar pals. The Who were touring the States at the time, so Pete Townshend and Keith Moon came on in Greensboro and West Palm Beach for 'Baby Don't You Do It', 'Little Queenie' and 'Can't Explain' amongst others. Joe Walsh also joined in at West Palm Beach. Other guests included Freddie King in Jersey City and Buffalo for the blues classics 'Have You Ever Loved A Woman' and 'Hideaway'; John Mayall for an instrumental shuffle in Long Beach; Todd Rundgren and Dickie Betts in New York for 'Little Queenie'; and Ronnie Wood in London for 'Steady Rolling Man' and 'Little Queenie'.

At the end of the first leg of the tour, Eric and the band joined RSO's latest signing in the studio for a sparkling session that was eventually released in 1976 as part of FREDDIE KING 1934-1976, which is a definite must have. Eric and his band then flew out to Jamaica to record their second album, and unsurprisingly, given the location, THERE'S ONE IN EVERY CROWD has a noticeable reggae influence. Peter Tosh, creative force and founder

TOP ROW LEFT TO RIGHT

Jesse Davis's self-titled album features Eric on 'Reno Street Incident', 'Tulsa County', 'Washita Love Child', 'Every Night Is Saturday Night', 'You Belladonna You', 'Rock And Roll Gypsies', 'Golden Sun Goddess' and 'Crazy Love'. ■ Eric plays on 'Alcatraz' and 'Beware Of Darkness' for Leon Russell's LEON RUSSELL AND THE SHELTER PEOPLE album. ■ BUDDY GUY AND JUNIOR WELLS PLAY THE BLUES features Eric on nine tracks including 'A Man Of Many Words', 'My Baby She Left Me' and 'Come On In This House'.

BOTTOM ROW LEFT TO RIGHT

Stephen Stills' '2' album features Eric on 'Fishes and Scorpions'. ■ Howlin' Wolf's THE LONDON HOWLIN' WOLF SESSIONS album features Eric on 'I Ain't Superstitious' and twelve other tracks. ■ Dr. John's SUN, MOON AND HERBS features Eric on six tracks.

TOP ROW LEFT TO RIGHT

Eric contributes to one track, 'Don't Worry Kyoko' for Yoko Ono's double album FLY. ■ James Luther Dickinson's DIXIE FRIED album features Eric on 'The Judgement'. ■ Bobby Keys self-titled album features Eric on several tracks.

BOTTOM ROW LEFT TO RIGHT

Delaney And Bonnie's D & B TOGETHER features Eric on 'Coming Home' and 'Groupie (Superstar)'. ■ Bobby Whitlock's self-titled album features Eric on 'Where There's A Will There's A Way', 'A Day Without Jesus', 'Back In My Life Again' and 'The Scenery Has Slowly Changed'.

■ Bobby Whitlock's RAW VELVET features Eric on 'The Dreams Of A Hobo' and 'Hello LA Bye Bye Birmingham'.

member of the Wailers and Bob Marley, came down to the studio adding a reggae sound with his distinctive guitar and vocals to 'Whatcha Gonna Do', for the CROSSROADS box set, and 'Burial', which remains unreleased.

Eric's own schedule in 1974 was too hectic for him to help out other musicians. He didn't play with anyone else until January 1975 when he cut several tracks with Arthur Louis, including a reggae version of Dylan's 'Knockin' On Heaven's Door'. However, controversy struck when Eric recorded a similar version of the same song and released it as a single at the same time as Louis' version. Eric had a worldwide hit, while Louis saw his record sink without trace. As compensation, Eric recorded one of Louis's songs 'Someone Like You' for his B–side and gave him a new song, 'Layla Part 2', which also featured Eric's guitar work, but was never released.

Eric's next session was with the Rolling Stones at Electric Lady Studios in July 1975. Eric had guested on SYMPATHY FOR THE DEVIL at Madison Square Garden, and the Stones returned the compliment by helping Eric out on a track for his next album. With all the Stones present, Eric and the band ran through eight takes of 'Carnival In Rio'. The finished master lasts for just over eight minutes, but remains unreleased.

The other major session Eric played in 1975 took place at Columbia Studios for Bob Dylan's DESIRE album. Eric had to hire a dobro and electric guitar as all his equipment had already been sent on to the next gig. He ended up playing on about six numbers, but Dylan was dissatisfied with

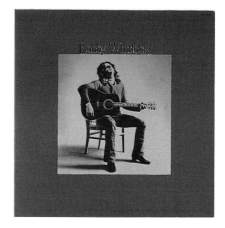

most of them and rerecorded everything the next day. 'Romance In Durango' was the only track featuring Eric that made it on to the album.

Santana played support on Eric's 1975 summer tour of the United States and Carlos Santana, a respected jazz-rock guitarist himself, frequently came on and improvised on an extended 'Eyesight To The Blind' that could be stretched out for a full fifteen minutes. Keith Moon from The Who, ever the party animal, bashed his way through 'Why Does Love Got To Be So Sad' in LA, and country-rock sensations, Poco, added their lilting harmonies to 'Let It Rain' at the Scope in Norfolk. Jazz guitar virtuoso, John McLaughlin, together with drummer Alphonse Mouzon, joined Carlos and Eric for 'Stormy Monday' at the Nassau Coliseum, New York.

Eric recorded his next album NO REASON TO CRY in April 1976, at The Band's amazing Shangri-La Studios, which looked straight out to sea. During the recording it was as if the rock fraternity had decided collectively to ensure Clapton's return was successful. Bob Dylan contributed a song, 'Sign Language' and The Band, Van Morrison, Billy Preston, Ronnie Wood and Georgie Fame all came down to help out. The album could easily have turned into a supersession, all flawless technique and no soul, but it is one of his finest albums of the seventies.

While in California, Clapton took great pleasure in turning out for Joe Cocker, Kinky Freidman, Rick Danko, Corky Laing, Ringo Starr and Stephen Bishop. He also found time to jam with the Crusaders at The Roxy

TOP ROW LEFT TO RIGHT

MUSIC FROM FREE CREEK, a compilation from various artists, features Eric as King Cool on 'Road Song', 'Getting Back To Molly' and 'No One Knows'. ■ LONDON REVISITED, a Muddy Waters and Howlin' Wolf album features Eric on 'Going Down Slow', 'Killing Floor' and 'I Want To Have A Word With You'. ■ Eric contributes to 'Eyesight To The Blind' and 'Sally Simpson' for the soundtrack version of The Who's TOMMY.

BOTTOM ROW LEFT TO RIGHT

Arthur Louis's FIRST album was only released in Japan. Eric contributed to 'Knockin' On Heaven's Door', 'Plum', 'The Dealer', 'Still It Feels Good', 'Come On And Love Me', 'Train 444' and 'Go Out And Make It Happen'. ■ Eric plays on Arthur Louis's extremely rare single 'Knockin' On Heaven's Door' released on the Plum label. ■ Eric guests on one track 'Romance In Durango' for Bob Dylan's DESIRE album.

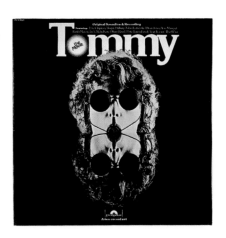

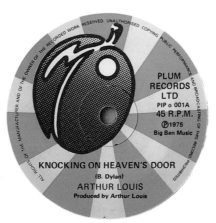

in LA, alongside Elton John, Stevie Wonder and Rick Danko.

Eric and the Rolling Stones have had a close affiliation since the early sixties when the Yardbirds took over their residency at The Crawdaddy club in Richmond. Occasionally, Brian Jones would even jam with the Yardbirds at the legendary club. The association continued, and on his return to England in May, Eric jammed with them in Leicester on 'Brown Sugar' and 'Key To The Highway'.

Eric decided to play seaside towns exclusively on his next UK tour, which also gave him a chance to have a mini-holiday. The tour ended in a holiday camp with an exclusive performance for patrons, most of whom had never heard of Eric Clapton, but by the end of the evening they felt he had the potential, with a little more practice, to go places. Van Morrison turned up at a few shows to sing 'Kansas City' and 'Stormy Monday'; he was managed by tour promoter Harvey Goldsmith at the time. But the most spectacular event was perhaps the opening show at the Crystal Palace Bowl, London where Larry Coryell, Ronnie Wood and Freddie King came on for a rousing encore of 'Further On Up The Road'.

Since the day he first caressed the neck of a guitar, Eric has absorbed many diverse styles and influences whilst still remaining faithful to his first love, the blues. During his infatuation with Don Williams, Eric joined the country superstar at London's Hammersmith Odeon, adding dobro to four numbers. He was clearly influenced by Williams at this time and admired

TOP ROW LEFT TO RIGHT

Eric plays the congas on some tracks for Dr. John's HOLLYWOOD BE THY NAME album. ■ Joe Cocker's STINGRAY album features Eric on 'Worrier'. ■ Eric contributes to ROTOGRAVURE, Ringo's solo album with the track 'This Be Called A Song'.

BOTTOM ROW LEFT TO RIGHT

Kinky Friedman's LASSO FROM EL PASSO album features Eric on 'Kinky' and 'Ol' Ben Lucas'. ■ Stephen Bishop's CARELESS album features Eric on 'Save It For A Rainy Day' and 'Sinking In An Ocean Of Tears'. ■ Eric's name mentioned in the credits of Roger Daltrey's ONE OF THE BOYS album, but he does not appear to play on the album.

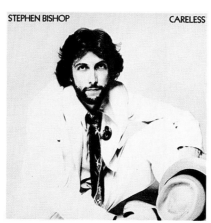

the playing of his guitarist Danny Flowers. After the show Don and his band went on to Eric's home for an all nighter.

Eric embarked on a US tour in November 1976. Freddie King was support and he would join the headliner most nights for the encore of 'Further On Up The Road'. A corking version of this number from Dallas was released on Freddie's memorial album, 1934-1976. After the tour, Eric was invited to play at The Band's farewell concert. A historic show to mark the end of their days on the road, The Band invited special guests to join in such as Joni Mitchell, Neil Young, Muddy Waters, Ringo Starr, Ronnie Wood, Ronnie Hawkins and, of course, Bob Dylan. Eric did 'All Our Pastimes' and 'Further On Up The Road' before joining in the grand finale of 'I Shall Be Released'. The obligatory jam with Eric, Neil Young, Robbie Robertson, Ringo Starr, Stephen Stills and Carl Radle followed.

The year 1977 started quietly with Eric contributing to Pete Townshend and Ronnie Lane's upcoming album. The only live gig was a small charity show in his local village hall on Valentines Day in front of five-hundred people backed by Ronnie Lane and his band Slim Chance. The remainder of the year was spent recording SLOWHAND and touring Europe and Japan. In contrast, 1978 was a much busier year; a huge US tour started on 1 February at the PNE Coliseum in Vancouver, and ended on 9 April at the Maple Leaf Gardens in Toronto. The reward was a top-ten album. On returning to England Eric appeared at Alexis Korner's 50th birthday party at Pinewood Studios. It was a nostalgic evening as the old faces from the British blues scene gathered together for the first jam in a long time. The event was recorded and filmed and later released in Europe as THE PARTY ALBUM with Eric playing on four songs.

A three-date stadium tour of Europe followed in the summer of 1978 with Bob Dylan headlining. In England, the concert attracted 180,000 people to Blackbushe Airport, and Eric joined Bob for a rousing version of 'Forever Young'. Dylan donated two songs, 'Walk Out In The Rain' and 'If I Don't Be There By Morning' to Eric's new BACKLESS album, which incidentally, also drew it's title from the folk singer. Backstage, Dylan gave full vent to an ego inflated by more than a decade of fawning adulation. Holding court like a medieval king, he demanded complete attention from his subjects. If you turned away for a second he'd immediately glare at you in a manner you were unlikely to forget. Eric seemed to think Bob had eyes in the back of his head, hence the title.

A European and UK tour took place in October 1978 with Muddy Waters as support. These were memorable shows giving many of Eric's fans a unique opportunity to see and hear the legendary blues giant, and Muddy would often join Eric on stage for the encores. Some of the concerts were filmed for the documentary, *Eric Clapton And His Rolling Hotel*, but the film does not show Eric at his best and has only been seen at a few film festivals. It is, however, an honest and revealing period piece, and includes some

FROM TOP DOWN

Corky Laing's MAKIN' IT ON THE STREET album features Eric on 'On My Way'.

■ Ronnie Lane and Pete Townshend's ROUGH MIX album features Eric on 'Rough Mix', 'Annie', 'April Fool' and 'Till The Rivers Run Dry'. ■ Freddie King's '1934-1976' features Eric on 'Sugar Sweet', 'TV Mama' and 'Gambling Woman Blues'.

hilarious scenes shot on the luxurious Orient Express, which had been hired to carry the band around Europe. The most amusing scene comes when a French railway official is granted an interview with Eric for French Railway News. Unbeknown to him, the person he interviews is a roadie posing as the World's Greatest Guitarist. The poor guy even had a photograph taken with the technician, which probably still hangs on his office wall to this day. The film concludes with a jam featuring George Harrison and Elton John on a spirited version of 'Further On Up The Road' recorded at Guildford Civic Hall. The year ended for Eric with the contribution of a guitar intro to 'Love Comes To Everyone', which appears on George Harrison's self-titled album.

Another busy year followed in 1979, most of which was spent on the road. The main event of the year was Eric's wedding to Pattie 'Layla' Boyd in Tuscon, Arizona, which was followed in May, during a break in the hectic touring schedule, by a reception for friends and family. In the massive marquee in his garden the various guests took to the stage for a superstar jam that no record company could buy. Imagine the sales of an album of Cream and Beatles standards featuring Eric Clapton, George Harrison, Paul McCartney, Ringo Starr, Jack Bruce, Denny Laine, Lonnie Donnegan and many others. Another extracurricular activity this year, with Danny Douma and Marc Benno, is of no special interest. However, he can be heard on every track of Marc's album, LOST IN AUSTIN along with most of his band.

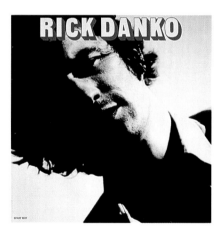

By 1980, Eric had an all-English band, which included Gary Brooker. The highlight of a short UK tour in May was Jeff Beck's appearance at the Civic Hall in Guildford for a hot rendition of 'Ramblin' On My Mind'. This was the first time the two had played together since Eric jammed with Jeff and the Yardbirds at the Marquee club in 1966. This year he also played on Phil Collins' If LEAVING ME IS EASY and John Martyn's COULDN'T LOVE YOU MORE.

Forty-seven dates in the United States had to be cancelled in 1980 as a result of Eric's burst ulcer. A full period of rest and recuperation was ordered during which Eric revealed a hitherto hidden passion for fishing. He did not appear in public again until September 1981, when he joined Jeff Beck for three numbers at the Amnesty International concerts in London at the Theatre Royal, Drury Lane. He did 'Crossroads', 'Further On Up The Road' and 'Cause We Ended As Lovers', before the poignant finale of 'I Shall be Released' led by Sting.

On the last date of the 1982 US tour at Miami's Sportatorium Muddy Waters joined Eric for 'Blow Wind Blow'. Sadly, this was to be their last appearance together before Muddy's death in 1983.

1983 and Eric was back in shape and raring to go. He embarked on a large US tour in February to tie in with the release of MONEY AND CIGARETTES. The tour came over to England and then Europe before it's conclusion back in the US. As was customary, one of the best shows took place in the old home town, Guildford, where the encores featured Phil Collins and Jimmy Page making a rare appearance since the demise of Led Zeppelin, which made them something special. The highlight of the 1983 US tour came in Chicago when Eric headed down to Buddy Guy's night club for some late-night jamming, which he always does when in town. When these two are on form, no one can touch them.

Eric also managed a couple of sessions early on in the year. He can be heard on THE CHALLENGE by Fleetwood Mac's Christine McVie, and 'Everybody's In A Hurry But Me', which appeared on Ringo Starr's OLD WAVE album. The latter is quite difficult to find, since it received only limited release in Canada and Germany due to lack of interest.

Much to everyone's surprise, Eric collaborated with Roger Waters in August, for the ex-Pink Floyd member's first tour. Many observers could not envisage Eric Clapton's laid-back blues guitar blending in with the psychedelic world of Roger Waters. But not only did Eric's guitar sound alive, but it was the old fiery Clapton again, unheard for so long.

Eric's 20th anniversary as a recording artist fell in 1983, and to celebrate it two special concerts were staged at his favourite venue, the Royal Albert Hall. Jimmy Page and Jeff Beck agreed to appear, and it was the first time the triumvirate of ex-Yardbird guitarists played together on stage since their demise in the sixties. Naturally, the concerts sold out instantly and became the most talked about event in town. Both nights were

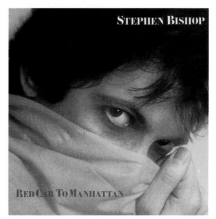

FROM TOP DOWN

Alexis Korner's THE PARTY ALBUM features Eric on 'Hey Pretty Mama', 'Hi-Heel Sneakers' and 'Stormy Monday Blues'. ■ Ronnie Lane's SEE ME album features Eric on 'When Lad Has Money', 'Barcelona' and 'Way Up Yonder'. ■ Eric's third collaboration with Stephen Bishop is for his RED CAB TO MANHATTAN album. Eric plays on two tracks, 'Little Moon' and 'Sex Kittens Go To College'.

in aid of charity, which is something Eric has become actively involved with over the years. Proceeds from the first night went to ARMS (Action Research into Multiple Sclerosis) and the second night was in aid of the Prince's Trust.

Charlie Watts, Bill Wyman, Stevie Winwood, Ray Cooper, Kenny Jones and Andy Fairweather Low joined the superstar line-up. Eric took to the stage first for his set. Amongst the numbers performed was a lively version of 'Rita Mae', which included a manic percussion solo by the inimitable Ray Cooper that almost stole the show. Ray later joined Eric's band in 1988 and performed his almost obligatory solo to the delight of audiences everywhere until his departure in 1992.

Stevie Winwood followed with a short set and was in turn followed by sets from Jimmy Page and Jeff Beck. Then everyone came back on stage for the four-song encore. The event was filmed and is available on video. Of particular interest is that Eric used many different guitars including the rare Gibson Explorer, which he had not played since 1975. The evening came to a heartbreaking end with Ronnie Lane, who is an MS sufferer, singing a couple of numbers.

'The World's Most Expensive Band', as this superstar ensemble became known, enjoyed themselves so much that they decided to repeat the whole exercise on a short tour of the US. Stevie Winwood could not make it but was replaced by Joe Cocker. The only other major change was Eric

TOP ROW LEFT TO RIGHT

Eric plays on John Martyn's classic track 'Couldn't Love You More', which appears on the GLORIOUS FOOL album. ■ Various artists play on THE SECRET POLICEMAN'S OTHER BALL; Eric contributes to "Cause We Ended As Lovers', 'Further On Up The Road' and 'I Shall Be Released'. ■ Gary Brooker's LEAD ME TO THE WATER album features Eric on the title track 'Lead Me To The Water' and 'Home Lovin''.

BOTTOM ROW LEFT TO RIGHT

Ringo's OLD WAVE album features Eric on 'Everybody's In A Hurry But Me'. ■ Christine McVie's self-titled album features Eric on 'The Challenge'. ■ Eric plays on all the tracks of Roger Waters' THE PROS AND CONS OF HITCHIKING album.

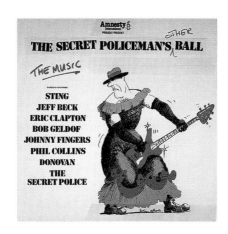
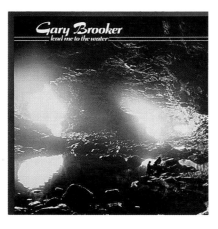

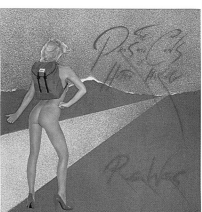

and Jeff Beck joining Jimmy Page on the Led Zeppelin anthem 'Stairway To Heaven'.

Whilst in LA, Eric and Jeff Beck went to the Baked Potato club for a jam with Lonnie Mack. Eric was due to join Lonnie for his upcoming album sessions, but had to cancel due to other engagements.

In July 1984 he joined his old friend Bob Dylan on stage at London's Wembley Stadium alongside Carlos Santana, Mick Taylor and Van Morrison for eight numbers. The whole concert was recorded but has never been released.

The major event of 1985 was, of course, Live Aid, which was broadcast to the world's largest ever television audience. Eric's set was so well received that even he was taken by surprise. Despite nerves he opened powerfully with 'White Room'. It's staccato wah wah showed he meant business, and by the end of the set he had won back a lot of old fans as well as gaining many new ones. He was joined by Phil Collins on drums at this historic event and he met Lionel Richie for the first time backstage, which led to an appearance on the massive DANCING ON THE CEILING album.

After his exceptional performance at Live Aid, Eric's profile was higher than it ever had been and BEHIND THE SUN became his best-selling album in years. He even made an appearance on the hugely popular *Late Night With Letterman* playing with the house band on such classics as 'Layla', 'White Room' and 'Knock On Wood'.

Another important development in 1985 was Eric's first serious soundtrack. He wrote and performed the music for a chilling thriller about nuclear waste that was shown on BBC television in November that year. There were six episodes of *Edge Of Darkness* and the soundtrack won him an award. Like session work, soundtrack commissions provide Eric with other avenues for his work.

Later in the year, Eric was invited by Carl Perkins to join in a special concert to celebrate thirty years of rockabilly. Other star guests included two of Perkins' greatest fans, George Harrison and Ringo Starr who had both sung his songs on Beatles' albums. The backing band was hand-picked by musical director/producer Dave Edmunds. Eric played and sang 'Matchbox' and 'Mean Woman Blues', and also provided some exceptional soloing on Blackie, his faithful strat. Towards the end of the show everyone joined in for a rock 'n' roll history lesson, running through such classics as 'Blue Moon Of Kentucky', 'That's Alright', 'Whole Lotta Shakin' Going On' and a wonderful all-out version of 'Blue Suede Shoes', which left an emotional Carl Perkins telling the audience it was the best he'd ever played on. This exceptional concert has been shown on television many times and has been released on video.

Eric ended the year by joining Buddy Guy and Junior Wells at Dingwalls in London for a great set, improvising until the early hours. A week later he played a set of R & B standards for charity in a small pub in

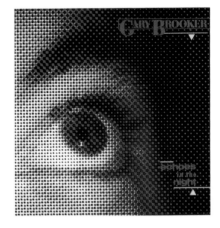
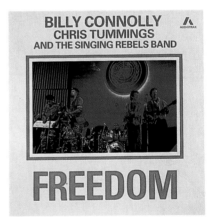

FROM TOP DOWN

Corey Hart's FIRST OFFENSE album features Eric on 'Jenney Fey'. ■ ECHOES IN THE NIGHT by Gary Brooker features Eric on one track, 'Echoes In The Night'. ■ The soundtrack to *Water* features an Eric song 'Freedom'. This rare pic sleeve single has Eric pictured with Billy Connolly and George Harrison in a still from the film.

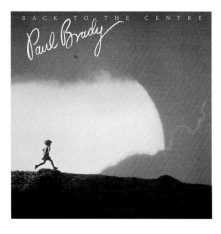

FROM TOP DOWN

Paul Brady's BACK TO THE CENTRE album features Eric on 'Deep In Your Heart'. ■ Liona Boyd's PERSONA album features Eric on 'Labyrinth'. ■ Eric joins Lionel Richie on the track 'Tonight Will Be Alright', which appears on the DANCING ON THE CEILING album.

Southend. And the following week he joined Dire Straits – and other guests including Nils Lofgren and Paul Young – for two of their Christmas concerts at London's Hammersmith Odeon, playing on 'Two Young Lovers', 'Cocaine', Solid Rock' and 'Further On Up The Road'.

Eric took note of the prevailing wind in 1986 – out went the jeans and in came the Armani and Versace suits and matching hairstyle. His first performance of the year was an invitation-only tribute to Ian Stewart, the Rolling Stones' pianist and friend who had recently died from a heart attack. Eric joined the Stones at London's 100 Club with Pete Townshend, Jeff Beck and Jack Bruce for some blues numbers such as 'Hootchie Cootchie Man', 'Little Red Rooster' and 'Down The Road Apiece'.

Eric parted company with his 1985 touring band and recruited the cream of the session world to help him record AUGUST in Los Angeles. Sessions took place in April and lasted approximately three weeks. It was a totally new sound, more polished and a lot more commercial. He collaborated on most numbers with Greg Phillinganes, Stephen Bishop and Phil Collins, who was also producer. Lamont Dozier contributed a couple of numbers and Tina Turner guested on another two, including the powerful duet, 'Tearing Us Apart'. The album also featured a horn section and a slick, deluxe sleeve with a serious looking Eric on the front and back. 'It's In The Way That You Use It', co-written with old friend Robbie Robertson and featured in Martin Scorcese's Color Of Money, was the natural choice for the first single. Interestingly enough, another number, 'It's My Life Baby', which also featured in the film, was never released by Eric. This blues tune finds him backed by the English band Big Town Playboys who play authentic R & B in small pubs and clubs. A great number, not that dissimilar to the arrangement of Ray Charles' 'Hard Times' on JOURNEYMAN, it seems destined to lie in a tape vault along with so many other neglected classics.

On 20 June 1986 the Prince's Trust celebrated it's 10th Anniversary in mind-blowing style with an amazing concert at Wembley Arena. The main part of the evening consisted of various artists taking the stage to perform one of their songs, backed by a superstar band that included guitarists Eric Clapton, Midge Ure and Mark Knopfler, with Phil Collins on drums, Elton John on piano, and Mark King on bass. Tina Turner, Rod Stewart, Paul Young, George Michael, Joan Armadtrading, Mick Jagger, David Bowie and Paul McCartney all took their turn in the spotlight. This unique show was recorded for later radio broadcasting, as well as being filmed for home video release. Among the many magic moments are Eric and Tina Turner crooning 'Tearing Us Apart'; Mick Jagger and David Bowie making their only ever live appearance together singing 'Dancing In The Street'; and Paul McCartney making his first return to the stage since Live Aid.

Jamming and guesting with other musicians became the norm in 1986. During his four-piece band tour Eric played at the prestigious

Montreux Jazz Festival in Switzerland. On the eve of the group's appearance, Eric jammed with one of his heroes, Otis Rush, and even got to sing 'Double Trouble'. In August he was invited up on stage at The Roof Garden in Kensington by Prince to play on a few Al Green numbers. Eric greatly admired Prince's music and his ability to turn his hand to just about any instrument. He was even caught performing '1999' during a break between takes of the unseen video for 'Tearing Us Apart'.

Eric contributed some wild guitar solos to four songs on Bob Geldof's album. 'I did a lot of work in a very short amount of time, because he was wise enough to catch me on my first and second takes, which is usually when I'm best'. His work on Geldof's album is essential listening as he was basically given carte blanche to do what he liked. The Dylan session that followed for the soundtrack *Hearts of Fire* was not so good 'Bob came into London, looking to get a band together. He seemed to be flying pretty blind. He knew he had to get some music for his film and it was so early on in the stage of the game that he did not know what he wanted'.

As soon as the Dylan session was over Eric flew to the States for rehearsals with Keith Richards, Robert Cray, Johnnie Johnson and Chuck Berry, for the latter's 60th birthday celebrations to be held at the Fox Theatre in St Louis. Chuck was his legendary, capricious self and things turned out pretty chaotic on the night. But it led to Eric's solo in 'Wee Wee Hours', which is simply stunning. He was pretty angry waiting so long in the wings to come on, and by the time he did all his pent-up frustration came out in the solo. 'I was very frustrated and it came out. I attacked the guitar a bit.'

Eric made two further guest appearances during his stay in the US; first with Lionel Richie at Madison Square Garden and the second on the *Nightlife* television show performing with the houseband. He flew back to England in November and played with Robert Cray in a small club. One song 'Phone Booth' came out as a free flexi disc with *Guitar Player* magazine and is now highly sought after by collectors.

He stayed home for a week before flying back to New York for a well-received, four-date club tour, for which Steve Ferrone replaced Phil Collins in the drum seat. Keith Richards made a surprise appearance at The Ritz during 'Cocaine' and 'Layla'. It was a set of shows that Eric loved. He finished the year off by recording the soundtrack to *Lethal Weapon* with David Sanborn in London. Quite a year and probably his most successful. He was a household name once again, regularly seen in the press.

1987 was to be equally busy as he consolidated the gains of the previous year. A small British and European tour kicked things off, with special-guest Mark Knopfler on leave from Dire Straits, in the line-up. The audiences were enraptured at the sight and sound of these two guitar greats playing together, and three of the now traditional concerts at London's Royal Albert Hall were recorded for a possible live album. In February, Eric

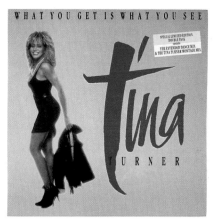

FROM TOP DOWN

Bob Geldof's DEEP IN THE HEART OF NOWHERE features Eric on 'Love Like A Rocket', 'August Was A Heavy Month', 'The Beat Of The Night', 'Good Boys In The Wrong'. ■ Eric joins with Tina Turner on the 12 inch single of 'What You Get Is What You See'. ■ John Astley's EVERYONE LOVES THE PILOT features Eric on 'Jane's Getting Serious'.

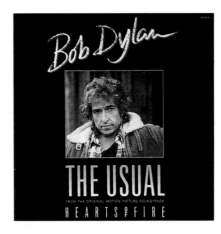

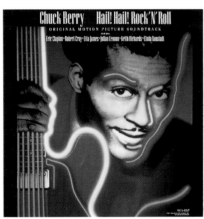

FROM TOP DOWN

Bob Dylan's 'The Usual' single features Eric.
■ Chuck Berry's HAIL HAIL ROCK 'N' ROLL
album features Eric on 'Wee Wee Hours'
and 'Rock 'N' Roll Music'. ■ George
Harrison's CLOUD NINE album features Eric
on 'Cloud Nine', 'That's What It Takes',
'Devil's Radio' and 'Wreck Of The
Hesperus'.

recorded three numbers with Jack Bruce, his old Cream partner, an event which had the tongues wagging once again about the old band reforming.

Eric took part in the Prince's Trust concerts at Wembley Arena again in 1987, the highlight of which was, without a doubt, the appearance of two Beatles together, George Harrison and Ringo Starr. Eric contributed some fine solos to 'While My Guitar Gently Weeps', as he had on the WHITE album and to 'With A Little Help From My Friends'. A few weeks later he joined Tina Turner at the same venue for 'Tearing Us Apart' though Eric stumbled in a couple of places. The song turns up on Tina's double live album with all mistakes edited out – the wonders of modern technology.

In September he recorded a new version of J.J. Cale's 'After Midnight' for a Michelob beer commercial. Filming took place in New York's Lone Star Café during the afternoon. As luck would have it, Roomful Of Blues were playing there that evening, so Eric decided to stick around for a jam. The sight of the incredible Ronnie Earl and Eric together on this little stage was every blues fan's dream.

On returning to England work began on a television special commemorating Eric's twenty-five years in the music business, centred around a specially staged concert with Buddy Guy. Both guitarists played out of their skins for over two hours at Ronnie Scott's club, although only a few numbers were filmed and the final mix was not what it could have been. 'I watched some of that and was very disappointed with the sound mix because you can hardly hear Buddy,' bemoaned Eric. He also joined the jazz-guitar wizard a few nights later at Dingwalls, but it was an awful meandering performance in comparison to the previous show. In fact, it was so bad that Jeff Beck, who was due to join in on the encores, left early without playing a note.

Eric popped up on two other albums in 1987. He can be faintly heard playing an acoustic on THEY DANCE ALONE by Sting and he is well to the fore on George Harrison's CLOUD 9. There is no problem hearing those trademark stratocaster licks on 'That's What It Takes', 'Devil's Radio' and 'Wreck Of The Hesperus', as well as on the album's title track. Harrison explained, 'when he comes over to play on my songs he doesn't bring an amplifier or a guitar, he says, "Oh, you've got a good Strat." He knows I've got one because he gave it to me!'

1988, being Eric's 25th anniversary in the music business, was another hectic year. The band was expanded to include Ray Cooper on percussion and two wonderful backing singers, Tessa Niles and Katie Kissoon. Mark Knopfler guested in the touring band, and Greg Phillinganes was replaced by Alan Clark, the keyboard player from Dire Straits. Greg left the band to be Michael Jackson's musical director on the BAD tour.

Eric recorded two soundtracks in between tours – *Homeboy* the Mickey Rourke film and *Peace In Our Time*, a British television documentary on World War II. He also squeezed in the annual Prince's

Trust concerts that were held at London's Royal Albert Hall, although these would be the last to feature old Slowhand. He actually headlined the shows and the band was supplemented for the occasion by Elton John. Support ranged from teen flavours-of-the-month, Wet Wet Wet and Black, to soft-rockers T'Pau through to sixties-stalwarts, the Bee Gees, Leonard Cohen and Joe Cocker. The celebrity backing band assembled for the event included Queen's Brian May, Midge Ure and Phil Collins. The all-star finale had everyone up on stage behind Joe Cocker singing his classic rendition of Lennon and McCartney's 'With A Little Help From My Friends'.

A few days later Eric returned a few favours when he turned out with Dire Straits, who had re-formed especially for the Live Aid-style extravaganza that celebrated the release of Nelson Mandela. An emotive version of 'Wonderful Tonight' capped a terrific performance.

Eric also played at an altogether different kind of charity event in 1988; a low-key concert in the grounds of a private estate alongside Gary Brooker, Phil Collins, Andy Fairweather Low and Mike Rutherford amongst others. The £50.00-a-head show stretched out for two and a half hours and among songs played were 'Abacab', 'Cocaine', 'Behind The Mask' and 'Whiter Shade Of Pale'.

On the massive US tour in September Eric found time on his days off to jam with Elton John and Little Feat in Los Angeles. At the tour's end, he went to New York and blundered through two Cream classics, 'Spoonful'

BELOW Robert Cray's 'Phone Booth' flexi-single with Eric.

TOP ROW LEFT TO RIGHT

Bob Geldof's 12 inch single 'Love Like A Rocket'. ■ Eric joins Tina Turner on 'Tearing Us Apart'. ■ Rare pic CD of Gayle Anne Dorsey's 'Wasted Country'.

BOTTOM ROW LEFT TO RIGHT

BRENDAN CROCKER AND THE FIVE O'CLOCK SHADOWS album features Eric on 'This Kind Of Life'. ■ Eric joins the Bunburys on their 7in and 12in versions of the single 'Fight'.

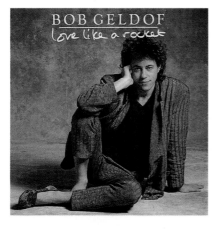

and 'Sunshine Of Your Love' with Jack Bruce. It was not a good performance, and confirmed what many had suspected for years – a Cream re-formation is not a good idea.

The traditional Albert Hall shows got 1989 under way. The shows once again featured Mark Knopfler, and a set-list spanning Eric's whole career including long-lost gems such as 'Bell Bottom Blues'. He went on to record a theme for the latest James Bond movie, *Licence To Kill,* but it was never released due to various disagreements between all parties (Duran Duran came in at the eleventh hour).

Bad luck struck again when Eric was booked to play guitar on the album BRENDAN CROCKER AND THE FIVE O'CLOCK SHADOWS. Just before recording was due to begin, he injured his finger playing cricket, and consequently could only contribute vocals. More successful was an appearance on Cyndi Lauper's 'A Night To Remember' and Zucchero's eponymous album.

Eric was also asked to contribute to the Elton John tribute album TWO ROOMS. A series of top international stars were each asked to pick a number by Elton and record it in their own style. Eric wisely chose 'The Border Song'.

While in New York mixing JOURNEYMAN Eric dropped into the Bottom Line to play some classic rock 'n' roll songs with Carl Perkins. A

BELOW Eric with Keith Richards at the Ritz in New York on 23 November 1986.
BELOW RIGHT Eric and Sting at rehearsals for the Secret Policeman's Other Ball in September 1981.

ABOVE Mick Jagger, Ron Wood, Eric and Keith Richards on stage during 'Little Red Rooster' at New York's Shea Stadium on 10 October 1989.

RIGHT Eric and Elton John together for a double headliner world tour in 1992.

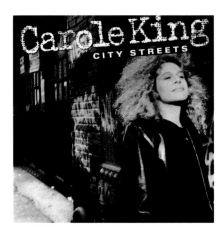  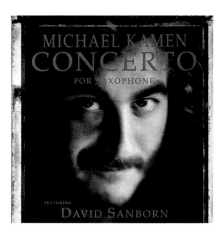

TOP ROW LEFT TO RIGHT

Carole King's CITY STREETS album features Eric on the title track 'City Streets' and 'Ain't That The Way'. ■ Cyndi Lauper's A NIGHT TO REMEMBER album features Eric on 'Insecurious'. ■ Michael Kamen's CONCERTO FOR SAXOPHONE AND ORCHESTRA album features Eric on 'Sandra'.

few weeks later he found himself on stage at the Armoury with an Elvis award for Best Guitarist, and joined in the all-star bash through 'I Hear You Knockin'' featuring Keith Richards, Vernon Reid, Jeff Healey, Tina Turner, Clarence Clemens and Bobby Keys. This memorable event was shown worldwide on television.

A summer tour of Africa followed, ending in Mozambique at Machava Stadium in front of an audience of 102,000. The year closed with a series of guest spots; first in Rome with Zucchero on 'Wonderful World', followed by an appearance New York with Elton John on ROCKET MAN. He then did three dates with the Stones on their huge 'Steel Wheels' tour in New York, Los Angeles and Atlantic City, during which he contributed a stunning solo on 'Little Red Rooster'. The latter show was broadcast live on pay-per-view television and radio.

Most of 1990 was spent touring the world and promoting the platinum-seller JOURNEYMAN. The usual quota of names dropped by; Daryl Hall in New York; Stevie Ray Vaughan in Detroit; Billy Preston in The Hague and George Harrison in Los Angeles. Halfway through the tour he was presented with a Living Legend Award at the Armoury in New York by Buddy Guy. The obligatory jam took place on a lengthy version of 'Sweet Home Chicago' with Bo Diddley, Stephen Tyler, Neil Schon, Dave Stewart, Lou Reed, Richie Sambora, Buddy Guy and Phil Palmer all on guitars.

1991 started with twenty-four nights at the Albert Hall. In contrast to the previous year he also found time to play on a few sessions. He can be heard on Buddy Guy's album DAMN RIGHT I'VE GOT THE BLUES alongside Jeff Beck. He also features on 'Mr Bluesman' from Richie Sambora's first solo album and on two tracks on Johnnie Johnson's excellent long player, JOHNNIE B BAD. He also joined sax-ace David Sanborn in the studio for a track on UPFRONT. But perhaps the most unexpected session Eric did this year was for Kate Bush's RED SHOES album, which was eventually released in late 1993.

The year ended with the historic tour of Japan co-starring George Harrison. Billed as 'Rock Legends' it was George's first outing since 1974. The shows lasted for two-and-a-half hours and covered the entire length of

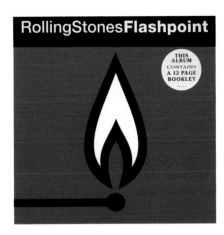

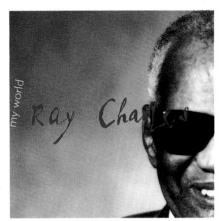

the ex–Beatles' career. Eric and his band provided back up, and played a short set of their own half way through each show, and, no, Eric did not do 'Layla'. An excellent double CD, LIVE IN JAPAN resulted.

1992 saw Eric continue his association with Elton John on 'Runaway Train', a single taken from the album THE ONE. He also contributed to the soundtrack of *Lethal Weapon 3,* just as he had done for the previous two films. A more unusual session, and very low key one, took place towards the end of 1992 for Thomas Jefferson Kaye's NOT ALONE album. He had released two albums in the mid seventies without much success and was not heard of again until now. The album also features other notables such as Steve Miller, Doctor John and Rick Danko. However, don't expect to hear any blistering EC guitar work, this is a release for diehards only.

1993 saw Eric contribute to two tribute albums, the first for his friend Jimi Hendrix and the second for Curtis Mayfield.

By 1968 Cream had the world at their feet, and from that time on Eric Clapton's name on an album automatically meant a boost to sales. He is not unaware of this and consequently he only does the sessions and makes the guest appearances that he really wants to, many of them going uncredited. Eric will no doubt continue to play with other people, compose film soundtracks and undertake any activity that enables him to take time out from the sometimes constricting treadmill of his own career.

TOP ROW LEFT TO RIGHT

Eric plays on the track 'Little Red Rooster' for the Rolling Stones's FLASHPOINT album. ■ Lamont Dozier's INSIDE SEDUCTION album features Eric on 'That Ain't Me'. ■ Ray Charles MY WORLD features Eric on 'None Of Us Are Free'.

ABOVE

David Sanborn's UPFRONT album features Eric on 'Full House'.

Elton John's THE ONE album features Eric on 'Runnaway Train'.

Eric joins Zucchero on his 'Wonderful World' single.

Jack Bruce's SOMETHIN ELSE album features Eric on three tracks.

FACING PAGE TOP Mark Knopfler and Eric Clapton at the Nelson Mandela concert at Wembley Stadium on 11 June 1988.

FACING PAGE BOTTOM Eric, Elton John, Bonnie Raitt and Curtis Stigers take a bow at the last of their Wembley Stadium concerts in 1992.

ABOVE Eric and friends at New York's Armoury for the Elvis Awards on 6 June 1990. Also pictured are Bo Diddley, Lou Reed, Dave Stewart, Phil Palmer and Nathan East.

RIGHT Eric and Lionel Richie get friendly on stage at New York's Madison Square Garden in 1986.

8 *The Bootlegs*

*I*t is important to note that bootlegs are illegal and no one, artist, composer, record company or publisher, receives any royalties. It is a criminal offence to manufacture and sell any bootleg or pirate recording in most major music markets.

The first bootleg of any note, Bob Dylan's legendary GREAT WHITE WONDER, appeared in 1969, featuring recordings made with The Band at Big Pink in Woodstock. It sparked off a tidal wave of bootlegs that shows no sign of abating nearly thirty years later. The Rolling Stones, Jimi Hendrix, The Beatles and every major artist since has had to contend with the release of pirate recordings over which they have no control.

Bootlegs consist of material obtained illicitly. This often takes the form of ropey live recordings made by a fan standing in the middle of an audience waving his walkman over his head. Other live bootlegs use tapes taken straight from the mixing desk. Most retailers of bootlegs will swear that the bootleg you are interested in is taken from the mixing desk; make sure that you listen before purchasing. Another, rarer form of bootleg, and one that is considered a must by the completist, features material recorded in the studio by the artist but deemed unfit for public release for one reason or another. Over the years, bootlegs have progressed from vinyl to compact disc, but this does not necessarily mean improved quality. There are some gems to be had, however, and an attempt will be made to run through the better Eric Clapton ones in this chapter, giving recording date, venue, quality and critical review.

Bootlegging, even though illegal, is a fairly easy process. Countries – mainly in Asia and the former Eastern bloc – that have not signed International Copyright Conventions all have pressing plants outside the

FACING PAGE

Derek And The Dominos STORMY MONDAY
An extremely rare vinyl bootleg album
recorded live at the Santa Monica Civic
Auditorium on 20 November 1970
during their US tour.

ERIC CLAPTON'S CREAM

Eric Clapton
Change of Address

Eric Clapton
The End Of Summer Night

ERIC CLAPTON
DEREK & the DOMINOS
—"STORMY MONDAY"

I.
DEREK'S BOOGIE
BLUES POWER
STORMY MONDAY I

II.
STORMY MONDAY II
LET IT RAIN

Special Guest:
DELANEY BRAMLETT

ERIC CLAPTON
DEREK & the DOMINOS
—"STORMY MONDAY"
TMQ 71082

TRADE MARK
OF QUALITY

Nov. 20, 1970 at the Santa
Monica Civic Auditorium
Cover ©1974 by Mr.
William G. Stout
413231

'74 William G. Stout

GEORGIA BLUE

ERIC CLA
BLUES

reach of Western law. Send a digital audio tape (DAT) to a pressing plant in Korea or one of the ex-Eastern bloc countries and the finished CDs will be sent back to you within weeks. Interestingly, in some countries in Europe, such as Luxembourg, Italy and Switzerland, bootleg CDs are sold openly in high street record shops. This is due to complex copyright laws that currently exist in countries that have not yet signed the Treaty of Rome. Basically, if an artist is recorded in concert in a country that has not signed the treaty, the bootleggers are within the law to sell the recordings made in that same country. Predictably, some of the better bootlegs are actually recorded in Britain or the States and to deter criminal prosecution, the pirates give incorrect or generally vague information on the sleeve such as 'live in Europe'.

But bootlegs do highlight an important niche market that the music business is content to ignore. While most fans are content with official releases and the occasional concert, other more dedicated followers want a record of everything; every studio session; every concert and every alternate version of a song. Obviously, record companies are concerned that if they were to release so many products the artist would become over-exposed and the market saturated, but they do so at the risk of ignoring their core market; those people who can be relied upon to buy absolutely everything by a particular artist. These fans go to see their favourite artist in concert and would dearly love a recording of that show as a permanent souvenir. As record companies won't release it, someone else does so illegally, and the realease will, more often than not, be of poor quality.

Record companies, or indeed the bands themselves, could easily stamp out bootlegging overnight by simply offering fans a chance to buy a copy of that night's performance by mail order. They would make money and ensure fans are not ripped off by some unscrupulous pirate. In fact some bands, such as Fish, are already offering such a service. However, it is too much to expect that this service will be made available by every artist.

As for Eric Clapton, he collects his bootlegs even though he is on record as saying, 'if bootleggers ruled the world we wouldn't make a living.'

RIGHT Cream and Blind Faith
STEPPING STONES Part 1
Single CD featuring some
soundboard tracks from
Cream's LA Forum show in
October 1968. Also has the
first part of a Blind Faith
concert in Gothenburg in June
1969.

FAR RIGHT Blind Faith
STEPPING STONES Part 2
Single CD featuring the second
part of the Gothenburg show.

RIGHT Cream CREAMER
Various soundboard tracks
from Cream's farewell tour of
the US. Recorded in Oakland,
San Diego and Los Angeles.

FAR RIGHT Eric Clapton
CHANGE OF ADDRESS
Single compilation CD
consisting of rare numbers by
Cream, Blind Faith, Derek
And The Dominos and Eric's
solo years.

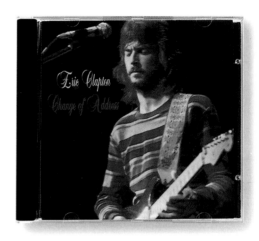

RIGHT Blind Faith
THE MORGAN REHEARSALS
Double CD from Blind Faith's
first studio rehersals.

FAR RIGHT Blind Faith
CROSSROADS
Single CD recorded at the
Santa Barbara Fairgrounds
Arena on 16 August 1969.
Poor quality.

RIGHT Blind Faith
GOTHENBURG 1969
Single CD recorded in
Gothenburg June 1969. Not
complete show.

FAR RIGHT Eric Clapton
THE UNSURPASSED ERIC
CLAPTON
Single CD of the rare alternate
mix of Eric's first solo album.

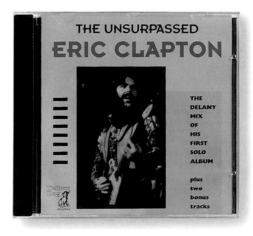

RIGHT
Derek And The Dominos
THE DOMINO THEORY Parts 1 & 2
A great two CD set of a
soundboard recording of the
23 October 1970 late show at
New York's Fillmore East. 'Let
It Rain', however is taken from
the official album
IN CONCERT and is from
a different show.

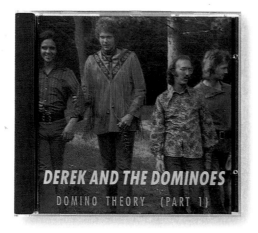 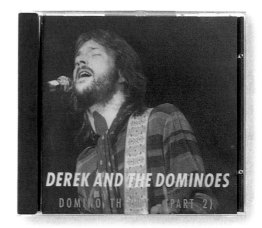

RIGHT Eric Clapton
A NIGHT AT THE CROSSROADS
Single CD recorded along the
1974 US tour. No recording
details known.
FAR RIGHT Eric Clapton
BRIGHT LIGHTS IN BLUES CITY
Single CD recorded on 13 July
1974 at New York's Madison
Square Garden .
Good quality soundboard, but
not complete show.

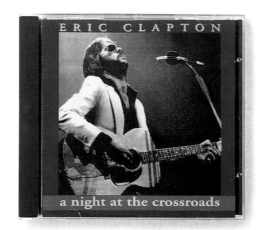 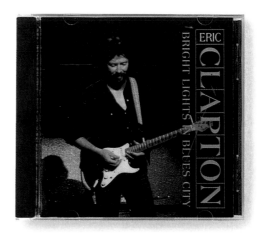

RIGHT Eric Clapton
E.C. LIVE AT LONG BEACH ARENA
Single CD recorded on 20 July
1974 at the Long Beach Arena.
Good quality soundboard, but
not complete show.
FAR RIGHT Eric Clapton
BLUES POWER
Single CD recorded on 10 July
at the Civic Centre in
Providence. Good quality
soundboard, but not complete.

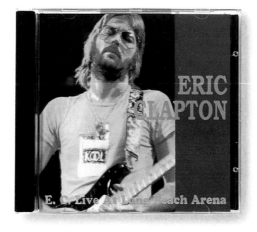 

RIGHT Eric Clapton
STORMY MONDAY BLUES
Single CD recorded on 14
August 1975 at the Los
Angeles Forum. Good quality.
FAR RIGHT Eric Clapton
THE END OF SUMMER NIGHT
Double CD recorded at the
last date on the 1975 US tour
at the Scope Arena in Norfolk.
Last three tracks are recorded
in Denver on the same tour.
Good quality but not complete.

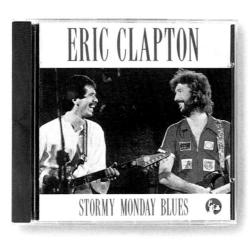 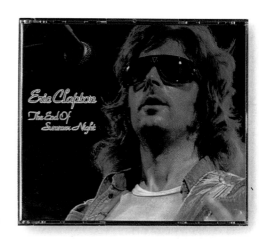

RIGHT Eric Clapton
MILK COW BLUES
Double CD recorded in April
1975 at Brisbane Festival Hall
and the Coliseum in Denver on
23 June 1974. Average sound
and incomplete.
FAR RIGHT Eric Clapton
ONE NIGHT IN DALLAS
Single CD recorded on 14
November 1976.
Great radio broadcast, but not
complete show.

RIGHT Eric Clapton
CLAPTOMANIA
Single CD recorded on 26
April 1977 at the BBC's TV
Studios in Shepherds Bush for
the *Old Grey Whistle Test*.
Awful sound.
FAR RIGHT Eric Clapton BLUES
YOU CAN'T LOSE
Single CD recorded on 27
April 1977 at London's
Hammersmith Odeon. Good
soundboard sound of a great
show, but not complete.

 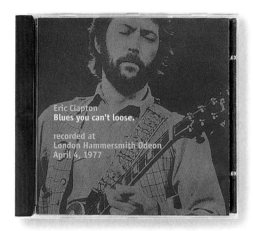

RIGHT Eric Clapton
AMERICAN TOUR '78
Single CD recorded on 11
February 1978 at the Santa
Monica Civic Auditorium as
well as on 14 November 1976
at the Convention Centre in
Dallas. Good quality radio
broadcast, but not complete
shows.
**RIGHT FAR RIGHT AND
BELOW RIGHT** Eric Clapton
DIRE CIRCUMSTANCES
Single CD recorded on 11
February 1978 at the Santa
Monica Civic Auditorium as
well as on 23 September 1988
at Irvine Meadows
Amphitheatre, Lugana Hills.
Awful, avoid even though it has
nice packaging.

RIGHT Eric Clapton
BLUE SHERIFF
Single CD copied from vinyl source. Recorded on 20 April 1983 at the Stadhalle in Bremen. Average sound.

FAR RIGHT Page, Beck, Clapton
THE NIGHT OF THE KINGS
Double CD recorded on 20 September 1983 at the Royal Albert Hall in London for the Ronnie Lane ARMS concert. Great radio broadcast of the majority of the show.

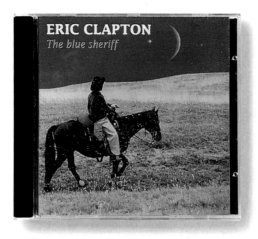
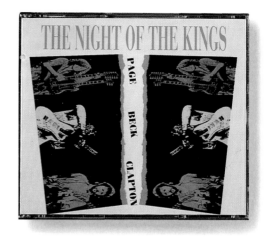

RIGHT Eric Clapton
ALTERNATIVE TRACKS
Rare Japanese double CD featuring outtakes from 461 OCEAN BOULEVARD, NO REASON TO CRY and BEHIND THE SUN. Appalling quality.

FAR RIGHT Eric Clapton
REZIPROCAL AFFECTION
Single CD recorded on 22 April 1985 at the Coliseum, Richmond. This amazing sounding CD was copied from a *King Biscuit* radio CD.

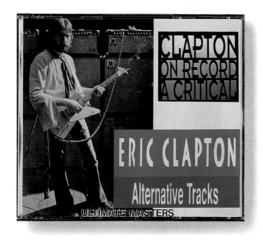

RIGHT Eric Clapton and Keith Richards LIVE AT THE RITZ
Double CD recorded on 23 October 1986 at The Ritz in New York. One of Eric's best shows but poorly recorded. Keith plays on 'Cocaine' and 'Layla'.

FAR RIGHT Eric Clapton
SAME OLD BLUES
Superb double CD recorded on 27 April 1987 at New York's Madison Square Garden. Essential.

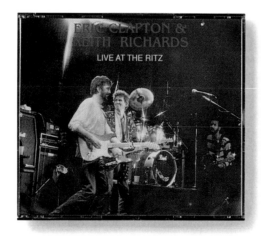

RIGHT Eric Clapton
GEORGIA BLUES
Single CD recorded in England and America in 1986 and 1987. Poor sound.

FAR RIGHT Eric Clapton
THE UNRELEASED LIVE ALBUM 1986-1987
Single CD recorded at various shows in England and America that was to be released as a double album officially by Warner. Avoid.

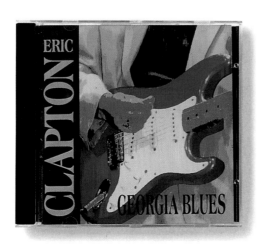

RIGHT AND FAR RIGHT
Eric Clapton
ON TOUR 1987 Parts 1 & 2
Great double CD recorded on
12 January 1987 at London's
Royal Albert Hall. Excellent
soundboard sound and
complete.

 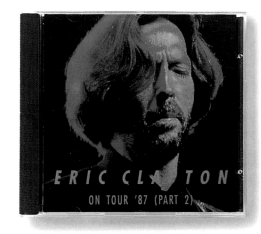

RIGHT Eric Clapton
CAUGHT IN THE ACT
Excellent double CD recorded
on 16 January 1987 at the
Ahoy Halle in Rotterdam. Very
good but not complete.
FAR RIGHT Eric Clapton
ONE FINE DAY
Rare Japanese double CD
recorded on 2 November
1988 at the Tokyo Dome and
the soundtrack to the Buddy
Guy/Eric Clapton jam at Ronnie
Scotts Club on 6 October
1987. Very good.

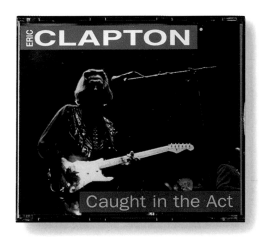 

RIGHT Eric Clapton
WEDNESDAY NIGHT AT THE
TOKYO DOME
Double CD recorded on 2
November 1988 at the Tokyo
Dome. Elton John and Mark
Knopfler join Eric. Very good
radio broadcast sound, but not
complete.
FAR RIGHT Eric Clapton
THE TWELFTH NIGHT
Double CD recorded on 3
February 1989 at Royal Albert
Hall. Great sound.

 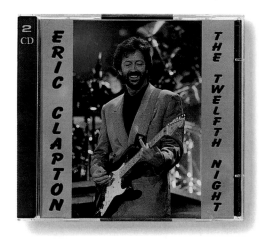

RIGHT AND FAR RIGHT
Eric Clapton LONDON AT NIGHT
Volumes 1 & 2
Excellent double CD recorded
on 24 January 1990 at London's
Royal Albert Hall. Great radio
broadcast sound and almost
the complete show.

RIGHT Eric Clapton
ROYAL ALBERT HALL 1990
Parts 1 & 2
Double CD recorded on
10 February 1990 at Royal
Albert Hall with the
National Philharmonic
Orchestra. Poor sound.
FAR RIGHT Eric Clapton
BLUES NIGHT
Rare Japanese double CD
recorded on 3 February 1990
at Royal Albert Hall with
Buddy Guy and Robert Cray.

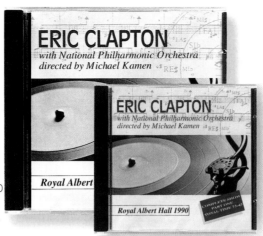

RIGHT Eric Clapton
BAD LOVE
Rare Japanese double CD
recorded on 24 January 1990
at London's Royal Albert Hall.
FAR RIGHT Eric Clapton
BLUES NIGHT
Double CD recorded on 25
February 1991 at Royal Albert
Hall with Albert Collins, Buddy
Guy, Robert Cray and Jerry
Portnoy.

RIGHT Eric Clapton
SONGS FOR LAYLA
Double CD recorded on 17
February 1991 and 24 February
1991 at London's Royal Albert
Hall. Great sound.
**FAR RIGHT AND BELOW
RIGHT** Eric Clapton, Mark
Knopfler, Elton John SUPERJAM
Single CD recorded at
Knebworth on 30 June 1990

RIGHT Eric Clapton MY BLUES
Recorded from the television
broadcast of *Unplugged*. Also
features various unreleased EC
blues numbers from various
sources. Excellent sound.
FAR RIGHT Eric Clapton
ROYAL ALBERT HALL 2-12
Rare Japanese double CD
recorded on 12 February 1992
at London's Royal Albert Hall.
Great audience recording.

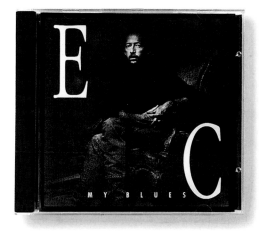
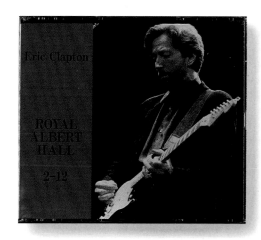

RIGHT Eric Clapton
ROYAL ALBERT HALL 2-17
Rare Japanese double CD
recorded on 17 February 1992
at London's Royal Albert Hall.
Average audience recording.
FAR RIGHT Eric Clapton
TEARS IN HEAVEN
Double CD recorded on 1
February 1992 at the
Brighton Conference Centre.
Excellent quality recording.

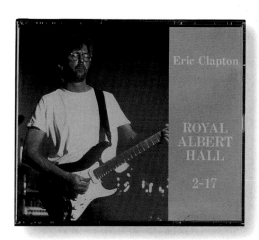

FAR RIGHT Eric Clapton
ANOTHER PAGE
Same as TEARS IN HEAVEN
except this was the first release
before being bootlegged by a
competitor!
FAR RIGHT Eric Clapton
WEMBLEY STADIUM
26 JUNE 1992
Rare Japanese double CD
recorded at the first of Eric's
three nights at Wembley
Stadium. Good audience
recording.

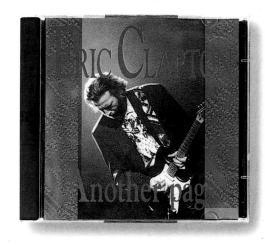

RIGHT Eric Clapton
LIVE AT THE ROYAL ALBERT HALL
12TH FEBRUARY 1992
Double CD with very good
sound. Complete show.
FAR RIGHT Eric Clapton
SLOWHAND BLUES
Japanese double CD recorded
on 7 March 1993 at London's
Royal Albert Hall. Excellent
blues-only show and very
good sound.

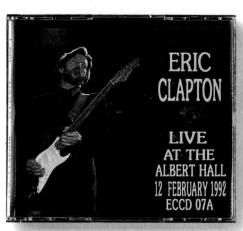

THE YARDBIRDS

	UK	US	
SINGLES:			
I WISH YOU WOULD/A CERTAIN GIRL	Columbia DB7283	Not released	June 64
GOOD MORNING LITTLE SCHOOL GIRL/I AIN'T GOT YOU	Columbia DB7391	Not released	October 64
FOR YOUR LOVE/GOT TO HURRY	Columbia DB7499	Epic 9790	February 65
ALBUMS:			
FIVE LIVE YARDBIRDS	Columbia 33SX1677	Not released	February 65
CD VERSION	Charly 182		
SONNY BOY WILLIAMSON AND THE YARDBIRDS	Fontana TL 5277	Mercury SR61071	January 66
REMEMBER...THE YARDBIRDS	Regal Starline SRS 5069	Not released	June 71
SHAPES OF THINGS	Charly Box 104	Not released	November 84
CD VERSION	Decal LIK BOX 1		

JOHN MAYALL'S BLUES BREAKERS

	UK	US	
SINGLES:			
I'M YOUR WITCHDOCTOR/TELEPHONE BLUES	Immediate IM012	Not released	October 65
LONELY YEARS/BERNARD JENKINS	Purdah 3502	Not released	August 66
PARCHMENT FARM/KEY TO LOVE	Decca F12490	Not released	September 66
ALBUMS:			
BLUES BREAKERS WITH ERIC CLAPTON	Decca SKL4804	London PS 492	July 66
Available on CD			
LOOKING BACK	Decca SKL5010	London PS 562	September 69
Available on CD			
PRIMAL SOLOS	Decca TAB66	London LC50003	July 83
Available on CD			

CREAM

	UK	US	
SINGLES:			
WRAPPING PAPER/CAT'S SQUIRREL	Reaction 591007	Not released	October 66
I FEEL FREE/N.S.U.	Reaction 591011	Atco 6462	December 66
STRANGE BREW/TALES OF BRAVE ULYSSES	Reaction 591015	Atco 6488	June 67
ANYONE FOR TENNIS/PRESSED RAT AND WARTHOG	Polydor 56258	Atco 6575	May 68
SPOONFUL PART I/SPOONFUL PART II	Not released	Atco 6522	September 68
SUNSHINE OF YOUR LOVE/SWLABR	Polydor 56286	Atco 6544	September 68
WHITE ROOM/THOSE WERE THE DAYS	Polydor 56286	Atco 6617	January 69
CROSSROADS/PASSING TIME	Not released	Atco 6646	January 69
BADGE/WHAT A BRINGDOWN	Polydor 56315	Atco 6668	April 69
SWEET WINE/OH LAWDY MAMA	Not released	Atco 6708	June 70
ALBUMS:			
FRESH CREAM	Reaction	Atco SD 33-206	December 66
MONO	593001		
STEREO	594001		
Available on CD			
DISRAELI GEARS	Reaction	Atco SD 33-232	November 67
MONO	593003		
STEREO	594003		
Available on CD			
WHEELS OF FIRE	Polydor 583031	Atco SD 2 700	August 68
Available on CD			
GOODBYE	Polydor 583053	Atco SD 7001	March 69
Available on CD			
BEST OF CREAM	Polydor 583060	Atco SD-33291	November 69
Available on CD (Japan only)			
LIVE CREAM	Polydor 2383016	Atco SD 33-328	June 70
Available on CD			
LIVE CREAM VOL. 2	Polydor 2383119	Atco SD 7005	July 72
Available on CD			

BLIND FAITH	**UK**	**US**	
SINGLE:			
INSTRUMENTAL JAM	Island promo	Not released	June 69
ALBUM:			
BLIND FAITH	Polydor 583059	Atco SD 33-304	August 69
Available on CD (UK version has two bonus tracks from the			
abortive Rick Grech solo album sessions and are not Blind Faith			
outtakes as the sleeve would have you believe.)			

DELANY AND BONNIE			
SINGLE:			
COMIN' HOME/GROUPIE (SUPERSTAR)	Atlantic 584308	Atco 6725	December 69
ALBUM:			
ON TOUR	Atlantic 2400013	Atco SD 33-326	June 70
Available on CD			

PLASTIC ONO BAND			
SINGLE:			
COLD TURKEY/DON'T WORRY KYOKO	Apple 1001	Apple 1813	October 69
ALBUMS:			
LIVE PEACE IN TORONTO	Apple 1003	Apple SW3362	December 69
SOMETIME IN NEW YORK CITY	Apple PCSP716	Apple SVBB3392	September 72
Available on CD			

ERIC CLAPTON			
SINGLE:			
AFTER MIDNIGHT/EASY NOW	Polydor 2383021	Atco 6784	October 70
ALBUMS:			
ERIC CLAPTON	Polydor 3383021	Atco SD 33-329	August 70
Available on CD			
HISTORY OF ERIC CLAPTON	Polydor 2659012	Atco SD 2-803	July 72
Available on CD (Japan only)			
RAINBOW CONCERT	RSO 2394116	RSO SO 877	September 73
Available on CD			

DEREK AND THE DOMINOS			
SINGLES:			
TELL THE TRUTH/ROLL IT OVER	Polydor 2058057	Atco 6780	September 70
Withdrawn September 70			
BELL BOTTOM BLUES/KEEP ON GROWING	Not released	Atco 6803	January 71
LAYLA/I AM YOURS	Not released	Atco 6809	February 71
LAYLA/BELL BOTTOM BLUES	Polydor 2058130	Not released	July 72
WHY DOES LOVE GOT TO BE SO SAD (LIVE)/	RSO 2090104	RSO 400	April 73
PRESENCE OF THE LORD (LIVE)			
ALBUMS:			
LAYLA AND OTHER ASSORTED LOVE SONGS	Polydor 2625005	Atco SD 2-704	December 70
Available on CD as original as well as a special 25th Anniversary			
box set containing 3 CDs with various jams and outtakes.			
IN CONCERT	RSO 2659020	RSO SO 2-8800	March 73
Available on CD			

ERIC CLAPTON AND HIS BAND   UK   US

SINGLES:

	UK	US	
I Shot The Sheriff/Give Me Strength	RSO 2090132	RSO 409	July 74
Willie And The Hand Jive/Mainline Florida	RSO 2090139	RSO 503	October 74
In limited edition picture sleeve with instuctions on how to do the hand jive.			
Swing Low Sweet Chariot/Pretty Blue Eyes	RSO 2090158	RSO 509	May 75
Knocking On Heaven's Door/Someone Like You	RSO 2090166	RSO 513	August 75
Hello Old Friend/All Our Pastimes	RSO 2090208	RS 861	October 76
Carnival/Hungry	RSO 2090222	RS 868	February 77
Lay Down Sally/Next Time You See Her	RSO 2090264	Not released	November 77
Lay Down Sally/Cocaine	Not released	RS 886	November 77
Wonderful Tonight/Peaches And Diesel	RSO 2090275	RS 895	March 78
Promises/Watch Out For Lucy	RSO 21	RS 910	October 78
If I Don't Be There By Morning/Tulsa Time	RSO 24	Not released	March 79
In picture sleeve			
Cocaine/Tulsa Time	Not released	RS 928	April 79
Tulsa Time/Cocaine	Not released	RS 1039	June 80
Blues Power (live)/Early in the Morning (live)	Not released	RS 1051	October 80
I Can't Stand It/Black Rose	RSO 74	RS 1060	February 81
Another Ticket/Rita Mae	RSO 75	RS 1064	April 81
In picture sleeve			
Layla/Wonderful Tonight (live)	RSO 87	Not released	February 82
In picture sleeve			
as 12in version	RSOX 87		
I Shot The Sheriff/Cocaine	RSO 88	Not released	May 82
In picture sleeve			
As 12in version	RSOX 88		
Bonus tracks: live version of 'Knocking On Heaven's Door' from the December 79 Budokan shows in Japan.			
I've Got A Rock And Roll Heart/Man In Love	Duck W9780	Duck 29780	January 83
In picture sleeve			
as 12in version	Duck W9780T		
Bonus tracks: 'Everybody Oughta Make A Change'			
The Shape You're In/Pretty Girl	Not released	Duck 29647	April 83
The Shape You're In/Crosscut Saw	Duck W9701	Not released	April 83
In picture sleeve			
as 12in version	Duck W9701T		
Bonus tracks:'Pretty Girl'			
picture disc	Duck W9701P		
Slow Down Linda/Crazy Country Hop	Duck W9651	Not released	May 83
In picture sleeve			
as 12in version	Duck W9651T		
Bonus track: live version of 'The Shape Your In'			
This was planned but withdrawn before release.			
Wonderful Tonight/Cocaine	RSO 98		April 84
In picture sleeve			
You Don't Know Like I Know/Knock On Wood	Duck 7-29113 (Australian)	Not released	November 84
In Australia only			
Edge Of Darkness/Shoot Out	BBC RESL178	Not released	January 85
Forever Man/Too Bad	Duck W9069	Duck 29081	March 85
as 12in version	Duck W9069T		
Bonus track: 'Something's Happening'			
See What Love Can Do/She's Waiting	Not released	Duck 28986	June 85
She's Waiting/Jailbait	Duck W8954	Not released	June 85
Behind The Mask/Grand Illusion	Duck W8461	Duck 28391	January 87
as 12in version	Duck W8461T		
Bonus track: 'Wanna Make Love To You'			
as 7in double pack	Duck W8461F		
Bonus tracks: live versions of 'Crossroads' and 'White Room' from 15 July 86 NEC show.			

	UK	US	
IT'S IN THE WAY THAT YOU USE IT/GRAND ILLUSION	Not released	Duck 28514	March 87
IT'S IN THE WAY THAT YOU USE IT/BAD INFLUENCE	Duck W8397	Not released	March 87
AS 12IN VERSION	Duck W8397T		
Bonus track: 'Same Old Blues' and 'Pretty Girl'			
TEARING US APART/HOLD ON	Duck W8299	Duck 28279	June 87
AS 12IN VERSION	Duck W8299T		
Bonus track: live version of 'Run' from 15 July 86 NEC show.			
WONDERFUL TONIGHT/LAYLA	Polydor POSP881	Not released	August 87
AS 12IN VERSION	Polydor POSPX881		
Bonus tracks:'I Shot The Sheriff' and a live version			
of 'Wonderful Tonight' from the Budokan 79 show.			
AS CD SINGLE	Polydor POCD881		
Bonus tracks: 'I Shot The Sheriff' and 'Swing Low Sweet Chariot'			
HOLY MOTHER/TANGLED IN LOVE	Duck W8141	Not released	November 87
AS 12IN VERSION	Duck W8141T		
Bonus tracks: 'Forever Man' and 'Behind The Mask'			
AFTER MIDNIGHT (1988 RERECORDED VERSION)/I CAN'T STAND IT	Polydor PO8	Polydor 887403	July 88
AS 12IN VERSION	Polydor PZ8		
Bonus track: 'Whatcha Gonna Do'			
AS CD SINGLE	Polydor PZCD8		
Bonus tracks: 'Whatcha Gonna Do' and an un-live version of			
'Sunshine Of Your Love' by Cream from 7 March 1968 at San			
Francisco's Winterland.			
PRETENDING/BEFORE YOU ACCUSE ME	Not released	Duck 22732	October 89
BAD LOVE/BEFORE YOU ACCUSE ME	Duck W2644	Not released	November 89
AS 12IN VERSION	Duck W2644T		
Bonus tracks: live versions of 'Badge' and 'Let It Rain' from			
15 July 86 NEC show.			
AS CD SINGLE	Duck W2644CD		
Bonus tracks: same as 12in			
BOX SET SINGLE	Duck W2644B		
Bonus tracks: exclusive live version of 'I Shot The Sheriff' from			
15 July 86 NEC show and a family tree.			
BAD LOVE/HARD TIMES	Not released	Duck 19980	January 90
NO ALIBIS/RUNNING ON FAITH	Duck W9981	Not released	March 90
AS 12IN VERSION	Duck W9981T		
Bonus tracks: live version of 'Behind The Mask' from 15 July 86			
NEC show.			
AS CD SINGLE	Duck W9981CD		
Bonus tracks: same as 12in			
BOX SET SINGLE	Duck W9981B		
With guitar badge and photos.			
NO ALIBIS/HOUND DOG	Not released	Duck 19848	April 90
PRETENDING/HARD TIMES	Duck W9970	Not released	May 90
AS 12IN VERSION	Duck W9970T		
Bonus track: 'Knock On Wood			
AS CD SINGLE	Duck W9970CD		
Bonus track: 'Behind The Sun'			
WONDERFUL TONIGHT (LIVE)/EDGE OF DARKNESS (LIVE)	Duck W0069	Not released	October 91
AS CD SINGLE	Duck W0069CD		
Bonus tracks: live versions of 'Layla Intro' and 'Cocaine' from the			
big band Royal Albert Hall 91 shows.			
LIMITED-EDITION COLLECTORS CD SINGLE	Duck W0069CDX		
Bonus tracks: exclusive live versions of 'I Shot The Sheriff' and 'No			
Alibis' from the big band Royal Albert Hall 91 shows.			
TEARS IN HEAVEN/TRACKS AND LINES	Not released	Duck 19038	January 92
TEARS IN HEAVEN/WHITE ROOM (LIVE)	Duck W0081	Not released	January 92
AS 12IN VERSION	Duck W0081T		
Bonus tracks: 'Tracks And Lines' and live version of 'Bad Love			

	UK	US	
TEARS IN HEAVEN/WHITE ROOM (LIVE)			
AS CD SINGLE	Duck W0081CD		
Bonus tracks: same as 12in			
LAYLA (LIVE UNPLUGGED)/TEARS IN HEAVEN (LIVE UNPLUGGED)	Duck W0134	Not released	September 92
LAYLA (LIVE UNPLUGGED)/TRACKS AND LINES	Not released	Duck 18787	September 92

ALBUMS:

	UK	US	
461 OCEAN BOULEVARD	RSO 2479118	RSO SO 4801	August 74
Available on CD			
THERE'S ONE IN EVERY CROWD	RSO 2479132	RSO SO 4806	April 75
Available on CD			
EC WAS HERE	RSO 2394160	RSO SO 4809	August 75
Available on CD with bonus full version of 'Driftin' Blues'			
NO REASON TO CRY	RSO 2394160	RSO 1-3004	August 76
Available on CD with bonus track 'One Night'			
SLOWHAND	RSO 2479201	RSO RS 1-3030	November 77
Available on CD			
BACKLESS	RSO 2479221	RSO RS 1-3039	November 78
Available on CD with bonus full version of 'Early In The Morning'			
JUST ONE NIGHT	RSO 2479240	RSO RS 2-4202	May 80
Available on CD			
ANOTHER TICKET	RSO 2479285	RSO RX-1-3095	February 81
Available on CD			
TIME PIECES – BEST OF ERIC CLAPTON	RSO RSD5010		March 82
Available on CD			
MONEY AND CIGARETTES	Duck W3773	Duck 23773	February 83
Available on CD			
TIME PIECES VOLUME 2 – LIVE IN THE SEVENTIES	RSO RSD5022		May 83
Available on CD			
BEHIND THE SUN	Duck W925166-1	Reprise 9.25166	March 85
Available on CD			
EDGE OF DARKNESS	BBC 12RSL178	Not released	November 85
Available on CD			
AUGUST	Duck WX71	Reprise 9.25476	October 86
Available on CD with bonus track 'Grand Illusion'			
THE CREAM OF ERIC CLAPTON	Polydor ECTV1	Not released	September 87
Available on CD			
CROSSROADS	Polydor ROAD1	Polydor 835 261-2	April 88
Available on CD			
JOURNEYMAN	Duck WX322	Reprise 9.45024	November 89
Available on CD			
24 NIGHTS	Duck WX373	Reprise 9.26420	December 91
Available on CD			
Available in a limited-edition box set.			
UNPLUGGED	Duck WX480	Reprise 9.45024	July 92
Available on CD			

SOUNDTRACKS:

	UK	US	
LETHAL WEAPON SOUNDTRACK	Warner	Warner	April 87
HOMEBOY SOUNDTRACK	Virgin		November 88
Available on CD			
LETHAL WEAPON 2 SOUNDTRACK	Warner	Warner	September 89
Available on CD			
RUSH SOUNDTRACK	Duck	Reprise	January 92
Available on CD			
LETHAL WEAPON 3 SOUNDTRACK	Warner	Warner	June 92
Available on CD			

OTIS SPANN
Stirs Me Up (single)
   Decca

OTIS SPANN
The Blues Of Otis Spann (album)
   Decca November 64
   Available on CD as 'Cracked Spanner Head'

CHAMPION JACK DUPREE
From New Orleans To Chicago (album)
   Decca April 66
   Available on CD

ERIC CLAPTON WITH JIMMY PAGE
Blues Anytime Vol.1,2,3,4 (album)
   Immediate 67
   Available on CD

ARETHA FRANKLIN
Lady Soul (album)
   Atlantic March 68
   Available on CD

THE BEATLES
The Beatles White Album (album)
   Apple November 68
   Available on CD

GEORGE HARRISON
Wonderwall Music (album)
   Apple November 68
   Available on CD

JACKIE LOMAX
Sour Milk Sea/The Eagle Laughs At You (single)
   Apple February 69
   Available on Is This What You Want? CD

JACKIE LOMAX
Is This What You Want? (album)
   Apple March 69
   Available on CD

JACKIE LOMAX
New Day (A side) (single)
   Apple May 69
   Eric does not play on B side
   Available on Is This What You Want? CD

BILLY PRESTON
That's The Way God Planned It (album)
   Apple June 69
   Available on CD

MARTHA VELEZ
Fiends And Angels (album)
   London June 69
   Available on CD

BILLY PRESTON
That's The Way God Planned It (single)
   Apple August 69

SHAWN PHILLIPS
Contribution (album)
   A&M January 70

VIVIAN STANAHALL
Labio Dental Fricative/Paper Round (single)
   Liberty February 70

DORIS TROY
Ain't That Cute (A side) (single)
   Apple February 70
   Eric does not play on B side

LEON RUSSELL
Leon Russell (album)
   A&M May 70
   Available on CD

JONATHAN KELLY
Don't You Believe It (single)
   Parlophone June 70

KING CURTIS
Teasin' (single)
   Atlantic July 70
   Available on History Of Eric Clapton CD (Japan only)

DORIS TROY
Get Back (B side) (single)
   Apple August 70
   Eric does not play on A side
   Available on 'Doris Troy' CD

DORIS TROY
Doris Troy (album)
   Apple September 70
   Available on CD

BILLY PRESTON
Encouraging Words (album)
   Apple September 70
   Available on CD

GEORGE HARRISON
All Things Must Pass (album)
   Apple November 70
   Available on CD

STEPHEN STILLS
Stephen Stills (album)
   Atlantic November 70
   Available on CD

ASHTON GARDNER AND DYKE
The Worst Of (album)
   EMI February 71

THE CRICKETS
Rockin' 50's Rock 'n' Roll (album)
   CBS February 71

JESSE DAVIS
Jesse Davis (album)
   Atlantic April 71
   Available on CD (Japan and Germany only)

JOHN MAYALL
Back to the Roots (album)
   Polydor June 71

LEON RUSSELL
Leon Russell And The Shelter People (album)
   Shelter June 71
   Available on CD

BUDDY GUY AND JUNIOR WELLS
Play The Blues (album)
   Atlantic July 71
   Available on CD

STEPHEN STILLS
Stephen Stills 2 (album)
   Atlantic July 71
   Available on CD

BOBBY WHITLOCK
Bobby Whitlock (album)
   CBS July 71

HOWLIN' WOLF
The London Sessions (album)
   RSR August 71
   Available on CD

DOCTOR JOHN
Sun Moon And Herbs (album)
   Atlantic November 71
   Available on CD (Japan only)

YOKO ONO
Fly (album)
   Apple December 71

GEORGE HARRISON
The Concert For Bangla Desh (album)
   Apple January 72
   Available on CD

JAMES LUTHER DICKINSON
Dixie Fried (album)
   Atlantic February 72

BOBBY KEYS
Bobby Keys (album)
   Warner July 72

BOBBY WHITLOCK
Raw Velvet (album)
   CBS December 72

VARIOUS ARTISTS
Music From Free Creek (album)
   Charisma May 73

HOWLIN' WOLF
London Revisited (album)
   Chess October 74
   US release only

FREDDIE KING
Burglar (album)
 RSO November 74
Available on CD

THE WHO
Tommy The Movie (album)
 RSO July 75
Available on CD (Japan only)

ARTHUR LOUIS
Knockin' On Heaven's Door/Plum (single)
 Plum August 75

ARTHUR LOUIS
First Album (album)
 Polydor August 75
Available in Japan only

BOB DYLAN
Desire (album)
 CBS December 75
Available on CD

DR. JOHN
Hollywood Be Thy Name (album)
 United Artists December 75
Available on CD

JOE COCKER
Stingray (album)
 A&M June 76
Available on CD

RINGO STARR
Rotogravure (album)
 Polydor October 76

KINKY FREIDMAN
Lasso From El Paso (album)
 Epic November 76

STEPHEN BISHOP
Careless (album)
 ABC December 76
Available on CD (Japan only)

ROGER DALTREY
One Of The Boys (album)
 Polydor May 77

CORKY LAING
Makin' It On The Street (album)
 Elektra May 77

RONNIE LANE AND PETE TOWNSHEND
Rough Mix (album)
 Polydor September 77
Available on CD

FREDDIE KING
1934-1976 (album)
 RSO October 77
Available on CD

RICK DANKO
Rick Danko (album)
 Arista January 78
Available on CD

THE BAND
The Last Waltz (album)
 Warner April 78
Available on CD

VARIOUS ARTISTS
White Mansions (album)
 A&M May 78
Available on CD

ARTHUR LOUIS
Knockin' On Heaven's Door/The Dealer (single)
 Island June 78

GEORGE HARRISON
George Harrison (album)
 Dark Horse February 79
Available on CD

MARC BENNO
Lost In Austin (album)
 A&M June 79
Available on CD (Japan only)

DANNY DOUMA
Night Eyes (album)
 Warner August 79

ALEXIS KORNER
The Party Album (album)
 Interchord March 80
Released in Germany only
Available on CD (Castle Communications)

RONNIE LANE
See Me (album)
 RCA July 80

STEPHEN BISHOP
Red Cab To Manhatten (album)
 Warner October 80
Available on CD (Japan only)

PHIL COLLINS
Face Value (album)
 Virgin February 81
Available on CD

GARY BROOKER
Home Lovin' (A side) (single)
 Mercury March 81
Eric does not play on B side

GARY BROOKER
Leave The Candle/Chasing The Chop (single)
 Chrysalis April 81

ARTHUR LOUIS
Still It Feels Good/Come On And Love Me (single)
 Main-street July 81

JOHN MARTYN
Glorious Fool (album)
 WEA October 81

SECRET POLICEMAN'S OTHER BALL
The Music (album)
 Springtime March 82

GARY BROOKER
Lead Me To The Water (album)
 Mercury March 82
Available on CD

RINGO STARR
Old Wave (album)
 Bellaphon June 83
Released in Germany, Canada and Brazil only

CHRISTINE MCVIE
Christine McVie (album)
 Warner January 84
Available on CD

ROGER WATERS
The Pros And Cons Of Hitch-Hiking
(album)
 Harvest May 84
Available on CD

COREY HART
Corey Hart (album)
 EMI June 84
Available on CD

GARY BROOKER
Echoes In The Night (album)
 Mercury September 85
Available on CD

PAUL BRADY
Back To The Centre (album)
 Mercury March 86
Available on CD

LEONA BOYD
Persona (album)
 CBS August 86
Available on CD

LIONEL RICHIE
Dancing On The Ceiling (album)
 Motown August 86
Available on CD

PRINCE'S TRUST
Prince's Trust 10th Birthday Party (album)
 A&M October 86
Available on CD

BOB GELDOF
Deep In The Heart Of Nowhere (album)
 Mercury November 86
Available on CD

TINA TURNER
What You See Is What You Get (single)
    Capitol March 87
    12in version only

JOHN ASTLEY
Everybody Loves The Pilot (album)
    Atlantic June 87
    Available on CD

PRINCE'S TRUST
Prince's Trust Concert 1987 (album)
    A&M August 87
    Available on CD

STING
Nothing Like The Sun (album)
    A&M October 87
    Available on CD

BOB DYLAN
Hearts Of Fire (album)
    CBS October 87
    Available on CD

CHUCK BERRY
Hail Hail Rock 'n' Roll (album)
    October 87
    Available on CD

GEORGE HARRISON
Cloud 9 (album)
    Dark Horse November 87
    Available on CD

JACK BRUCE
Willpower (album)
    Polygram 88
    Available on CD

BOB GELDOF
Love Like A Rocket (A side) (single)
    Mercury
    Eric does not play on B side.

BUSTER SOUNDTRACK
Buster (album)
    Virgin 88
    Available on CD

TINA TURNER
Live In Europe (album)
    Capitol March 88
    Available on CD

JOHN MAYALL
Archives to the Eighties (album)
    Polydor August 88
    Available on CD

ARTHUR LOUIS
Knockin' On Heaven's Door (album)
    PRT July 88
    Available on CD

BUCKWHEAT ZYDECO
Taking It Home (album)
    Island August 88
    Available on CD

GAIL ANNE DORSEY
The Corporate World (album)
    WEA October 88
    Available on CD

JIM CAPALDI
Some Come Running (album)
    Island December 88
    Available on CD

THE BUNBURYS
One Moment In Time (album)
    November 88
    Available on CD

BRENDAN CROKER
And The Five O'Clock Shadow (album)
    Silvertone 89
    Available on CD

THE BUNBURYS
Fight (single)
    Arista January 89

CAROLE KING
City Steets (album)
    Capitol April 89
    Available on CD

STEPHEN BISHOP
Bowling In Paris (album)
    Atlantic September 89
    Available on CD

PHIL COLLINS
But Seriously (album)
    Virgin November 89
    Available on CD

CYNDI LAUPER
A Night To Remember (album)
    CBS November 89
    Available on CD

ZUCCHERO
Zucchero (album)
    London November 89
    Available on CD

VARIOUS ARTISTS
Nobodys Child (album)
    Warner 90
    Available on CD

VARIOUS ARTISTS
Knebworth (album)
    Polydor August 90
    Available on CD

MICHAEL KAMEN
Concerto For Saxophone And Orchestra
    Warner September 90
    Available on CD

THE ROLLING STONES
Flahpoint (album)
    RSR Records October 90
    Available on CD

BUDDY GUY
Damn Right I've Got The Blues (album)
    Silvertone July 91
    Available on CD

RICHIE SAMBORA
Stranger In This Town (album)
    Phonogram August 91
    Available on CD

LAMONT DOZIER
Inside Seduction (album)
    Atlantic August 91
    Available on CD

JOHNNIE JOHNSON
Johnnie B Bad (album)
    Elektra September 91
    Available on CD

DAVID SANBORN
Upfront (album)
    Warner March 92
    Available on CD

ELTON JOHN
The One (album)
    Rocket June 92
    Available on CD

THE BUNBURYS
Bunbury Tails (album)
    Polydor October 92
    Available on CD

JACK BRUCE
Somethinels (album)
    CMP February 93
    Available on CD

RAY CHARLES
My World (album)
    Warner 93
    Available on CD

THOMAS JEFFERSON KAYE
Not Alone (album)
    Hudson Canyon July 93
    Available on CD

VARIOUS ARTISTS
Stone Free: A Tribute to Jimi Hendrix
    Reprise October 93
    Available on CD

Index

ABBREVIATIONS
Boot: bootleg
CD: compact disc
Comp: compilation
CT: cassette
FM: film
LP: long-playing disc
Maxi: 12inch maxi-disc
Other: promo material, live performance, etc.
PD: picture disc
ST: soundtrack
VO: video
Note: Song titles in quotes are singles, unless
    otherwise stated.

A

'Abacab': Other 197
'After Midnight' 69, 147, 148, 196; Other 68;
    PD 69
'All Our Pastimes': Other 189
Allman Brothers Band 72, 73
ALTERNATIVE TRACKS: Boot 210
AMERICAN TOUR '78: Boot 209
ANOTHER PAGE: Boot 213
'Another Ticket': Other 122
ANOTHER TICKET: Album 120;
    Maxi/Other 122
ANTHOLOGY OF BRITISH BLUES VOLS.
    1 AND 2: Other 181
'Anyone For Tennis' 41
Armatrading, Joan 194
ARMS charity 130, 192; Boot 210;
    Other 128, 130
AUGUST: Album 144, 194; Other 143

B

'Baby Don't You Do It': Other 185
BACKLESS: Album 109, 124; Other 108, 189;
    PD 109
'Bad Love' 150, 152; Maxi/Other 153
BAD LOVE: Boot 212
'Badge' 84, 152, 181; Other 45, 153
Baker, Ginger 24, 30, 33, 38, 39, 44, 48, 49,
    60, 61, 109, 181
Band, The 98, 100-101, 187, 189, 190
Beatles, The 15, 43, 101, 109, 164, 178,
    180, 181
Beck, Jeff 20, 109, 121, 128, 130, 148, 164,
    180, 191-194, 210
'Before You Accuse Me' 150; Maxi 153;
    Other 162
'Behind The Mask' 144; Maxi 143; Other 197
BEHIND THE SUN: Album 136-13, 193;
    Boot 210; Other 138, 140
'Bell Bottom Blues': Other 70, 198
Benno, Marc 190
Berry, Chuck 19, 90, 145, 195, 196
Betts, Dickie 185
Big Town Playboys 194
Bishop, Stephen 187, 188, 191, 194
'Black Rose': Other 122
Blake, Peter 160
Blind Faith 61-76, 84, 181
BLIND FAITH: Album 61, 182; Other 61, 62, 63
'Blow Wind Blow' 120; Other 191
'Blue Moon Of Kentucky': Other 193
BLUE SHERIFF: Boot 210
Blues Breakers 21-22, 180
BLUES BREAKERS FEATURING ERIC
    CLAPTON: Album 24
BLUES NIGHT: Boot 212
BLUES POWER: Boot 208
BLUES WORKS 1963-1965: LP/Comp 20
BLUES YOU CAN'T LOSE: Boot 209
Bonzo Dog Band 90
Booker T & the MGs 164
'Boom Boom' 17
'Born Under A Bad Sign': Other 48
Bowie, David 194
Boyd, Joe 180
Boyd, Pattie 69-70, 73, 75, 76, 85, 86, 95, 97,
    106, 109, 110, 124, 139, 142, 190
Bramlett, Bonnie and Delaney 66
BRENDAN CROCKER AND THE FIVE
    O'CLOCK SHADOWS: Album 197, 198

Brennan, Terry 13
BRIGHT LIGHTS IN BLUES CITY:
    Boot 208
Brock, Dave 13
Brooker, Gary 118, 191, 192, 197
Brooks, Bobby 158
Broonzy, Big Bill 13
Brown, James 41
Brown, Pete 33
'Brown Sugar': Other 188
Browne, Nigel 158
Bruce, Jack 23, 30, 33, 38, 39, 43, 44, 47, 48,
    49, 109, 180, 181, 190, 194, 196, 198, 201
Bunburys 197
'Burial' 186

C

Cale, J.J. 67, 148, 196
'Can't Explain': Other 185
Capaldi, Jim 82, 184
'Carnival In Rio' 99, 186; Other 96, 97
Cash, Johnny 184
Cash, Rosanne 140
Casser, Brian 15
'Cat's Squirrel': EP 37
CAUGHT IN THE ACT: Boot 211
'Cause We Ended As Lovers' 192; Other 191
Chandler, Chas 41
CHANGE OF ADDRESS: Boot 207
Charles, Ray 34, 101, 194, 201
Chas and Dave 130
'Choker' 181
'Circus has Left Town': Other 162
CLAPTOMANIA: Boot 209
Clapton, Conor 142, 144, 145, 160-161
Clark, Alan 196
Clayton, Sir Cedric 183
Clemens, Clarence 200
'Cocaine' 104; Other 107, 148, 194, 195, 197
Cocker, Joe 130, 165, 187, 188, 192, 197
Cohen, Leonard 197
Collins, Albert 155, 164, 212
Collins, Phil 127, 130, 136, 142, 144, 147, 148,
    165, 191, 193, 194, 197
Color Of Money: ST 194
Colyer, Ken 17
Connery, Sean 100
Connolly, Billy 193
Cooder, Ry 127
Cooper, Ray 162, 192, 196
Coryell, Larry 101, 188
Cox, Jimmy 74
Cray, Robert 145, 150, 155, 156, 159, 195,
    197, 212
Cream 24, 30-49, 84, 87, 160, 166, 180,
    181, 201
'Cream On Top': Other 47
CREAMER: Boot 207
Crickets 183
Cropper, Steve 163
'Crossroads' 84, 180; Other 47, 48, 191
CROSSROADS: Boot 207; CD 147-148;
    Other 148, 186
Curtis, King 183

D

D & B TOGETHER (Delaney/Bonnie):
    Album 186
Daltrey, Roger 188
Danko, Rick 101, 187, 188, 190, 201
Davis, Jess Ed 101, 185
Deacon, John 165
Del Santo, Lory 145
Delaney and Bonnie 63, 181, 182-183, 186
Delaney and Bonnie and Friends 66-69, 182
Derek and the Dominos 69-76, 84, 147,
    183, 184
'Devil's Radio' (Harrison) 196
Diamond, Neil 106
Dickinson, James Luther 186
Diddley, Bo 13, 200, 203
DIRE CIRCUMSTANCES: Boot 209
Dire Straits 139, 194, 197
DISRAELI GEARS: Album 34-38, 39; Other
    40, 41

'Dizzy Miss Lizzy': Other 64
Donnegan, Lonnie 109, 190
'Don't Think Twice': Other 164
Doors, The 39, 43
Dorsey, Gayle Anne 197
'Double Trouble': Other 195
Douma, Danny 190
Dowd, Tom 38, 73, 91, 101, 127, 180
'Down The Road Apiece': Other 194
Dozier, Lamont 194, 201
Dr John 106, 184, 201
'Draggin' My Tale' 181
Dreja, Chris 10, 12, 14, 16, 21
Dunn, 'Duck' 127, 140
Dupree, Champion Jack 23, 180
Dylan, Bob 76, 97, 98, 99, 100-101, 106,
    107, 108, 145, 147, 184, 187, 189, 193, 195,
    196, 204

E

E.C. LIVE AT LONG BEACH ARENA:
    Boot 208
Earl, Ronnie 196
East, Nathan 142, 162, 203
EC WAS HERE: Album 95; Other 94
Edge 142
'Edge of Darkness' 142
EDGE OF DARKNESS: Album 142
Edmunds, Dave 140, 193
Elliman, Yvonne 87, 90, 92, 107
Elliott, Jack 13
Elvis awards: Best Guitarist 200, 203
ERIC CLAPTON & THE YARDBIRDS:
    Comp 20
Eric Clapton And His Rolling Hotel: FM
    189-190
Eric Clapton Stratocaster Signature Series
    guitar 142
ERIC CLAPTON: Album 67; Other 68
ERIC CLAPTON'S CREAM: Boot 206
ERIC CLAPTON'S RAINBOW
    CONCERT: Album 84
Ertegun, Ahmet 61

F

'4 Till Late': Other 37
461 OCEAN BOULEVARD: Album 87, 124;
    Boot 210; Song book 87; Other 85, 86, 87,
    91, 93
Fabroni, Rob 101
Fairweather Low, Andy 130, 162, 192, 197
Faithfull, Marianne 58
Fame, Georgie 98, 187
Farewell tour, US 46-47
Ferrone, Steve 162, 195
Flowers, Danny 189
'For Your Love' 19, 20
'Forever Man' 138; Maxi 139; VO 138
'Forever Young': Other 189
Forrester, Roger 91, 109, 124, 126, 158, 161
Fox Theatre, St. Louis 195
Frame, Pete 153
Franklin, Aretha 44, 72, 180
FREDDIE KING 1934-1976 (King): Album
    185, 189
Free 181
'Freedom': Other 193
'Freight Loader' 181
FRESH CREAM: Album 33; Boot 206; Other
    7, 36
Friedman, Kinky 187, 188

G

'Get Ready': Other 90
'Getting Back To Molly' 187
'Give Me Back My Dynamite' (Troy) 183
'Golden Ring' 108
'Good To Me As I Am To You' 180
'Got To Hurry' 20
GEORGIA BLUES: Boot 210
Gilmore, David 165
Gitlis, Ivry 58
Goldsmith, Harvey 101, 188
Gomelsky, Giorgio 15-16, 19
GOODBYE: Album 48; Other 44, 45

Gordon, Jim 69, 184
GOTHENBURG 1969: Boot 207
Gouldman, Graham 19
Graham, Bill 43
Graham Bond Organisation 24, 30
GREAT WHITE WONDER: Boot 204
Grech, Rick 60, 61, 182, 184
Grimes, Hamish 17
Guy, Buddy 21, 139, 155, 158, 159, 164, 178,
    181, 184, 191, 193, 196, 200, 212

H

Hall, Daryl 200
Hammer, Ralph 82
'Happy Birthday': Other 101
Harlech, Lord 82
Harrison, George 65, 66, 69-70, 76, 95, 140,
    148, 150, 164, 180-184, 190, 193, 196, 200-
    201
'Have You Ever Loved a Woman' 74; Other
    185
Hawkins, Roger 127
Hawkins, Ronnie 189
Hazeldean Foundation, Minneapolis 124
Healey, Jeff 200
Hearts of Fire: ST 147, 195
'Hello Old Friend': Other 96
Hendrix, Jimi 41, 75, 165, 166, 180, 181;
    tribute album 201
'Hey Hey': Other 162
HISTORY OF ERIC CLAPTON: Album 76
Hiseman, Jon 181
Holly, Buddy 181, 183
'Holy Mother': Maxi 143
Homeboy: ST 147, 196
'Honey In Her Hips' 17
'Hootchie Cootchie Man': Other 194
Hooker, John Lee 13
'Hound Dog' 150
House, Son 33
Howlin' Wolf 41, 69, 183-184, 185

I

'I Am Yours' 74
'I Can't Stand It': Other 122
'I Feel Free' 34, 35; Other 39
'I Hear You Knockin'': Other 200
'I Shall Be Released' 192; Other 189, 191
'I Want To Know' 180
'I Wish You Would' 15, 18
'I'm So Glad' 36; Other 37
'I've Got A Rock And Roll Heart':
    Maxi/Other 125
IN CONCERT (Derek and the Dominos):
    Album 74; Boot 208
'It's In The Way That You Use It':
    Maxi/Other 143; ST 194
'It's My Life Baby': ST 194

J

Jagger, Mick 109, 181, 184, 194, 199
James, Skip 33
Jersey City concert 185
Jimi Hendrix Experience 43
John, Elton 148, 150, 155, 158, 164, 188, 190,
    194, 197, 198, 199, 200, 201, 203, 211, 212;
    tribute album 198
JOHN MAYALL'S BLUES BREAKERS
    WITH ERIC CLAPTON: Album 22
Johnny Cash Show 184
Johns, Glyn 106-107
Johnson, Johnnie 156, 159, 195, 200
Johnson, Robert 10, 33, 162, 166
Jones, Brian 58, 188
Jones, Kenny 130, 192
Jones, Mick 150, 152
Jones, Paul 180
JOURNEYMAN: Album 152, 194; Other
    153, 200
'Just Like a Prisoner' 136
JUST ONE NIGHT: Album 110; Other 120

K

'Kansas City': Other 188
Kaye, Thomas Jefferson 201

Kelly, Jonathan 183
'Kentucky Racehorse' 190
'Key To The Highway': Other 188
Keys, Bobby 186, 200
King, Albert 127
King, B.B. 13, 41, 164, 180
King, Freddie 13, 21, 101, 185, 188, 189
King, Mark 194
King Biscuit: Boot 210
Kirk, Roland 60, 181
Kissoon, Katie 162, 196
'Knock On Wood': Other 193
Knopfler, Mark 139, 144, 148, 158, 194, 195,
    196, 198, 203, 211, 212
Korner, Alexis 189, 191
Kossoff, Paul 181

L

'Lady of Verona' 145
Laine, Denny 190
Laing, Corky 187, 189
Landau, Jon 45
Lane, Ronnie 130, 189, 191
'Last Night' 101
Lauper, Cyndi 198
Lawley, Sue 155
'Lay Down Sally' 104; Other 107
'Layla' 84; Maxi/Flex/CD 71; Other 71, 136,
    Other 148, 150-152, 193, 195
LAYLA AND OTHER ASSORTED LOVE
    SONGS: Album 72, 74, 184; CD 73; Other
    75, 97
'Layla Part 2' 186
Leavell, Chuck 162
Led Zeppelin 181, 193
Lee, Albert 109, 110, 118, 127
Lennon, John 58, 64-66, 181-182
'Let It Rain' 84; Other 153, 187
Lethal Weapon: ST 145, 147, 195
Lethal Weapon 3: ST 201
Levenson, Bill 147
Levy, Marcy 91, 92, 109, 140
Lindsay Hogg, Michael 58
Little Feat 197
'Little Moon' (Bishop) 191
'Little Queenie': Other 90, 185
'Little Red Rooster' (Stones) 201; Other 155,
    184, 194, 199, 200
'Little Wing' 84; CD/Other 73
Live Aid 76, 136, 140, 154, 193
LIVE AT THE RITZ: Boot 210
LIVE AT THE ROYAL ALBERT HALL:
    Boot 213
LIVE CREAM: Other 46
LIVE CREAM VOLUME II: Album 46
LIVE IN JAPAN: Album 164; CD 201
Lofgren, Nils 194
LONDON AT NIGHT: Boot 211
LONDON REVISITED (Waters/Wolf):
    Album 187
LONDON SESSIONS: Album 184
'Lonely Stranger': Other 162
Loog-Oldham, Andrew 16
LOST IN AUSTIN (Benno) 190
Louis, Arthur 186, 187
'Love Comes To Everyone' (Harrison) 190
'Love Like A Rocket' (Geldorf) 195; Maxi 197
'Love Me Do' (Beatles) 15
'Love Minus Zero': Other 164
Lovin' Spoonful 38

M

MacLaine, Shirley 100
Madison Square Garden, New York 42, 78, 89,
    99, 163, 164, 186, 195, 203
Magical Mystery Tour (Beatles): FM 58
MAKIN' IT ON THE STREET (Laing):
    Album 189
Manuel, Richard 100
Markee, Dave 110
Marley, Bob 87, 186
Martyn, John 104, 191, 192
Mason, Robin 13
'Matchbox': Other 184, 193
May, Brian 197

Mayall, John 20-21, 23, 24, 30, 180, 185
Mayfield, Curtis: tribute album 201
McCartney, Paul 190, 194
McCarty, Jim 10, 12, 21
McGuinness, Tom 13, 15
McLaughlin, John 187
McVie, Christine 191, 192
McVie, John 23
'Mean Woman Blues': Other 193
Michael, George 194
Miles, Billy 74
Miles, Buddy 181
'Miles Road' 181
MILK COW BLUES: Boot 209
Miller, Steve 201
'Mini Opera' (The Who): FM 58
Misterioso, L'Angelo 181
Mitchell, Joni 106, 189
Mitchell, Mitch 58, 181
MONEY AND CIGARETTES: Album 127,
    191; Other 125, 126, 128
Montreux Jazz Festival, Switzerland 195
Moon, Keith 90, 99, 185, 187
Morgan Studios, London 181
Morrison, Van 101, 187, 188, 193
Mothers of Invention 41
Mouzon, Alphonse 187
'Mr Bluesman' (Sambora) 200
Muddy Waters 13
Murphy, Shaun 140
Murray the K Show 38
MUSIC FROM FREE CREEK: Comp 187
'My Baby She Left Me' (Guy/Wells) 185
'My Father's Eyes': Other 162
MY BLUES: Boot 209
MY WORLD (Charles): Album 201

N

'1999': Other 195
Nack, Lonnie 193
Nassau Coliseum, New York 89, 187
National Philharmonic Orchestra 155, 158, 212
NEC, Birmingham 136, 144, 163
NIGHT EYES (Douma): Album 190
Nightlife 195
Niles, Tessa 162, 196
Nine Below Zero 165
Nizami, Ganjavi 73
'No Alibis': Other 153
'No One Knows' 187
NO REASON TO CRY: Album 99, 100-101,
    187; Boot 210; CD 101; Other 98, 104
'Nobody Knows You When Your Down and
    Out' 74
'None Of Us Are Free' (Chharles) 201
NOT ALONE (Kaye) 201

O

'Ol' Ben Lucas' (Friedman) 188
Old Grey Whistle Test 106; Boot 209
'Old Love' 150
OLD WAVE (Starr): Album 192
Oldaker, Jamie 87, 127, 140
Olympic Studios 106
ON TOUR (Delaney and Bonnie):
    Album 63, 66
ON TOUR 1987: Boot 211
ON TOUR WITH ERIC CLAPTON:
    Album 67
ONE FINE DAY: Boot 211
ONE MORE CAR, ONE MORE RIDER:
    see AUGUST
ONE NIGHT IN DALLAS: Boot 209
ONE OF THE BOYS (Daltrey): Album 188
Ono, Yoko 58, 64-65, 182
Ormsby-Gore, Alice 80, 85
Ormsby-Gore, Frank 85

P

Page, Jimmy 20, 128, 130, 148, 180, 191, 192,
    193, 210
Palmer, Ben 13, 14, 20, 23, 38-39, 180
Palmer, Phil 200, 203
Palmer, Tony 48, 100
'Paper Round' (Stanshall) 183
Pappalardi, Felix 38
Parker, Ray 82
Patterson, Meg 84-85
Peace for Christmas charity concert 66, 182
Pearce, Roger 17

Perkins, Carl 140, 184, 193, 198
Petty, Tom 164
Phantom, Slim Jim 140
Phillinganes, Greg 142, 194
'Phone Booth' (Cray) 197; Flex 195
Picket, Wilson 72
Pink Floyd 130
Plastic Ono Band 64-66, 182
PLAY THE BLUES (Guy/Wells): Album 184
'Plum' (Louis) 187
Poco 187
Portnoy, Jerry 159
Powell, Enoch 102
Powerhouse, The 180
'Presence of the Lord' 61, 84; Other 63
Preston, Billy 69, 100-101, 180-181, 182, 184,
    187, 200
PRIMAL SOLOS: Album 22, 24
'Prime Cuts': Other 96
Prince 195
'Prince Of Peace' (Russell) 182
Prince's Trust 130; concerts 146, 150, 192, 194,
    196, 197
'Promises': Other 109
PROS AND CONS OF HITCHIKING
    (Waters): Album 130; Other 127

R

Radle, Carl 69, 87, 189
Raitt, Bonny 203
RAMBLING ON MY MIND: Album 24
RAW VELVET (Whitlock): Album 186
Ready Steady Go 14, 33, 39
Redding, Otis 19, 34
Reed, Jimmy 13
Reed, Lou 164, 200, 203
Reid, Vernon 200
Relf, Keith 10, 12, 14, 16, 21
'Reno Street Incident' (Davis) 185
Renwick, Tim 165
REZIPROCAL AFFECTION: Boot 210
Richards, Keith 58, 181, 195, 198, 199, 200,
    210
Richie, Lionel 139, 195, 203
'Right Now' (Preston) 182
'Rita Mae': Other 192
'Road Song' 187
Robert Stigwood Organisation 124
Robertson, Robbie 98, 101, 189, 194
'Rock and Roll Gypsies' (Davis) 185
Rock 'n' Roll Hall of Fame 48, 49, 166
Rock Against Racism 102
Rocker, Lee 140
ROCKET MAN (John): Album 200
ROCKIN' 50'S ROCK 'N' ROLL (Holly):
    Album 183
'Roll Away The Stone' (Russell) 182
'Roll It Over' (Derek and the Dominos) 70
'Rollin' And Tumblin': Other 162
Rolling Stone 45; Covers 91, 130; 'Random
    Notes' 91
Rolling Stones 15, 16, 19, 43, 58, 99, 155, 178,
    181, 186, 194, 200
'Romance In Durango' (Dylan) 99-100, 187
Ronnie Scott's 196
Roomful of Blues 196
Roosters, The 13-14
'Rough Mix' (Lane/Townshend) 189
ROUGH MIX (Lane/Townshend): Album
    189
ROYAL ALBERT HALL 1990: Boot 212
ROYAL ALBERT HALL 2: Boot 213
'Run So Far' 150
'Runaway Train' (John) 164, 201
Rundgren, Todd 159
Rush, Otis 21, 195
Rutherford, Mike 154, 165, 197

S

'Sally Simpson' (Who): ST 187
Sambora, Richie 200
'Same Old Blues' 130; Other 154
SAME OLD BLUES: Boot 210
Samwell-Smith, Paul 10, 12, 14, 16, 19, 21
'San Francisco Bay Songs': Other 13
Sanborn, David 195, 200, 201
Santana 97, 100, 187
Santana, Carlos 97-99, 187, 193
Schon, Neil 200

Scorcese, Martin 106
SECRET HISTORY: Boot 206
Secret Policeman's Other Ball 198
SEE ME (Lane): Album 191
Sharp, Martin 40
'She's Waiting': Other 136, 142
Shea Stadium, New York 163, 199
'Sign Language' (Dylan) 100-101, (Dylan) 187
'Signe': Other 162
Sims, Dick 87
'Ski-ing' 181
Slick, Earl 140
Slim Chance 189
SLOWHAND: Album 107, 124, 189; Other
    104, 107
SLOWHAND BLUES: Boot 213
'Smile': Other 96
Smith, 'Legs' Larry 90, 91
Smythe, Colin 158
'Snake Drive' 181
'Solid Rock': Other 194
SOME TIME IN NEW YORK CITY (Ono):
    Album 64, 182
SOMETHIN ELSE (Bruce): Album 201
SONGS FOR LAYLA: Boot 212
Spampinato, Joey 159
Spann, Otis 23, 180
Spector, Phil 70
Spencer Davis Group 180
Spinetti, Henri 110
Spooky Tooth 181
'Stairway to Heaven' (Led Zeppelin) 130, 193
'Standin' Around Crying': Other 155
Stainton, Chris 110, 127, 140
Stanshall, Vivian 180
Starr, Ringo 76, 140, 184, 187, 189, 190, 193,
    196
'Steady Rolling Man': Other 185
'Steel Wheels' tour (Stones) 200
STEPHEN STILLS (Stills): Album 183
STEPPING STONES PART 1: Boot 207
STEPPING STONES PART 2: Boot 207
Stewart, Dave 200, 203
Stewart, Ian 194
Stewart, Rod 102, 194
Stigers, Curtis 203
Stigwood, Robert 30, 33, 60-61, 90, 91
'Still It Feels Good' (Louis) 187
Stills, Stephen 69, 181, 183, 185, 189
Sting 191, 196, 198
Stock, Ray 15
'Stone Free': Other 165
STORMY MONDAY: Boot/Flex 204
'Stormy Monday': Other 101, 187, 188
'Stormy Monday Blues' (Korner) 191
STORMY MONDAY BLUES: Boot 208
'Strange Brew' 41
'Sugar Sweet' (King) 189
'Sunshine Of Your Love': Other 43, 47, 48, 63,
    198
SUPERJAM: Boot 212
'Sweet Home Chicago': Other 158, 165, 200
'Sweet Wine': Other 37
'Swing Low Sweet Chariot': Other 91
'Symphony for the Devil': Other 99
SYMPATHY FOR THE DEVIL (Stones):
    Album 186

T

24 NIGHTS: Album/VO 160; Other 160,
    161
25th Anniversary Tour 148, 149
T'Pau 197
Tampa Stadium, Florida 97
Taylor, Mick 193
Taylor, Roger 165
'Tearing Us Apart' (Turner) 194, 196; PD 145;
    VO 144, 145, 195; Other 194, 197
'Tears In Heaven' 161; VO 164; Other 162
TEARS IN HEAVEN: Boot 213
'Teasin' (King) 183
'Tell The Truth' (Derek and the Dominos) 70
Terry, George 87, 107
'That'll Be The Day' (Holly) 183
'That's Alright': Other 193
'That's The Way God Planned It' (Preston) 182
THAT'S THE WAY GOD PLANNED IT
    (Preston): Album 182
'That's What It Takes' (Harrison) 196

'The Beat Of The Night' (Geldof) 195
'The Border Song' 198
'The Burning of the Midnight Lamp':
    Other 165
'The Challenge' (McVie) 192
THE CHALLENGE (McVie): Album 191
The Color Of Money: ST 147
THE CREAM OF ERIC CLAPTON: Album
    146; Other 146
'The Dealer' (Louis) 187
THE DOMINO THEORY: Boot 208
'The Dreams Of A Hobo' (Whitlock) 186
'The Eagle Laughs At You' (Lomax) 182
THE END OF SUMMER NIGHT: Boot 208
The Hit: ST 147
'The Judgement' (Dickinson) 186
'The Kind Of Life' (Crocker) 197
THE LAST WALTZ: Album/FM/Other 106
THE LONDON HOWLIN' WOLF
    SESSIONS (Wolf): Album 185
THE MORGAN REHEARSALS: Boot 207
THE NIGHT OF THE KINGS: Boot 210
THE ONE (John): Album 201
THE PARTY ALBUM (Comp): Album 189,
    191
THE PROS AND CONS OF HITCHIKING
    (Waters) 192
THE RAINBOW CONCERT: Comp 184
THE SECRET POLICEMAN'S OTHER
    BALL: Comp 192
'The Scenery Has Slowly Changed'
    (Whitlock) 186
'The Shape You're In': Maxi/PD/Other 125
THE SHAPES OF THINGS: CD comp 19
'The Usual' (Dylan) 196
THE TWELFTH NIGHT: Boot 211
THE UNRELEASED LIVE ALBUM:
    Boot 210
THE UNSURPASSED ERIC CLAPTON:
    Boot 207
THE WORST OF (Gardner/Dyke):
    Album 183
THE YARDBIRDS: LP comp 20
THEIR SATANIC MAJESTIES
    (Rolling Stones) 39
THERE'S ONE IN EVERY CROWD:
    Album 91-93, 95, 101, 185-186; Other 93
THEY DANCE ALONE (Sting): Album 196
'This Be Called A Song' (Starr) 188
'Thorn Tree in the Garden' 74
'Till The Rivers Run Dry'
    (Lane/Townshend) 189
Titelman, Russ 161
Tommy 95; ST/Other 185
'Too Lovely To Leave Alone' 97
Topham, Anthony 'Top' 16
Tosh, Peter 91, 185-186
Townshend, Pete 82, 84, 90, 91, 142, 155, 184,
    185, 189, 194
Traffic 60
'Train 444' (Louis) 187
'Tribute To Elmore' 181
Troy, Doris 183, 184
Tull, Jethro 58
'Tulsa County' (Davis) 185
TURN UP DOWN: Album 118
Turner, Tina 144, 145, 194-197, 200
'TV Mama' (King) 189
TWO ROOMS (various): Album 198
'Two Young Lovers': Other 194
Tyler, Stephen 200

U

U2 136
'Under My Thumb' (Rolling Stones): Other 61
UNPLUGGED: Album 161-164, 166;
    Other 162
Unplugged: FM 161; Boot 213
UPFRONT (Sanborn): Album 200, 201
Ure, Midge 194, 197

V

Vaughan, Jimmie 155, 158
Vaughan, Stevie Ray 158, 200
Velez, Martha 182
Vernon, Mike 13, 23
Voorman, Klaus 64, 182, 184

W

Wailers 91
'Walk Out in the Rain' (Dylan) 108, 189
Walker, T-Bone 13
Walsh, Joe 185
'Wanna Make Love To You': Maxi 143
Warner's Holiday Camp 101
'Washita Love Child' (Davis) 185
'Wasted Country' (Dorsey): CD/PD 197
Water: ST 147, 193
Waters, Muddy 106, 109, 120, 148, 155, 180,
    189, 191
Waters, Roger 127, 130, 191, 192
Watts, Charlie 130, 184, 192
'Way Up Yonder' (Lane) 191
WEDNESDAY NIGHT AT THE TOKYO
    DOME: Boot 211
'Wee Wee Hours': Other 195
Wells, Junior 139, 184, 193
WEMBLEY STADIUM: Boot 213
'West Coast Idea' 181
West Palm Beach concert 185
Wet Wet Wet 197
'What You Get Is What You See': Maxi 195
'What's Shakin' 180
WHAT'S SHAKIN: Album 180
'Whatcha Gonna Do' 186
WHEELS OF FIRE: Album 43; Other 42
'When Lad Has Money' (Lane) 191
'When Pinkie Get's The Blues' see 461
    OCEAN BOULEVARD
'Where There's A Will There's A Way'
    (Whitlock) 186
'While My Guitar Gently Weeps' 181;
    Other 196
Whitaker, Robert 42
White, Alan 64, 182
WHITE ALBUM (Beatles): Album 58, 181
WHITE MANSIONS: Comp 190
'White Room': Other 43, 47, 136, 150, 193
'White Trash' 190
'Whiter Shade Of Pale': Other 197
Whitlock, Bobby 69, 74, 75, 185
'Whole Lotta Shakin' Going On': Other 193
Who, The 38, 58, 185
'Why Does Love Got To Be So Sad': Other 187
Wile, John 124
William, Larry 13
Williams, Don 104, 188-189
Williams, Jerry 136, 150
Williamson, Sonny Boy 17-18, 178-180
'Willie And The Hand Jive': Other 85, 90
Winston Legthigh and the Dirty Macs 58
Winter, Johnny 164
Winterland, San Francisco 46, 102
Wintershall concert 154
Winwood, Stevie 60-62, 130, 180, 181, 184
'With A Little Help From My Friends': Other
    196, 197
Wonder, Stevie 82, 184, 188
'Wonderful Tonight' 107, 161; Maxi 120;
    Other 107, 109, 120, 148, 197
'Wonderful World' (Zucchero) 200, 201
WONDERWALL MUSIC (Harrison):
    Album 181
Wood, Ronnie 82, 98-101, 106, 164, 184-189
'Worrier' (Cocker) 188
'Wrapping Paper' 33, 35; Other 37
'Wreck Of The Hesperus' (Harrison) 196
Wyman, Bill 109, 130, 184, 192

Y

Yardbirds, The 13-19, 130, 178-180, 188
'Yer Blues' (Beatles): FM 58; Other 64, 181
York, Pete 180
'You Belladonna You' (Davis) 185
'You Don't Know Like I Know': Other 127
'You Give Me Joy Joy' (Troy) 183
'You're Too Good To Die You Should Be
    Buried Alive' (Wood) 100
'You've Got Me Thinking' (Lomax) 182
Young, Neil 104-106, 164, 189
Young, Paul 194

Z

Zanuck, Lili 161
Zappa, Frank 41
Zucchero 200
ZUCCHERO: Album 198
ZZ Top 165

Acknowledgements

Author's acknowledgement

This book would not have been possible without the following people to whom I am eternally grateful: Roger Forrester, Di Puplett, Joe McMichael, Bill Levenson at PolyGram, Virginia Lohle at Star File in New York, John Peck, Andreas Seghers, L'Imagerie Rock Graphics in Studio City, California and Mark Hayward at Vinyl Experience/UFO Records. I would also like to thank Karen Daws for her patience over the last year when most of my weekends were spent staring at a computer screen. As always, hello to Guy and Mady Roberty, Rose Clapp, Pat McDonald and Heather Klasson.

Publisher's Acknowledgements

Dragon's World would like to thank the following for their individual contributions to this book: Roger Forrester; Mark Hayward from Vinyl Experience; Denise at Winterland for the loan of badges and T-shirts; Debra Jacobson and Mary Smith from L'Imagerie Gallery, 12117 Ventura Blvd, Studio City, CA 91604-2515 for the loan of tickets and posters, they have a mail order service for their rock concert posters; Virginia Lohle at Star File photo agency; London Features International and Retna Photo Library; Barry Plummer and John Peck for their photographs; Graham Bush for special photography; Bill Levenson at PolyGram International, Michael Mazzarella at Atlantic Records and Dixie Hollier, Greg Geller and his assitant Jo at Warner for their help in tracking down US catalogue numbers; Stuart Green for text styling; James Rubinstein; Keith Bambury; Lesley Gilbert; and Carole King.

The author and publisher gratefully acknowledge the assistance of the following record companies in the preparation of the illustrated discography: Apple, Arista, Castle Communications, Charly, Chrysalis, EMI, MCA, PolyGram, RCA, Silvertone, Sony, Virgin and Warner. Every effort has been made to obtain permission for the use of illustrations reproduced wherever possible. We apologize for any unintentional errors, omissions or infringements of copyright. These will be corrected in future editions.

Photographic Credits

LONDON FEATURES INTERNATIONAL LTD: 14, 16, 31, 39, 59, 65, 141, 156 BOTTOM, 199 BOTTOM, Kevin Mazur 49, P. Ollerenshaw 202 BOTTOM.

John Peck: 2, 5, 119, 129, 137, 150 LEFT, 154, 159 TOP, 163 TOP RIGHT, 165.

Barry Plummer: 110.

RETNA PICTURES LTD: 21, 38, 159 BOTTOM, Adrian Boot 106, 198 RIGHT, Larry Busacca 198 LEFT, Henry Diltz 157, Steve Granitz 163 TOP LEFT,

KING COLLECTION 11, 12, Janet Macoska 92 TOP, Chuck Pulin 163 BOTTOM, Michael Putland 34, 61, 81, 88, 89 BOTTOM, 92 BOTTOM LEFT AND RIGHT, Patrick Quigly 150 RIGHT, Ray Stevenson 48.

STAR FILE: 13, 73, 75, 90, 179, 203 BOTTOM, Mickey Adair 140 TOP, Jim Cummings 66, Harry Goodwin 32, Bob Gruen 89 TOP, 128 TOP, Steve Judson 9, Joel Levy 199 TOP, Chuck Pulin 203 TOP, David Seely 151, Barie Wentzell 83, Vinnie Zuffante 128 BOTTOM, 166, 202 TOP.

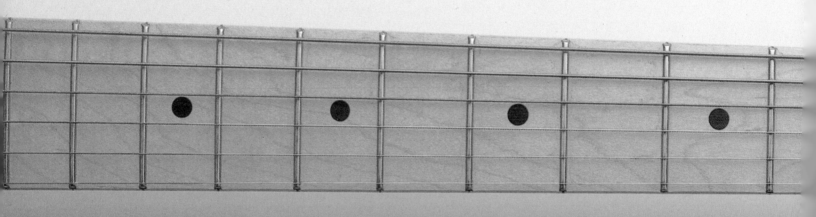